The Improvement Process

How America's Leading Companies Improve Quality

Dr. H.J. Harrington

Chairman of the Board pro tem,
American Society for Quality Control
Project Manager, Q A
IBM Corp., San Jose

Quality Press
American Society for Quality Control
310 West Wisconsin Avenue, Milwaukee, Wisconsin 53203

McGraw-Hill Book Company

New York   St. Louis   San Francisco   Auckland   Bogotá
Hamburg   Johannesburg   London   Madrid   Mexico
Milan   Montreal   New Delhi   Panama
Paris   São Paulo   Singapore
Sydney   Tokyo   Toronto

*This book is dedicated to my best friend,
loyal associate, constant companion,
and always willing listener and
adviser: My loving sweet Marguerite.*

Library of Congress Cataloging-in-Publication Data

Harrington, H. J. (H. James)
 The improvement process.

 Bibliography: p.
 Includes index.
 1. Quality control.   I. Title.
TS156.H34   1987   658.5′62   86-7359
ISBN 0-07-026754-5

1234567890   DOC/DOC   8932109876

ISBN 0-07-026754-5

The editors for this book were Martha Jewett and Nancy Young,
the designer was Naomi Auerbach and the supervisor
was Teresa F. Leaden. It was set in Baskerville by Harper Graphics.
Printed and bound by R. R. Donnelley & Sons Company.

Contents

8. System Improvement   135

9. Supplier Involvement   155

10. Systems Assurance   175

11. The Long and Short of It   182

Foreword

Following almost every football season, there are a host of articles predicting that this year's champion has the makings of a dynasty. But complacency almost inevitably strikes, and this year's champ becomes next year's chump.

The story of the American economy parallels the world of football. The U.S. dominated the post World War II scene, for almost 30 years. And then we slumped.

In the early 70s, U.S. management techniques were being called our most valuable export by numerous respected thinkers. Today, we are groping for solutions. All of our pet theories are being thoroughly reexamined. Many are being scrapped.

And reexamine we must, for some 70 percent of our industries, from the highest of high-tech to the lowest of low-tech, are under life-threatening challenge. And the challenges and challengers are growing in number. Korea, Brazil, Indonesia, and China are mounting attacks that may one day equal those coming from Japan.

In part, we did get complacent in the absence of world-class competitors. But the story is more profound, leading to the need to reassess the drive mechanism of our entire economic progress over the past 100 years.

The Europeans were historically the craftspeople, from Holland to Germany. Among them, the British were the inventors, taking far more than their share of the scientific prizes. And the United States? We were in many ways the Japanese of a century or so ago: the copiers and the perfecters of mass production. In fact, mass production was even the key to our war-time successes. With rare exceptions, such as Patton, the cornerstones of American victories were more ships, more planes, more tanks, more guns, and fuller logistics pipelines.

Today the residue of mass thinking still dominates—and haunts—American business. The "capacity mentality" or the "tonnage mentality" has dominated steel, autos, earth-moving equipment, and machine tools. It has also more recently dominated even semiconductors.

We still rate ourselves principally on size. The Fortune 500 is business's Holy Grail. Though the list offers many measures, only size is remembered.

American Airlines, following a recent United Airlines strike, celebrated a month in which their passenger miles exceeded those of number 1, United. It makes national news. What if American had the most profit (which it usually does) from providing a superior service (it is usually rated number 1 or number 2, sharing honors with Delta, in passenger satisfaction)? Those success indicators are of far less note, internally or externally.

Times are not "a-changin,'" for the U.S. economy. They have changed. Mass is no longer the principal means of success. Quality, measured in the customer's terms, is. New studies show decisively that better relative customer-perceived quality, not lower prices, is the prime determinant of long-term market share gain, not to mention return on sales, equity, and investment.

Quality, not volume, will become number 1 for the U.S.—in the manufacturing and service sector alike—or else. Or else we must prepare to lose control of our destiny, as we lose our manufacturing (and then technology) base, and suffer a long-term decline in standard of living. (Already, the 25 to 34-year-old male suffered a 26 percent real wage decline between 1973 and 1983.)

Jim Harrington's fine book is an outcropping of the necessary quality revolution *beginning* to sweep America. Quality is now a feature in newspaper and television daily reporting, and it has spawned a whole industry of consultants and quick-fix books. I emphasize the flash news (the umpteenth 3-minute prime-time story on Japan as number 1) and the quick-fix book phenomenon, because Harrington's effort is the antithesis of both. It is neither flashy nor does it have a quick-fix orientation. To the contrary, the IBM quality manager and president of the American Society for Quality Control makes it clear that the only approach to quality that will succeed is one that makes it *the* predominant way of life in the corporation.

The answer is not statistics, not circles, not suggestion systems, not badges and medals, not czars, not systems, not Fourth of July proclamations. It is all of these things and much, much more.

Harrington's book holds out the carrot. Residing in nooks and crannies are statistics that show the awesome promise of a thorough quality commitment. In one place he estimates that the cost of (poor) quality is no less than 25 percent of assets and 25 percent of people. He lets us in on the results of leading firms' progress. A Tektronix division cut inventory by 75 percent, floor space from 15,000 to 7,000 square feet, work in process by 50 percent, overall manufacturing cycle time from 30 to 40 days to 12 days, and customer delivery by a whopping 86 percent, from 14 to 15 weeks to 2! Motorola's president, William Weisz, has had the audacity to declare an objective of no less than 10-fold quality improvement in just 5 years. Hewlett-Packard's president, John Young, declared in 1979 that HP would cut product failures to one-tenth of today's level in 10 years.

Thus the opportunity is monumental—and numerous cases from leading companies demonstrate that it is achievable.

The Harrington book takes us step-by-step through the process of building in quality thinking as a way of life. It provides detailed checklists, the basics of statistical analysis, and even outlines of questionnaires for top management and hourly people alike.

For instance, Harrington recommends starting with a top management steering council. He includes a possible opening speech to the group, the outline of a 3-day off-site retreat, and questions to use in creating a compelling "needs analysis."

Other chapters incisively but thoroughly assess the pluses and minuses of the vast array of circle programs (quality circles, task forces, department-level improvement teams) and recognition/incentive systems (Scanlon plans, team incentives, suggestion systems, employee share-ownership programs).

I found four sections especially useful. Each represents a marked departure from standard treatises on quality.

Harrington goes far beyond lip service in describing what it takes to get management—at all levels—truly committed, the *sine qua non* of a thoroughgoing change of attitude toward quality. He makes it clear, for instance, that you are not living the quality message until it is reflected in your calendar:

> Now step back and take a look at your calendar. Are you spending as much time controlling the quality of your department's output as you are investing in cost and schedules? If not, you should adjust your priorities. If you don't have time for quality and don't value it enough to be interested in it, how can you expect your employees to? This applies to every level of management, as well as to the employees. Plant managers hold production status meetings in which quality, schedules, and costs are reviewed. Normally, schedules are addressed first, then cost, and then quality—if there is time. Time after time, a problem with schedules uses up more than its share of the meeting; as a result, quality is not discussed. If quality is really the most important factor, than it should be first on every agenda. The order of the

meeting agenda is a tell-tale sign that shows what management is most concerned about.

Likewise, he focuses on the radical new role for the first-line supervisor. The first-line supervisor, in a truly participative environment, loses power (in the traditional sense) and is even more stuck in the middle than ever—a new set of demands, a new set of measures, top management climbing all over his back, yet less traditional power. The first-line supervisor remains the key to success and is usually not the focus of quality discussions or texts. Harrington provides a pleasant exception.

The discussion of participation is also thoughtful and thorough. Harrington describes it philosophically and practically. The jumping off point is: "Error-free performance does not start with any new statistical method or problem-solving technique. It starts with each person having a thorough understanding of the job and having the confidence that he or she can do it correctly." Details of training programs and performance evaluations, for instance, are included.

A powerful chapter on supplier involvement also marks the text. The role of suppliers still remains underattended in most quality improvement discussions. The chapter covers supplier seminars, supplier surveys, and supplier rating schemes, in addition to discussing policy issues relating to a decision to go with fewer suppliers and the nature of achieving true partnership with one's suppliers.

The most compelling of Harrington's departures, though, is his emphasis on systems and process improvements. So many programs focus exclusively on "them" (the first-line employee), the ten-person team (the circle in one form or another), and individual incentives (for instance, suggestion programs). Harrington contends, correctly I believe, that

> The only way improvement gains can be effectively and permanently imbedded in the fiber of a company is through changing the systems that control the company's operations. It is not the employees who cause the majority of errors; they are just unwilling pawns who operate in the environment often controlled by obsolete and cumbersome operating systems. It is not the managers who cause the errors; their only error is allowing the company to operate with systems that have not been fine-tuned for today's needs. As we try to eliminate errors, we must not attack people. They are not the problem. What needs to be attacked and restructured are the operating systems that control and govern the company's performance.

Harrington's IBM experience has been decisive here. That firm's extraordinary quality improvement progress in the past 5 years has largely stemmed from a determination to grab hold of the often unseen, unchampioned processes which lock in so much of day-to-day behavior.

Harrington's sections on process analyses and process improvement teams are worth the price of admission alone.

Oh how I fret! Quality *must not* become the buzz-phrase of the 80s. We either retool our entire management structures in the direction of quality-first orientation—or else.

I am increasingly strident in my tone as I crisscross the country. Few are complacent any more. That's good. Most are experimenting. That's good. But, all too few have

- Come to grips with the revolutionary and thoroughgoing change in approach required (a focus on quality, not volume)
- Seen the size of the target of opportunity
- Understood that the pace of change must be radically accelerated despite the frenzy of change-oriented behavior that has already been going on
- Realized that people and managing systems, not capital (e.g., robots and automation), are the success key

I fervently hope that Harrington's readers will not only benefit from the thoroughness of his effort but will also "smell" the fundamental nature of the challenge for change that he mounts. This is a book for board members and first-line employees alike. All of our jobs are on the line.

Thomas J. Peters

Preface

How would you like to increase profits by 50 percent? To turn the mounds of scrap that sit throughout your manufacturing facility into shippable product? To increase your corporate output by 20 percent without building one new building or buying one new piece of equipment? To expand your R&D activities by 20 percent without adding one new engineer? To cut overtime in accounting from 30 percent to 2 percent? To see employees with smiles on their faces every day, rather than only at 4 p.m. on Friday?

It all sounds too good to be true. But many companies around the world are reaping fantastic benefits because their management teams have set new company performance standards and because management has taken the time and invested the effort to train the total company population in how to improve performance. They have made *the improvement process* part of their company's personality.

If you put the improvement process into effect, your company may not harvest *all* the benefits I have mentioned, or maybe it will harvest even more. Based on results achieved by companies such as IBM, Xerox, Memorex, and 3M, your company will become more productive, creating products and services far beyond your highest expectations. And you will discover that the money spent to make the improvement process part of your company's personality was one of the best investments you ever made.

James E. Preston, president of Avon, reported, "Last year, we spent about $300,000 on education and the implementations of QPIP (quality and productivity improvement process), but we recorded savings totaling more than $10 million, all directly attributable to QPIP."

John A. Young, president of Hewlett-Packard, when discussing the quality and improvement process at HP, stated, "Yokagawa/Hewlett-Packard efforts won it the esteemed Deming prize in 1982. During the

5 years it strove for the award, YHP has cut manufacturing costs on its own products by 42 percent and inventory by 64 percent. Failure rates went down 60 percent and R&D cycle time was cut by more than a third." In discussing improvement in the U.S. he continued, "Today we have a lot of success stories to tell. Our field failure rates have been decreasing more than 20 percent a year. In fact, many parts of our business will meet my factor-of-10 (improvement) goal in less than 10 years."

John Akers, president of IBM Corporation, believes that quality improvement will save IBM billions of dollars over the coming years.

There is a direct relationship between quality and productivity—they complement each other; they do not detract from one another. Starting your company on its quest for quality will provide you with a process that improves productivity, decreases product cost, and increases your share of the market.

As we entered the 1980s, it was obvious to most managers that something was wrong with the present U.S. management system and the curriculum being taught in business schools around the country. Recession, inflation, foreign competition, government regulation, and taxes had put a tight squeeze on American business. We were well on our way to becoming a second-rate industrial power. The values that had made America great had seemingly shifted. Short-range profits were more important than long-range gain. Maximization of assets was taking priority over customer's needs. Management theory replaced experience, and company loyalty was a thing of the past. We forgot that management is an art and not a science. American management had been looking for a set of rigid formulas that would ensure successful business. This attitude has only one sure result—ultimate failure of the company—for there is no one foolproof, step-by-step way to manage a company. If there were, we would not need managers; it could all be done with computers.

The only sure thing we have is the knowledge that things will change. As managers, we must be flexible and willing to meet those changes. We need to develop management systems that support the company's values, show true concern for employees, and remind us that we are not in business just to provide a product or service, but that our real purpose is to satisfy the customer's needs both today and tomorrow. The improvement process is just one item in the toolbox of management activities that can help to satisfy these requirements. Although it is laid out here in a step-by-step manner, its implementation must be tempered with a knowledge of the customer, the employees, and the company's personality.

Dr. H. James Harrington

Acknowledgment

Corporate America has been going through an era of discovery. In the late 1970s, American management realized that American business was not keeping pace with the quality and productivity growth rates of many other countries around the world. This realization brought about a renewed dedication to increased quality and productivity on the part of American management.

This book is the result of a 5-year study of the actions taken by over fifty American companies to improve the quality of their products and services. Numerous companies, both small and large, were studied to discover what was tried and what was effective.

Most of the companies studied based their improvement process on the teachings of one or more of today's foremost authorities on quality. They are, in alphabetical order: Philip B. Crosby, W. Edwards Deming, Armand V. Feigenbaum, Kaoru Ishikawa, and Joseph M. Juran. Although their teachings differ in content, each has many excellent points that should be included in every improvement process. As American business started to use these ideas, it had a tendency to integrate and combine them to meet special requirements, thereby developing new concepts and improved techniques. This book provides an overview of the ideas and methods that are, in the writer's opinion, the most advanced and effective.

Particular recognition is gratefully given to these five great quality professionals and to the companies that provided the data upon which this book is largely based.

As Sir Isaac Newton once said, "I stand on the shoulders of giants."

1

Why Improve?

INTRODUCTION

Following World War II, America found itself in the unique position of having the only major undamaged manufacturing system. The rest of the world's complexes were bombed out or obsolete. There was a huge demand for customer products to fill the void created over the war years, when the world's production capability was directed toward the war effort. American firms flourished in the seller's market. We fell under the delusion that all we had to do was stamp a product "Made in U.S.A." and it would sell anywhere in the world.

In our desire to meet this new customer demand, we expanded our production areas, invested in new equipment, and pushed to be sure that equipment utilization factors were high. We saw the mounds of scrap parts grow bigger and bigger and bigger; but we reasoned that the technology was getting more complex and that decreased first-time yield was the expected outgrowth of this evolution. To offset part of this cost, we invested heavily in developing, implementing, and managing repair processes. We carefully laid out the new manufacturing process with strategically located repair areas to minimize delay in putting the product back into the manufacturing cycle. We selected our very best employees to staff these repair areas because it is always much more difficult to do the job over than it is to do it right originally. Short-term repair was preferable to long-term prevention.

Defective products became a way of life. We even told our suppliers (indirectly, of course) that we didn't expect them to ship us defect-free parts, that it was all right to ship out parts at a 1 percent acceptable quality level (AQL), which means that the purchaser has agreed to accept 1 percent defective parts. As a result, some suppliers purposely added scrap parts to their shipped product because it was a way to sell those otherwise useless parts. The 1984 U.S. government outlay for goods and services was about $785.0 billion. A 1 percent AQL means that they could have accepted $7.8 billion worth of waste and scrap.

Why do we do this? Why don't we expect 100 percent good parts? We don't pay our suppliers with 1 percent counterfeit money. Why should we accept anything less than 100 percent good parts?

LIMITED GOALS

For years, business people have set limited goals, strangely reluctant to look beyond the immediate need to what was actually possible. Why is it that we set performance goals for ourselves and our employees and when they are reached, say "That's good enough"? We then turn our attention and efforts in a new direction, content with keeping the performances of our original product or activity close to the original goal we had set. Today, in this worldwide business arena, the product that was good enough yesterday barely squeaks by today and will be inadequate tomorrow. We must continue to improve if we want to stay in business. Just ask yourself why quality has become the latest advertising theme for American-made products, when quality used to be taken for granted in the same products. A recent issue of *Fortune Magazine* predicted one-third to one-half of the 30,000 American automobile suppliers will go out of business in the next few years. Historically we've said, "Quality costs money," while our competition overseas has been saying, "Quality *makes* money." And they've been proving it.

JAPANESE QUALITY STANDARDS

Following World War II, Japanese industries were not content to say they were good enough. They said they were not good enough, that they could be better. Upper management people committed themselves to finding ways to improve productivity and quality. They sent out management teams that searched the world over for the magic formula that would transform their industry from one that had a reputation for producing cheap copies of American products to one that could compete from a price and quality standpoint in the European and U.S. markets—because they were no longer able to compete in the cheap labor-intensive markets. They filmed, they sketched, and they listened to industrial leaders in the United States and Europe. They went home to digest, modify, and apply what they had learned. They were quick to grasp concepts such as statistical quality control and total quality control. Japanese managers demonstrated their commitment to quality by providing opportunities to their employees to study these new techniques during working hours.

I believe the real secret Japanese management teams found from their worldwide survey was that *the most successful companies have extremely high standards for their products and their people.* They were companies that were not satisfied with the state of the art, were not satisfied with their product performance, and were constantly trying to provide their customers with better products at lower cost. They provided their customers with products that not only met requirements but exceeded them, setting new standards for their industries. They saw that in many cases substandard products were expensive to manufacture and customers were unwilling to purchase them, even at bargain prices. They saw that companies whose processes produced continuously high-quality products every time benefited in three ways:

- Lower manufacturing costs
- Higher profit margins
- Larger shares of the market

A detailed analysis proves there is a direct relationship between return on investment (ROI) and product quality. High-quality products yield about 40 percent more ROI than low-quality products.

Japanese management leaders methodically set about to raise their performance standards for their employees. In the process, the employees' own expectations were raised for the products and services they themselves purchased. As product performance and customer expectations rose, fewer companies outside of Japan were able to compete effectively in the Japanese market. Better quality resulted in increased demand for Japanese products around the world. In "Strategy and Structure of Japanese Enterprise," Toyohiro Kono points out that culture is not the key factor in successful Japanese companies. They all have common business traits: innovative, long-term goals, competition-oriented, administratively centralized, respect for employees, and close contact with customers. Spurred on by the excellence of Japanese-made products, people around the world began to realize that the most expensive products are not always the best and that the cheapest products will not be the least costly in the long run.

Figure 1.1 shows graphically how Japanese quality forged ahead and how we are starting to recover. It also shows what is happening to the quality level of Asia's "Four Tigers" (Hong Kong, Singapore, South Korea, and Taiwan). Although their rapid quality growth occurred later than Japan's, today they are producing many products with quality levels equal to or better than similar products from the U.S., Europe, or Japan. In addition, the Four Tigers' labor rates are significantly lower, making it very difficult for other countries to compete with them. Although what will happen in the future is anybody's guess, one thing seems certain: If the U.S. and Europe do not change their attitude about quality, they will become second-rate industrial powers and Asia will dominate.

QUALITY—THE WORLDWIDE BATTLEGROUND OF THE 80S

The big "war" of the 80s is not a military war; it is an industrial war, and the spoils of this war are customers around the world. American industry is under attack, not just from Japan but from all of Asia and

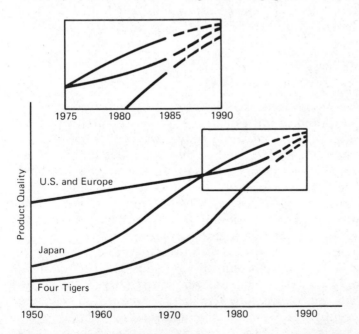

Figure 1.1   Product quality levels. (The curves for the U.S. and Europe and for Japan are based on the work of Dr. J. M. Juran.)

Europe. For many products, the standard of excellence is no longer set by the United States.

The great battle we all have to fight is against the creeping paralysis penetrating much of this country's value system. I call it the "don't give a damn" or "you're lucky it's that good" attitude. An attitude of indifference produces indifferent results. The cancer of indiffernce is becoming prevalent throughout the United States, and it is the disease we must fight to bring quality of product, service, and work life up to the competitive standards of this decade.

John A. Young, president of Hewlett-Packard, was asked by President Reagan to head a group to look at ways of improving the ability of American industry to compete both at home and abroad. In his report to the President and his cabinet, Young stated, "The ability of American industry to compete in world markets has eroded over the past 2 decades. The decline is evidenced in record trade deficits, declining world market share in technology industries, decreasing return in our manufacturing sector, slow productivity growth, and stagnant real wages."

Fortunately, things have begun to change in American business. A 1985 *Business Week* survey of 301 senior executives in large U.S. manufacturing companies facing Japanese competition revealed that the following steps are being taken to make their companies more competitive. They are:

- Investing in more efficient plants and equipment (27 percent)
- Improving the quality of service to customers (23 percent)
- Investing more in research and development (23 percent)

President Ronald Reagan pointed out the change in American business when he wrote, "Increasingly, business leaders respond to consumer expectations by improving the quality, safety, and effectiveness of their products."

The results of corporate America's efforts to improve have helped to reestablish our customers' faith in American products. In October 1985, Gallup conducted a consumer survey for the American Society for Quality Control (ASQC). This survey indicated that only 27 percent of consumers expected no improvement in the quality of American products, a gain of 250 percent over a 1980 survey conducted for ASQC. In the 1985 survey, only 33 percent of consumers surveyed stated that foreign-made products were equal to or better than American-made products, an improvement of over 227 percent.

These are significant improvements, but not good enough. This data indicates that we could still lose 33 percent of our internal market, and if we cannot win at home, how can we win in the international arena?

The facts describe a customer victimized by companies that designed obsolescence into their products and/or planned for repair rather than performance. These companies lived by the creed, *caveat emptor*—let the buyer beware.

THE CUSTOMER IS KING

In today's buyers' market the customer is king. What your customer wants is value. Value—that's a key word. It stands for quality and reliability at a reasonable price. In the competitive market it is imperative that each employee understands the importance of the customer. At IBM Austin, an employee card containing the following information emphasized this point.

> Customers are:
> - The most important people in any business.
> - Not dependent on us. We are dependent on them.
> - Not an interruption of our work. They are the purpose of it.
> - Doing us a favor when they come in. We are not doing them a favor by serving them.
> - A part of our business, not outsiders.
> - Not just a statistic. They are flesh-and-blood human beings with feelings and emotions, like ourselves.
> - People who come to us with their needs and wants. It is our job to fill them.
> - Deserving of the most courteous and attentive treatment we can give them.
> - The lifeblood of this and every other business. Without them we would have to close our doors.
>
> *Don't ever forget it!*

As John A. Young puts it, "Satisfying customers is the only reason we're in business." Customers are the lifeblood of a business, the most valuable asset. No customers means no business. No business means no jobs. Customers in the service industries are being turned off and turned out, not by price but by apathy, carelessness, and downright discourtesy. Customers are turning to foreign products because our managers and statisticians are willing to accept errors as random necessities, something to be lived with. We make excuses rather than progress. An attitude of good enough is not good enough today, and if we do not change, the tombstones marking our industrial plants will read "We thought we were good enough."

GOOD ENOUGH IS NOT GOOD ENOUGH

The time has come to change our standards. We can no longer live with the defect levels we have accepted in the past. Our companies need to make fewer errors and permit fewer defects. Materials and components need to be purchased to meet the job requirements. Poor training of employees, inferior supervision, and one-way communication must be corrected. It is time to stop accepting mediocre performance as acceptable and even rating it as "exceeds expectations" at times. Thomas J. Watson, Sr., the first president of IBM, said, "It is better to aim at perfection and miss than it is to aim at imperfection and hit it." It is time to embark on a new philosophy of expecting things to go right, not wrong. Your employees will try to live up to your expectations if you communicate with them and set the example. If you accept poor work, you'll get poor work. If you don't set the standards, your employees will set their own and they will be lower than they could be otherwise.

Because we are behind in some areas doesn't mean that we should give up; on the contrary, it should provide us with new challenges. We are a nation that cannot be counted out until the last bell of the fifteenth round. We started behind when we entered World War II, but we won the arms race. We were behind in the space race when Sputnik was launched, but we were the first to put a man on the moon. There is no reason why we cannot win this industrial encounter. All we have to do is stop accepting errors as if they were the norm and get angry when we see the billions of dollars that are wasted in our manufacturing and service industries because we (*all* of us) don't really try to do things right every time. We stop far short of our true potential, saying that's "good enough." We must not allow good enough to *be* good enough any longer.

America's productivity growth rate has been dropping since 1970 and has been a major factor in our worsening trade balance. On June 10, 1983, at the White House Conference on Productivity, President Reagan said,

> Improving productivity in this country lies at the heart of building and sustaining our economic recovery. It has been of major concern to me since the beginning of my presidency because greater productivity growth is necessary for us to achieve full employment, price stability, and sustained economic growth. It is a vital part of our efforts to improve our competitive position in world markets and create more job opportunities for an expanding American labor force, and it is essential if we are to raise incomes and maintain stable prices. Productivity growth is also tied to real economic growth and improving standards of living.

One of the very best ways to improve productivity is through improving the excellence of everything we do, thereby eliminating waste and providing our customers with world-class products and services.

In many areas, we still set the world standard for excellence but that should not give us a sense of confidence. If we don't continue to improve, some competitor will not be satisfied with his product and improve it, taking our customers away. Remember, when we stop improving, we start to lose ground. When we have so much experience that we think we have nothing left to learn, we start to slip backward, an unknown author once wrote.

There is no doubt about it: Our leadership has eroded—not because we lost our technological lead (most, if not all, major quality technological advancements were made by Americans) but because U.S. management did not stay abreast and accept and put to use the technologies that were developed here.

American management knows the importance of excellence but in many cases does nothing to improve. As Tom Peters, coauthor of *In Search of Excellence*, put it, "Everybody talks quality, but most of that is lip service. I'm not terribly sanguine about the prospects of big business becoming very vital from an entrepreneurial standpoint."

Everyone knows that it's better to win than to lose, to be good rather than bad, to do it right rather than wrong. So what's new? We live with such statements as: "No one makes errors on purpose" and "No one can be right every time" and "To err is human, to forgive divine." (Well, if that is true, we certainly have a lot of divine managers!) We can do error-free work. The only question is for how long. To produce error-free work for 30 seconds is easy, an hour is a little harder, and a week may not be possible now. But if we try, we can do it. We just have to set goals that improve the duration of our acceptable performance.

THE IMPROVEMENT PROCESS

The journey toward excellence is a never-ending road. Some people, because they see no end to their road, never take the first step. Others accept the challenge of the new day and continue down the road, forever improving, and looking forward to tomorrow's challenge. These are the people who will make the real contributions to humanity. These are the people who say: "Good enough is not good enough. I can do better."

Managers need a map to help lead their company down the quality road and keep it from running into dead ends. This road map is called the "improvement process." It is not a program since programs normally run for a definite period of time. It is a process—an ongoing, continuous commitment. It is a new way of thinking about all activities—from those on the manufacturing floor to the way the president runs his office to the way the janitor sweeps it. It is designed to bring about a new, more productive character to the business and has been used by hundreds of companies. The improvement process described in this book is the result of a study made of a number of major corporations and improvement processes taught by a number of quality consultants. Such companies as IBM, Hewlett-Packard, 3M, and Polaroid were examined. They all were greatly influenced during the 80s by quality professionals such as Mr. Philip B. Crosby, Dr. W. Edwards Deming, Dr. Armand V. Feigenbaum, Dr. Kaoru Ishikawa, and Dr. Joseph M. Juran. In the 40s, America had its war heroes, and in the 60s the astronauts were our role models. In the 80s, quality leaders, such as these, should be the heroes because their contributions to America's future and prosperity may be even greater than the previous social models.

When Avon's president, James E. Preston, was asked why they started their improvement process, he said, "It was a question of dollars and sense. Money was being spent that should have been saved. Lapses in quality were costing us money and customers." He added, "An analysis in the U.S. of these accounts revealed to us that nonconformance to measured quality standards in our products and services was costing the Avon division tens of millions of dollars annually."

The improvement process is an effective means of bringing about positive changes that save money for both the company and the customers. Oliver C. Boileau, president of General Dynamics Corporation, said about their improvement process, "For instance, the Fort Worth division had savings of $43.8 million for 1983–84."

In a memorandum dated July 31, 1985, to the heads of executive departments and agencies of the U.S. government, President Ronald Reagan wrote, "I know you have as one of your highest priorities completion of the next phase of our management improvement journey— improved delivery of public services through higher quality, improved timeliness, and lower cost to the taxpayers." President Reagan is setting a goal of improving government productivity by 20 percent with improved quality of services over the next 6 years.

2

The Improvement
Process

INTRODUCTION

When we stop improving, we start to slip backward. Too often we say
to ourselves: "I've always done it this way and it worked, so it must be
good enough." But that is no longer true, if it ever was. We cannot afford
to be stagnant.

Many companies around the world are content with getting by when
they should be getting better. Their management and employees are
satisfied with the present quality. Unfortunately when employees become
content, they stop improving. What needs to be developed is a construc-
tive level of dissatisfaction. Employees and management alike need to
believe they can be and do better.

How do you make a drastic change in the thinking of your company?
You can't command it. A poster campaign won't do. It will not occur
overnight or as the result of a productivity program. The trick is in
making the improvement process part of the company's operating system. It should be a part of everything we do, the way we think, and,
more important, the way we act.

Thomas J. Watson, Jr., past president of IBM, said, "We believe that all organizations should pursue all tasks with the idea that they can be accomplished in a superior fashion."

The improvement process is a group of activities that complement each other and provide an environment conducive to improving performance for employees and management alike. It provides a focus on an aspect of the business that is normally addressed only when it is out of control or when customers are irate. It is a process that helps us to accept change and continuing improvement as a necessary way of life.

The improvement process works for IBM, with 405,000 employees and a 1985 gross income of $50.1 billion. It works for Lewis Machining, which has 5 employees and grosses $1 million. It works for the military, and it works for the private sector. It works for the manufacturing plant, and it works for the service industry. The improvement process is good management practice that, when followed, will change the management characteristics and personality of your company.

TEN BASIC ACTIVITIES

The following ten improvement activities should be made part of the basic fiber of all companies, large or small. This list is the result of a study of many successful improvement processes already implemented by such companies as AT&T, Avon, Corning Glass, General Motors, Hewlett-Packard, IBM, Polaroid, and 3M.

1. Obtain top-management commitment
2. Establish an improvement steering council
3. Obtain total management participation
4. Secure team participation
5. Obtain individual involvement
6. Establish system improvement teams (process control teams)
7. Develop supplier involvement activities
8. Establish a systems quality assurance activity
9. Develop and implement short-range improvement plans and a long-range improvement strategy
10. Establish a recognition system

The improvement process is designed to change the personality, not the culture, of the company. A company's culture is molded from its heritage, its background, and the total intellectual and artistic content in its manner, style, and thought. Culture also includes the basic beliefs of a company and the foundation upon which it was built. Personality, on the other hand, as defined by Webster is "the quality or state of being a person—the capacity for choices, experiences, and liabilities of an individual person—a comparable complex characteristic of a group or nation." To alter the personality of a company, its leaders must be receptive to change. The problem is not in a company's heritage. It is management's preoccupation with short-term gains at the expense of company, employees, and, in the long run, profits.

1. *Top-management commitment.*   A company takes on the personality of its top management. Without top management's sincere belief that the company has the ability to do better than has been done in the past, there is no point in even starting the improvement process. The improvement process starts with top management, progresses at a rate proportionate to their demonstrated commitment, and will stop soon after they lose interest in the process. James E. Preston, president of Avon Products, Inc., said, "We need a continual effort to outdo what has already been done by ourselves and others—to do it better than ever before."

2. *Improvement steering council.*   The improvement steering council is a group of senior managers and/or their representatives and labor that takes the process outlined in this book and customizes it to fit the company's environment. There is no one process that meets the improvement needs of all companies. In fact, corporations such as IBM, Hewlett-Packard, and General Dynamics find that each of their locations has slightly different needs and characteristics. The improvement steering council serves as the process design engineer, preparing the company for the improvement process and directing the implementation of the process.

3. *Total management participation.*   The total management team is responsible for implementing the improvement process. It requires the active, demonstrated involvement of every manager and supervisor in the organization, from the company president to the supervisor of accounts payable. Why start with management? F. James McDonald, president of General Motors Corporation, points out, "If management thinks people don't care, it's likely that people won't care. But, far more important, if people think that management doesn't care—then it's almost certain that no one else will, either." Every manager needs to be trained to understand the new company standards and the associated improvement techniques. This training should start at the top and wash away old bad habits from each level of management before it reaches the next level—the "waterfall effect."

4. *Employee participation.*   Only when the total management team is trained, involved, and participating in the improvement process are you ready to involve the employees. This is accomplished by the first-

line manager (supervisor) of each department forming a department "improvement team." As the leader of this team, the manager is responsible for training the team to use improvement techniques he or she has already learned. The key point to be made was explained by John R. Opel when he was president of the IBM Corporation: "Everyone in IBM has customers, either inside or outside the company, who use the output of his or her job; only if each person strives for and achieves defect-free work can we reach our objective of superior quality." The purpose of the improvement team is to define the department's output and implement a system that will continuously improve the output. To start the process, the team must work with the customers to be sure their needs are understood in the department and to determine how to measure the department's success in meeting those needs. Once customer needs are defined and measured, activities can begin to improve the department's performance.

5. *Individual involvement.*   As important as group activities are, we cannot forget the individual. We need to develop systems that will give all individuals a means whereby they can contribute, be measured, and be recognized for their personal contributions to improvement.

Frank Cary, past chairman of the board of the IBM Corporation, wrote, "Our reputation for quality is only as good as our last machine or our last customer call. As IBMers, none of us can be satisfied with a quality rating of 95 percent or 99 percent or anything less than 100 percent. We should expect all our products to be defect-free."

6. *System improvement teams (process control teams).*   Every repeatable activity is a process—including activities such as accounts payable and information services—which can be controlled using the same techniques that are used in a semiconductor process. The key is to flow-diagram the process, then design in measurements, controls, and feedback loops. As we will see, each process, even though it spans many individual departments and even different functional organizations, must have a single individual held accountable for the success and total operation of the process.

Besides solving process-related problems, this is the team that will plan and implement our "just-in-time" stocking system. Edward J. Kane, director of quality for the IBM Corporation, provides an example of how system improvement teams solve problems at IBM. He stated

> The billing process consists of 14 major cross-functional activities which are logically related but physically dispersed among 255 marketing branches and 25 regional offices, a similar number of field service locations, and several headquarters operations and manufacturing sites. The work is cross-functional and nonsequential within any function. It is tied together by a complex information system. Overall, 96 percent of the invoices are ac-

curate, but because of the high cost of adjusting those that are incorrect, 54 percent of the total resource was devoted to cost of quality. Some of that cost is for prevention and appraisal (98.5 percent of the invoices delivered to the customer are correct), but most all the errors can be attributed to failure of some kind. This is testimony to the need to prevent errors rather than fix them after the fact.

The system team consists of individual representatives from each area involved in the process. The team works across functional lines to ensure that the most effective operating system is in place and that an improvement in one part of the process does not have a negative effect on the total process.

7. *Supplier involvement activities.* In modern countries, few companies are immune from partial dependency on outsiders. No successful improvement process can ignore the contributions that could be made by suppliers.

8. *Systems assurance.* For years, we had independent groups focusing their attention on measuring and reporting quality in the manufacturing process. Organizations such as product assurance and quality assurance directed their resources toward finding problems and ensuring their correction; the result has been reactive management that neglected more important preventive activities and the need for excellence of output in the nonproduct areas. Quality assurance resources devoted to product problem solving should be redirected to system controls that help upgrade operations so problems do not occur. We need to treat the disease, not the symptoms, and in most cases the disease is located in the systems controlling the business.

9. *Short-range quality plans and a long-range quality strategy.* Each company needs to develop a long-range quality strategy. The company then needs to be sure that the total management team understands the strategy to the point that they can develop step-by-step short-range plans (1 to 3 years) to ensure that their groups' activities support the long-range strategy. These short-range plans should be included in the annual strategic operating plan, and each group should be measured throughout the year on how well they are meeting these commitments—the same as they are measured on costs, schedules, and expenditures. "Quality improvement is being applied to all areas of our business. Specific quality objectives and strategies must be included within each unit's 5-year business plan," explains F. James McDonald.

10. *Recognition system.* The improvement process is an attempt to change the way everyone thinks about errors. There are two ways we can reinforce these desired changes: Punish everyone who fails to do the job right every time, or reward individuals and groups when they meet a goal or make a significant contribution to the improvement pro-

cess. The better way is to recognize the employees (remember, managers are employees also) for their successes, while encouraging them to strive for ever-higher levels of achievement.

The improvement process is a way to stamp out errors in both the white- and blue-collar areas. Phil Crosby, one of the world's leading quality consultants, feels that both service and manufacturing companies can be looked at in much the same way. He puts it this way: "The waste in the service companies goes out in baskets and in manufacturing companies in barrels." James E. Preston concurs: "Even our creative groups now realize that the quality improvement process has a positive effect on creative output."

DOES THE PROCESS WORK?

Does the improvement process always work? When implemented properly, Yes. When it fails, it is usually because

- Management misused it.
- Management didn't participate in it.
- Management feels that the employee, not management, is the problem.
- Management is unwilling to make a long-term commitment.
- Management does not make it part of the business activity.

Does the improvement process work? Just ask Harry E. Williams, vice-president of operations for Stacoswitch of Costa Mesa, California. In 1981 his company started an improvement activity and by the end of 1984 they saw

- Poor-quality cost drop 44 percent.
- An 8 percent increase in direct unit output.
- A 27 percent increase in sales.
- Manufacturing scrap drop to almost zero.
- Shipment value increase 36 percent.
- A personnel reduction of 30 percent in eleven operations departments achieved without layoffs.
- Gross profits rise 124 percent.
- Accept rates improve in all areas. (In the fab shop, accept rates were raised from 75 percent to 96 percent and in the mold shop from 72 percent to 98 percent. Output went up by 17 percent, while direct labor costs were reduced by 50 percent.)
- Overtime reduced by 91 percent.

The city of Dallas saved $12.5 million through employee participation, enhanced communication, innovation, and action. IBM Boulder's Pride Process enhanced copier reliability and reduced magnetic-tape failure costs, resulting in a $1.8 million saving in 1 year.

Oliver C. Boileau, president of General Dynamics Corporation, offers another example: The company's Fort Worth division reduced manufacturing nonconformance costs by 58 percent—and saved $37 million over 4 years. In one of those years, the percentage of F16s delivered with zero defects more than doubled. Why? "Their pursuit of improving quality," says Boileau.

TEN FUNDAMENTAL REQUIREMENTS

Ten fundamental requirements make the improvement process successful. These ten essentials are

1. Acceptance of the customer as the most important part of the process
2. Management's long-term commitment to make the improvement process part of the management system
3. Belief that there is room to improve
4. Belief that preventing problems is better than reacting to them
5. Management focus, leadership, and participation
6. The performance standard of zero errors
7. Participation by all employees, as both groups and individuals
8. Improvement focus on the process, not the people
9. Belief that suppliers will work with you if they understand your needs
10. Recognition for success

When you put it all together, does it work? Well, James E. Olson made his position very clear during his October 1985 Fortune Forum address when he said, "One of the things we are learning is that it pays off handsomely to focus continually on quality improvement in every aspect of our business. And I'm here to offer testimony—if anyone needs it— that such an approach works."

3

Top-Management Action

INTRODUCTION

Today's executives know that the business systems they mastered in the 60s and 70s are no longer the world-beaters they used to be. They also realize that change has to start with and be supported by top management. Zhao Ziyang, Premier of The People's Republic of China, showed his leadership in this area when he stated, "Product quality represents a main indicator of the level of technology and administration of an enterprise or a country. To constantly improve quality and push economic development forward has been an issue calling for an immediate solution." He added, " 'Quality first' is our long-term strategic policy in our economic construction."

A journey around the world starts with that first step outside the door. We are about to take that first step toward the ultimate goal of error-free performance. Before you start on any significant trip, there are several things you normally take into consideration. If it is a place to which you have never been before, it is a good idea to buy some books, to read about the places you will see and the culture of the people you will encounter. But most of all, it requires that you make the commitment of time, effort, and money. All this should happen before you take the first step out the door. The same kinds of things must be considered before you decide to commit your company to the improvement process.

IMPROVEMENT NEEDS ANALYSIS

Company presidents have the ultimate responsibility for the success or failure of their companies. Stockholders invest in their management abilities and hold them solely accountable for the profit picture. Today, quality is a big part of that picture in many companies. Hewlett-Packard is one. Its president, John Young, puts the matter bluntly: "We decided to address cost and international competition by aiming at the quality issue."

Now is the time to decide whether to commit your company, its funds, its effort, and its time to improving its performance. To help you in making this important commitment, spend some thoughtful time answering all the questions in the following "improvement needs analysis."

		YES	NO
1.	Are you getting a larger share of the potential market each year?	____	____
2.	Are your scrap and rework costs less than 1 percent of your sales?	____	____
3.	Do you meet production schedules?	____	____
4.	Are you meeting cost targets?	____	____
5.	Are you using *only* parts that meet specifications?	____	____
6.	Is your direct absenteeism rate less than 3 percent and your indirect rate less than 2 percent?	____	____
7.	Is your annual rate of turnover less than 5 percent?	____	____
8.	Are you able to attract the best people to your company?	____	____
9.	Are you spending the correct amount of money on educating your employees when you consider what errors are costing the company?	____	____
10.	Do people in your company meet their commitments 90 percent of the time?	____	____
11.	Do you really understand your customers' expectations concerning your products or services?	____	____
12.	Would you like to improve the morale of your employees?	____	____
13.	Are your overhead costs growing faster than your profits?	____	____

	YES	NO
14. Do you think that the people in your company can do better work than they are doing?	___	___
15. Is your receiving inspection rejecting more than 1 percent of the parts that come into your company?	___	___
16. Is more than 5 percent of your direct work force engaged in inspecting product?	___	___
17. Is the overtime of your indirect work force more than 5 percent?	___	___
18. Do you feel that manufacturing costs and time could be reduced, but you don't know how to do it?	___	___
19. Are you getting hate mail (complaints) from your customers when you would like to be receiving love letters (commendations)?	___	___
20. Has your company's productivity growth rate increased at less than the inflation rate over the past 10 years?	___	___
21. Have your stock dividends increased at a rate that is less than the inflation rate over the past 5 years?	___	___
TOTALS	___	___

Questions 1 through 12 and 14 and 18 should all have been answered Yes. All other questions should have been answered No. Give yourself one point for every question that was answered correctly, and use the following guidelines to determine if you should implement the improvement process:

Number of correct answers	Status or recommendation
21–19	You have a good system; there is no need for special improvement; continue what you have been doing.
18–15	You should evaluate implementing the improvement process.
14–11	The improvement process would help your company.
10–0	Improvement must be a high-priority activity.

EXECUTIVE INPUTS

The success of the improvement process is highly dependent on the support of the top-management team. Thus, before deciding to make the improvement process part of the company's management culture, the president must solicit the input of key members of the management team and organized labor. The president should be careful to guide the discussion away from the performance of the particular group that the executive is responsible for and keep it directed at the total company. The executive should understand that the president is thinking about implementing an across-the-board improvement process that will provide better input for everyone, thereby making it easier for them to do their jobs more efficiently. If one executive feels exceptionally strongly that his or her group is already performing at peak efficiency, that may be the person who should chair the improvement steering council so that the rest of the company can benefit from his or her experience in organizing to do the job right every time.

In any case, quality is a top-management responsibility. As F. James McDonald, president of General Motors, put it, "You can't escape the simple fact that top management is ultimately responsible. He or she has to go home at night and look in the mirror and answer the question, 'Did what I've said and done today reinforce the quality ethic—or not?' That's the acid test."

POTENTIAL SAVINGS

One last step before the final commitment to implement the improvement process is to make an estimate of potential savings. This is probably best accomplished by looking at poor-quality cost data described in Chapter 4 in the section entitled "Measure Today's Needs and Progress." If your company doesn't have a poor-quality cost system, you can estimate that between 15 and 30 percent of your annual revenue is lost in poor-quality cost and an additional 30 percent of your white-collar cost is the result of errors or the cost of checking their output to ensure they are not delivering errors to the next person in the company. In many companies that have not implemented the improvement process, the cost of poor quality originally accounted for about 25 percent of the assets, 25 percent of the people, and 40 percent of the space and inventory. That's a big target, and many companies are going after it. IBM is one. John Akers, president of IBM, believes "Quality improvement will reduce quality costs by 50 percent over the coming years. For us, that translates into billions of dollars of added potential profit and quality leadership in our industry."

In addition to this cost saving, the improvement process will decrease absenteeism, improve productivity, and improve morale. Better output quality should also have an effect in capturing a larger share of the market.

The savings come from every area. Oliver C. Boileau, president of General Dynamics Corporation, observes, "The productivity and quality improvement process has really impacted the engineering design release system at our Convair division. The number of errors made on drawings released to the manufacturing line has decreased from 41 percent in 1981 to 11 percent currently [1985]."

To achieve these savings, it will cost the company about 1 percent of the product cost to develop and install the improvement process during the first year. After that initial investment, the maintenance cost for the program will be negligible.

COMPANY PRESIDENT PARTICIPATION

One more thing must be considered: the impact of the improvement process on the company president. If the improvement process is really going to work, it must have more than the president's support—it needs his or her active participation as well. The president must become actively involved in the process and have a detailed understanding of how it works. The president must personally measure its progress and recognize people that contribute or fail to contribute to the success of the process. Managers and employees may believe what the president says, but they often wait to see if actions support the words. F. James McDonald points out, "Achieving true quality maturity is totally the responsibility of top management in our company. Others may carry it out to one degree or another, but those at the top must be willing to go the whole route."

MANAGEMENT SURVEY

One very effective way to determine if the general management team sees a need to improve is through a management opinion survey. The design of the survey helps specify where the management team feels the company is and how much it should improve. Typical survey questions might be

	MIN.			AVG.			MAX.
1. How well do individuals cooperate?							
Cooperation is	1	2	3	4	5	6	7
Cooperation should be	1	2	3	4	5	6	7
Level of inportance	1	2	3	4	5	6	7
2. How well do departments cooperate?							
Cooperation is	1	2	3	4	5	6	7
Cooperation should be	1	2	3	4	5	6	7
Level of importance	1	2	3	4	5	6	7

3. How good is service within the company?

Service quality is	1	2	3	4	5	6	7
Service quality should be	1	2	3	4	5	6	7
Level of importance	1	2	3	4	5	6	7

4. How concerned is management about work quality?

Quality concern is	1	2	3	4	5	6	7
Quality concern should be	1	2	3	4	5	6	7
Level of importance	1	2	3	4	5	6	7

5. How concerned are employees about their work quality?

Quality concern is	1	2	3	4	5	6	7
Quality concern should be	1	2	3	4	5	6	7
Level of importance	1	2	3	4	5	6	7

6. How good is employee morale?

Morale is	1	2	3	4	5	6	7
Morale should be	1	2	3	4	5	6	7
Level of importance	1	2	3	4	5	6	7

Other issues you may want to probe include productivity, communications, and organization.

The value of the opinion survey depends on frank and honest responses. This is why responses must be kept confidential. An outside firm may be needed to combine and analyze the data. Survey analysis should look at two factors:

1. The real value of the "is" answers. Should anything be done?

2. The mathematical difference between the "is" and "should be" answers. Ideally, the sum of all the differences should be very close to zero.

A large company should survey only upper and middle management. They should provide sufficient data. A complete opinion survey of management and employees will be discussed later in this chapter.

THE IMPROVEMENT CZAR

Now that all the facts are in hand, the president of the company needs to make a decision. If that decision is to include the improvement process as part of the total management system, the first thing the president must do is to demonstrate commitment to this change in business strategy by appointing an "improvement czar." This person will be responsible for implementing the improvement process through all areas of the company.

The improvement czar should be a person with stature, respected by the entire management team and by all the employees. Preferably, the czar should be at least in a functional management position and probably *not* from the quality assurance function. The czar should be an individual who sets a good example and high standards, a person who believes that the company can do better. He or she must want to take a leadership role in an activity having a long-lasting impact on the company management system.

The job of improvement czar is not a permanent position. It will last for about 2 to 3 years, but by that time the improvement process will become part of the management system and the personality of the company.

PERFORMANCE STANDARD

Now the company president has to embark on a long-term process of continuous improvement. He or she needs to establish the standard of excellence that will be used to measure the company's performance. A standard of error-free performance is the only acceptable one.

John R. Opel, past president of the IBM Corporation, stated, "Quality is not the exclusive province of engineering, manufacturing or, for that matter, services, marketing, or administration. Quality is truly everyone's job. Each function, each individual in IBM must assume the responsibility for a defect-free operation."

We pay people to do the job correctly, not to make errors and create even more work for themselves and others. To err may be human, but to be paid for it is divine. Our business world has accepted errors as a way of life. We live with them, we plan for them, and we make excuses for them. They have become part of the personality of our business. Our employees quickly recognize our standards and create errors so that they will not disappoint us.

Frank Squires, a leading quality consultant, said in December of 1977

The questions most asked by management are, in order of frequency:

How many?	(quantity)
How much?	(cost)
How good?	(quality)

Management is not against quality. Quantity just has higher priority. Management's order of importance has been quantity, cost, and quality. They must change these priorities. For the U.S. to survive in the world market, management must put quality first.

Unfortunately Frank was right at the time he wrote this statement and in most companies around the world, nothing has changed. Top management has to set a single standard that puts quality ahead of schedule and cost. If the quality problem is solved, schedule and cost problems will also disappear.

QUALITY POLICY

The foundation for an improvement process is a statement of "quality policy" that clearly and concisely says what is expected of all employees, as well as the products or services that are delivered to the customers. This quality policy should be released over the president's signature. To delegate this action to a vice president or another executive detracts from the meaning and the priority it will have in the working environment.

The quality policy should be worded so that it applies to each employee activity, not just to the quality of the product or service provided by the company. It should also clearly state the quality performance standards for the company and should cover the total aspects of the quality system, not just the defective parts. That sounds like a big order, and it is. Nevertheless, a good quality policy must be short and easy to remember.

Let's take a look at a typical quality policy to see if it meets these requirements (see Figure 3.1).

JOHNSON PLASTICS, INC.

Quality Policy

WE WILL DELIVER ERROR-FREE COMPETITIVE PRODUCTS AND SERVICES ON TIME TO OUR CUSTOMERS THAT MEET OR EXCEED THEIR EXPECTATIONS.

Definitions

We = The company as a whole and each individual employee
Competitive = Provide the customer with more value for the investment than the competition does
Customer = The next person that receives our output, inside or outside of the company

Implementation

To implement this policy means that all employees will understand what their customers expect and that they will provide the customers with products or services that meet or exceed their expectations. All requirements must be continuously evaluated and upgraded to reflect changing customer expectations. All work will be performed to requirements.

Dr. John E. Johnson
President, Johnson Plastics, Inc.

Figure 3.1 A Model Quality Policy

1. *Is it concise?*
   Yes. The policy, definitions, and implementation statement are confined to one page.

2. *Does it apply to each employee?*
   Yes, each employee has some value added to the part of the operation being performed in his or her area. The policy clearly states that it applies to an individual's value-added activities.

3. *Does it set the performance standard?*
   Yes, it states that the company expects error-free output from each employee. It does not state that the company expects each employee to be infallible, but rather allows each employee the chance to detect errors and correct them before the output is delivered to the customers. Nevertheless, the ultimate aim would be for everyone to perform his or her assigned tasks correctly every time—not just deliver error-free products or services to their customers.

4. *Does it cover the total aspects of quality?*
   Yes. In yesteryear, when we spoke of quality, we talked about the quality of the shipped product. Today, there is a "big Q" to quality. There is a quality of schedule, of price, and of performance.

   a. *Quality of schedule.* We can provide the best-performing item in the world, but if we do not deliver it to our customer when it is needed, it is useless.

   b. *Quality of price.* What good is a product if your customer cannot afford to buy it? Included in the quality of price is the quality of worth. Even if your customers can afford to buy your product, they may feel that it is not worth the price because your competitors produce something that will peform the same function at a lower price.

   c. *Quality of output.* This includes both product and service. Today, with greater and greater portions of our resources being used in the service industry, less than one-third of the American labor force is involved in producing durable goods. Even then, a large portion of this third is supporting the manufacturing process people—activities such as accounting, personnel functions, maintenance, and management. A ratio of five support people to one production worker is common in high-technology areas.

5. *Was it released over the president's signature?*
   Yes.

When this policy is put in the hands of both management and employees, it will provide some guidance in implementing the improvement process.

If you don't have a quality policy for your company, now is the time to have the president release one. And if you do have one, take the time to review it to be sure that it meets the requirements described in this chapter.

COMPANY DIRECTIVES AND POLICIES

Upper management must take a leading role in drafting company directives related to quality and continuous improvement. Company direction on important matters should not be left to chance or quick interpretation by management or employees. Clear, concise, written direction should be provided by the president of the company. Every manager should be held accountable for compliance to all company directives and policies. For example, a "no layoff" policy should be prepared early in the improvement process. It might read as follows: "No one will be laid off because of a productivity or quality improvement. People whose jobs are eliminated will be retrained for an equivalent or more responsible job. This does not mean that it may not be necessary to lay off employees because of a business downturn."

Quality improvement may sometimes call for major policy changes. One example is the Hughes Aircraft Maverick Project. As a result of an Air Force audit and joint Hughes-Air Force disassembly inspection of a Maverick missile, the Air Force suspended acceptance of Maverick units. Hughes suspended all assembly operations in its plant of 7000 people a week later. It was not until 4 months passed that the first "built-in-quality" Maverick hardware was submitted for mandatory government inspection. Five things caused this problem (root causes of the poor quality):

1. Complacency because of a high success rate on delivered products
2. Emphasis on schedule
3. Detection-oriented management style and not enough prevention
4. Erosion of capacity (ineffective use of capital, aging equipment, tools, etc.)
5. Manufacturing system designed to sift defects out rather than build quality in

As a result of this analysis of causes, management made two fundamental policy statements:

1. People who perform the job must understand their work and assume responsibility for the quality of their product.

2. A mechanism must be established to monitor effectiveness of the performer and provide changes and tools for them to continually improve the quality of their work.

MANAGEMENT AND EMPLOYEE OPINION SURVEY

After the company has committed itself to the improvement process, a complete management-employee opinion survey can be conducted. The survey's purpose is to set the baseline for measurement and to help identify improvement opportunities. It also serves as a communication link between employees and first-line management to higher-level management. The opinion survey provides another means to help management develop sensitivity and awareness. Through awareness of the team's overall attitudes, management can anticipate problems before they occur and take action to prevent them from developing.

The opinion survey should be approached carefully, keeping in mind that it will be repeated a number of times to measure trends. The survey questions should cover eleven areas. They are

1. Overall satisfaction with the company
2. The job itself
3. Salary
4. Advancement opportunities
5. Management
6. Counseling and evaluation
7. Career development
8. Productivity and quality
9. Work environment
10. Handling of concerns
11. Company benefits

In addition, a section for write-in comments enables the employee to provide more detailed information and address concerns not covered.

Possible questions might be

1. Everything considered, how would you rate your overall satisfaction with the company?
    a. Completely dissatisfied
    b. Very dissatisfied
    c. Dissatisfied

    d. Neither satisfied nor dissatisfied
    e. Satisfied
    f. Very satisfied
    g. Completely satisfied

2. How do you like your job—the kind of work you do?
    a. Very poor
    b. Poor
    c. Average
    d. Good
    e. Very good

3. How would you respond to the statement: "My job makes good use of my skills and abilities"?
    a. Strongly disagree
    b. Disagree
    c. Neither agree nor disagree
    d. Agree
    e. Strongly agree

4. How would you rate your salary considering your duties and responsibilities?
    a. Very poor
    b. Poor
    c. Average
    d. Good
    e. Very good

5. How do you rate the job being done by your immediate manager?
    a. Very poor
    b. Poor
    c. Average
    d. Good
    e. Very good

6. How much trust and confidence do you have in your immediate manager?
    a. Very little or none
    b. A little
    c. Some
    d. Quite a bit
    e. A great deal

7. What seems to be management's biggest concern?
    a. Costs
    b. Schedules
    c. Quality

8. What seems to be management's least concern?
    a. Costs

b. Schedules
c. Quality

It is imperative that confidentiality and anonymity are maintained if survey results are to be meaningful. Care must be exercised when the survey form is being filled out, during the data-analysis cycle, and when results are reported to the management team. Special care should be taken in providing feedback to small units.

To help define problem areas, each manager should be provided with a report showing how his or her people responded. This report should compare the department to the company and to the total function.

Each manager should conduct a "feedback session" in which the results of the survey are presented to the employees. These sessions are important because

- The employees will be curious about the results in general and how the department compares to the rest of the company in particular.
- It provides management with an opportunity to discuss employee concerns.
- It provides an excellent way to receive ideas and suggestions.
- It shows that management is serious about the results.
- It allows the team to develop corrective action.

IBM, which has been conducting regular opinion surveys since the late 1950s, saw the following gains after implementing the improvement process:

- Job performance   22%
- General satisfaction   12
- Skill utilization   14
- Personal development   13
- Communication upward   18
- Communication downward   16
- Job content   10
- Job involvement   6
- Morale index   9

The improvement process cannot take credit for all the gains, but the rate of improvement *was* unusually high, indicating that the improvement process did have some effect.

FROM THE TOP

Improvement and change start with top management. They must clearly communicate to lower management and their employees the importance they place on quality. For example, in the April 1983 edition of *Think* magazine, John R. Opel had this to say about quality:

> Quality is essential. It is:
> - Key to competitiveness,
> - Key to our business goals, and
> - Not just another 'hot button.'
> - We have the will, the means, and what it takes.
> - We are continuously raising and beating targets.
> - Error-free performance is attainable.
> - The savings estimated are in the hundreds of millions of dollars.

This does not apply just to business, but also to government. President Ronald Reagan stated

> Historically, American craftsmen have shown great personal pride and interest in developing quality goods and services. Today, we must reinforce our pride of workmanship by renewing that commitment.
> Improving the quality of American goods and services depends upon each of us. Individual workers, business managers, labor leaders, and government officials must all work to promote a standard of excellence in the public and private sectors.

He also stated, "Consumers, by seeking quality and value, set the standards of acceptability for products and services by voting with their marketplace dollars, rewarding efficient producers of better quality products and performance."

4

The Improvement Steering Council

INTRODUCTION

A key element in the improvement process is a well-thought-out creative design that is supported with an ambitious but realistic implementation strategy. The group responsible for the design and its implementation is the improvement steering council.

FIRST EXECUTIVE MEETING

With the selection of an individual responsible for being the focal point for the improvement activities (the improvement czar), you are ready to begin the next activity, the formation of an improvement steering council. To start this phase of the process, the president should call top executives and union officials together to discuss the quality profile of the company and what action is to be taken. Such a meeting could go something like this: The president of Johnson Plastics, Inc., John E. Johnson, starts the meeting by saying "Ladies and gentlemen, I have asked you here because I am concerned about the quality of the products we are shipping to our customers and the quality of the services we provide to ourselves. I have talked to each of you about this individually, so I know that most of you share my concerns. I am sure that the very effective rumor mill has already informed you that I have asked Frank Parker to take a special assignment on my staff to implement an improvement process throughout the company—and that includes your sales organization, Mr. Easton."

Ray Easton, the vice president of sales and marketing for the company, has been jotting down some notes about the meeting he had just left to come to this one. Ray quickly looks up, closes his notebook, and says, "I am with you, John."

Johnson continues, "I suppose all of you have been waiting for the second shoe to fall, and here it is. We are good and I'm proud of the accomplishments we have made over the years. I believe that we have one of the best teams in our type or any other type of business, but— and that's a big but—we can be much better than we are. Our profits are high, our order backlog is good, and our sales price is in line with our competition, but it is costing us a lot to put out our products. We should be able to boost our profit by over 90 percent if we can stop making so many needless errors. At about half the meetings I hold, someone reports that things did not get done on schedule because something wasn't considered or because someone didn't get some needed information or someone provided the wrong data or the activity is taking longer than was originally estimated.

"Just 6 months ago, marketing estimated that the market demands for the next 12 months for our 920 units would be 10,000 units per month, plus or minus 2000 units. Today, we are producing 12,000 per month, working 15 percent overtime and double shifts, and we could sell 25,000 units per month if we had them."

Ray Easton quickly speaks up, saying, "That unit took off like a sky-rocket. No one could have predicted that the customer acceptance level would be that high."

John continues, "Ray, I'm not trying to pick on you. I could give similar examples of errors from every function in this room, and that includes me. Some of them have had long-term financial impact on the company, and others have been just minor inconveniences. The problem we have is that we are beginning to accept errors as the normal way of doing business. The management personality of our company has degraded to the point that it is passive in many cases when we should be irate. Most of us have developed two standards, one for our personal life where we expect everything to go right. For example, if your doctor treated you for pneumonia and you had appendicitis, you wouldn't stand for it. You would first tell him what you thought of his abilities and then you would call your lawyer. While at work, you reason that everyone makes errors, so you expect them and plan for them.

"Each of you should get mad when you see the waste, scrap, and rework around the company, just as you would if accounting left the first digit off your paycheck. We cannot accept any level of errors to be considered normal for this company.

"To start this new process off, I am setting a single performance standard for the company, a standard that I expect each employee will strive to meet. The performance standard for each employee is to do each assignment in a manner that will provide error-free output, not 95 percent or 98 percent or even 99.5 percent, but 100 percent error-free. Now I realize that 100 percent error-free performance is hard to attain, but the point is that we must continuously strive to do each assignment better today than we did yesterday and better tomorrow than we are doing today until we have reached error-free performance. It is not impossible—individuals, departments and, yes, even whole plants have accomplished it for minutes, hours, days, or weeks. Errors are caused by poor equipment, lack of attention, insufficient job-related knowledge, poor time standards, and improper attitude. It can be done. I read where Bill Weisz, chief operating officer for Motorola, Inc., reported, 'The Mount Pleasant, Iowa, operation has achieved more than 5 years of continuous 100 percent delivery to schedule month after month. More than 100,000 orders and 250,000 mobile radios have been shipped without a single miss of scheduled dates. Perfection has been achieved.' As I look back, we missed shipments three times in the last 2 months because of a quality problem in the design or at a supplier.

"In order to get the improvement process started, I am forming an improvement steering council, and I expect each of you to assign one individual from your organization to become an active member of this council. The improvement steering council will be chaired by Frank Parker.

"The threefold mission of the improvement steering council is to

1. Develop a company-wide strategy to implement the improvement process
2. Provide direction and guidance for the implementation
3. Adjust the process to meet changing business needs"

Mary Cross interrupts, saying, "That sounds like they are running the company. I don't think that we should delegate a job like that to our subordinates."

"I agree," says John. "But you note that I said they would develop a company-wide strategy that can be used to implement the improvement process. We will all be deeply involved, and that is the reason I am forming an executive improvement team. Each of you is a member of that team, along with your representative to the improvement steering council. The executive improvement team will meet every other week to review progress and ensure that the activities are being given proper priority." A big moan goes up all around the table.

Tom Weston, vice president of research and development engineering, asks, "John, that doesn't include me, does it? I can see why manufacturing needs this program, but it really does not apply to my organization."

"This isn't a program. It's the management style that will be used by every manager, and it's the performance standard that is acceptable for every area in the company. Your organization is no exception," says John. "But I bet if you ask Rich [Rich Favor, vice president of manufacturing], he would tell you that you released the 915 unit without considering how it could be built and then tried to redesign it while it was in production. Just take time to look at your engineering change budget. That's your cost of doing the job over and over and over again. I understand that you are averaging seven changes per print during the product's life cycle. I think that's too many, don't you?"

"Yes, but . . . ," replies Tom Weston.

"No buts about it," interrupts John. "We all have our crosses to bear. Yours is engineering changes. Rich's is scrap and rework. Production control causes us to miss shipments because parts are not shipped from our suppliers on time, and then when they do get here quality assurance rejects them. The next thing I hear is that we are using the part anyway because they are off-specs. Last month I was told that 35 percent of the lots we reject in receiving inspection are off-spec'ed and used. There has to be something wrong."

"John," Mary Cross speaks up, "this looks like a QA problem. Why don't we let Bob Duwright, our vice president of quality, take care of it and report back to us on what he is doing to solve it?"

"That's the attitude that got us into our present position," states John. "QA has problems and I expect them to solve the ones they cause and report to us on product-related problems that *we* missed, but what I'm talking about goes beyond the limits I have placed on quality assurance. This activity applies to everyone in the company. For every job we are doing, I want us to develop a system that prevents problems from occurring, not detect and report them after they have occurred. If the rest of us were doing the right job of managing the business, we could almost do away with quality assurance. Each manager should assure the quality of his or her area's output. We have too many quality assurance managers and too few quality managers."

John pauses for a moment. The room is quiet and so he continues: "I know that some of the things we will be doing over the next few months will be new and strange to some of you. I am not going to ask you to accept these new concepts without questioning them; likewise, I expect you not to reject them without giving them a fair chance to develop and mature in our environment. You are all good managers today; if you weren't, you wouldn't have the jobs you have. What I want from my management team is to go beyond good. I want us to be the very best. Now I expect full cooperation and support from each of you in this important assignment. I will hold the first meeting of the executive improvement team at this same time next week. I will expect each of you to attend, with your improvement steering committee representative. You should plan on your representative to the improvement steering committee spending at least 12 hours per week helping to develop the improvement process for our company for the next 90 days. The executive improvement team activity is a top-priority activity so if any of you cannot attend, I would like him or her to call me beforehand and explain what has higher priority. We have three driving factors in our business today. They are quality, cost, and schedule. In today's environment, quality must come first, for if we can correct our quality problems, schedule and cost will almost take care of themselves."

EXECUTIVE IMPROVEMENT TEAM

To move into the active phase of the process, the president of the company should notify all the top executives that they are to become active members of the executive improvement team that he will be chairing. The executive improvement team is responsible for reviewing and approving the improvement strategy (developed by the improvement steering council, as explained below) and implementing the approval activities in their own organizations. They will review the status of the improvement process and approve all major financial and/or manpower expenditures. Regular participation in this team expresses the importance attached to the improvement process by top management.

IMPROVEMENT STEERING COUNCIL

The improvement steering council is appointed by the top executives of the company to represent them in developing and implementing the improvement process. The improvement czar serves as the company president's representative to the council and will normally serve as its chairman.

The Mission of the Council

The mission of the improvement steering council is to design the improvement process, develop guidelines, establish educational modules, measure progress, and assist in implementation. The council ensures the process is being implemented effectively throughout the business.

The Makeup of the Council

All functions in the company must be represented on the improvement steering council since each function has interfaces within the organization that affect the productivity and quality of other areas. The council members should be people who lead in the implementation of new ideas, understand the need for improvement, are respected by the other members of the group, support the concept of error prevention, and get mad when they see wasted effort and material. The team members

- Represent their respective functions on the improvement steering council and must have the authority to commit that function to implement the improvement process developed by the council
- Serve as the focal points for the improvement process in their own functions
- Coordinate activities, communicate process development status to management, and measure progress

The improvement steering council must be large enough to represent each functional area but still small enough to be effective. The council will be a part-time assignment for all council members except its chairman, who will become deeply involved in all aspects of the improvement process.

If you have a union shop, it is highly desirable to have one or two union representatives as members of the improvement steering council so that the union is deeply involved in developing and implementing the improvement strategy. This will also allow the union to see the advantages that the improvement process has for the employees.

Off-Site Working Session

The first working meeting of the improvement steering council should be a 3-day session at which members become familiar with the improvement concept and can openly discuss the company's quality problems. It should be held off-site. This session is best led by an experienced improvement consultant. This initial 3-day session is very important because it will serve to strengthen the team's interfaces and their understanding of each other's problems. Figure 4.1 shows a typical agenda for the 3-day meeting.

Although not mandatory, it is preferable that the executive improvement team also attend this 3-day kickoff meeting because it will supply the key people with the knowledge they need to embark on the voyage they are about to undertake. They also can take part in developing the initial strategy. Finally, their participation will also impress on the members of the improvement steering council the importance of their assignment.

Following the initial session, the improvement steering council should meet frequently as a group and every other week with the executive improvement team. During this period, they will be developing the strategy that will be used to implement the improvement process in the company.

Following the implementation phase, the improvement steering council will meet as appropriate, based on individual situations. It is important

---

1. Opening—Company president
2. Why improve?—Selected company vice president
3. Competitive status—Company vice president of marketing
4. World trends in quality—Consultant
5. Review of the improvement process—Consultant
6. Force-field analysis on what prevents the company from being as good as it could be—Consultant
7. Evening assignments in work teams to develop action plans related to item 6—Three or four groups
8. Present and discuss group recommendations—Groups
9. Review improvement tools—Consultant
   a. Poor-quality cost
   b. Statistical tools
   c. Problem-solving methods
   d. White-collar improvement
   e. Process controls
10. During the evening, divide into small working groups to review a case study and establish a recommended plan
11. Present and discuss group recommendations—Groups
12. Presentation of a successful improvement process—Representative from another corporation
13. Develop an action plan for the next 3 months—Improvement steering council
14. Summary—Improvement czar
15. Closing—Company president

Figure 4.1 Typical agenda for a 3-day off-site meeting.

to recognize that although the improvement steering council is responsible for developing the overall company strategy, it is the individual department manager who is responsible for developing the detailed plan that will be used in each department to ensure systematic improvement using the recommended strategies as appropriate.

COUNCIL ACTIVITIES

In fulfilling its mission, the improvement steering council is responsible for the following activities. Each individual activity will be discussed in some detail in the sections that follow.

1. Define the seven basic improvement rules for excellence
2. Develop and help implement the company improvement strategy
3. Measure today's needs and progress
4. Develop and maintain the awareness program
5. Establish and maintain the improvement educational process
6. Assist management and employees in implementing the improvement process
7. Review each function's annual strategic improvement plan
8. Develop and implement recognition and award plans
9. Be the focal point for sharing success stories
10. Resolve system problems that adversely affect the improvement process
11. Establish and maintain an interface with other improvement activities, both in and out of the company
12. Develop and implement the just-in-time stock management system

Define the Seven Basic Improvement Rules for Excellence

Most people think that they understand quality and excellence, but very few people will agree on a common definition of either term. One of the very first things the improvement steering council must do is to define some of the basic improvement rules and concepts that the company will use as building blocks in its improvement process. The improvement steering council needs to develop and have the executive improvement team approve the following basic improvement rules:

1. What is the definition of quality?
2. What is the definition of excellence?
3. What is the ultimate objective?
4. What is the strategy to obtain excellence?

5. What methods will be used to obtain it?
6. Who is responsible?
7. What measurement is used?

The First Basic Rule.   Defines quality. Quality is a personal thing, and everyone defines it in his or her own way. Philip Crosby defines it as "conformance to requirements." Dr. W. Edwards Deming says that "quality control does not mean achieving perfection. It means the efficient production of the quality that the market expects." Dr. Joseph M. Juran defines quality as "fitness for use." Dr. Armand V. Feigenbaum calls quality "the total composite product and service characteristics of marketing, engineering, manufacturing, and maintenance through which the product and service in use will meet the expectations of the customer."

The American Society for Quality Control and the American National Standards Institute define quality as "the totality of features and characteristics of a product or service that bear on its ability to satisfy a given need." *Webster's Third New International Dictionary* defines it as "degree of excellence." I like to define it as "meeting or exceeding customer expectations at a cost that represents value to them."

When it comes right down to it, the word can mean just about anything our customer wants it to mean. However it is defined, customers around the world want more of it. In analyzing the yearly public-buying survey prepared by Yankelovich, Skelly and White, an opinion-research firm, there is a definite trend indicating the customer is willing to pay more for better quality. Kikkoman President Katsumi Mogi of Japan states, "You have to know what the consumer wants as well as what he needs, then you must satisfy him with quality."

The first place the steering council should look for guidance is in the company quality policy. Let's look at the sample quality policy described in Chapter 3:

> We will deliver error-free competitive products and services on time to our customers that meet or exceed their expectations.

This quality policy commits each employee to provide the customer with competitive quality products and/or services on schedule and includes not only the end product or service that is delivered outside the company but also the service or product provided to other employees within the company. Furthermore, since quality is everybody's job, the quality definition must encompass this total concept. Limiting it to the factory floor is a sure way to increase costs, reduce productivity, and, eventually, bring failure to your company.

Keeping this broader customer perspective in mind, one definition of quality might be: "Meeting or exceeding the customers' expectations, at a price they can afford, and when they need your product or service."

The Second Basic Rule.   Defines excellence. Starting from the definition of quality just described, we define excellence as "surpassing customer expectations at a price that represents value to them and delivering consistent performance without repair or excuses."

The Third Basic Rule.   Defines the ultimate objective of improvement. Companies around the world have adopted a very simple objective: elimination of errors (or error-free performance). Certainly, we need milestones along the way for encouragment and evidence of progress but our ultimate goal should always be error-free performance. It's a challenge that makes us better than we were and provides the incentive to be better than we are.

The term "errors" was selected instead of "defects" because errors apply to everyone—the factory worker, the repairman, the engineer, the manager. In today's environment, a major portion of our thrust for excellence must be directed at the support operations since they account for a major portion of our total expenditures. In most cases, the savings that can be made in these support areas far outweigh the gains that can be made in the manufacturing environment. The manufacturing activities have been measured and controlled for years, but the service areas have gone virtually untouched.

The Fourth Basic Rule.   Describes the strategy to obtain excellence. All improvement is made in small steps by correcting individual problems. Thus, the strategy might be to be better today than we were yesterday, and to be better tomorrow than we are today.

The Fifth Basic Rule.   Prescribes the method used to obtain excellence. In many companies that have adopted the improvement process, the method chosen is total involvement of all employees to obtain the balance between preventing problems from occurring and evaluating problems that do occur to correct them and prevent them from recurring. (In most companies, there is a need to spend much more effort in preventing problems so that less effort can be spent in correcting them.)

The Sixth Basic Rule.   Identifies the responsible parties. As we have seen, in the improvement process quality is truly everybody's responsibility. No individual, no department, no organization is immune. But when problems do occur, remember, fix the problem—not the blame.

The Seventh Basic Rule.   Tells what the measurement of improvement is. Improvement is measured by the reduced cost required to provide the customer with excellent products and services. Lee Iacocca said, "If you do the job right the first time, you get both quality and productivity." That results in improved quality and decreased cost.

Develop and Help Implement the Company Improvement Strategy

The next step is to develop and implement a strategy for the improvement process in your company, keeping in mind that the process must be thorough, yet versatile enough to allow it to be applied to all areas of the company.

The process recommended in this book is based on activities that have been proven effective in a number of successful companies. I know of no instance in which these activities, when implemented as described in this book, have not produced spectacular results. It is easiest to implement the improvement process in companies that already have a sophisticated management team and well-educated employees; normally, these companies want to improve an already healthy organizational climate and financial bottom line. The improvement process will have a greater effect, however, on companies that are having problems competing in today's marketplace. In both cases, the financial returns are tremendous.

Each company has its own needs. There are different needs within the individual division, location, plant, and even department. The process that is right for you has to be based upon your product or service, the personality of your company, its leaders, and your competitive position. In some cases more drastic action is required to bring about an extensive restructuring of the habit pattern within the organization. For example, it is obvious that much more drastic action was required to change the habit pattern for the American automotive industry in the early 1980s than is required today to change the habit pattern in the hotel industry. Why? The hotel industry has kept pace with the competition, and the automotive industry fell behind.

In a large company, an overall improvement process should be prepared by the improvement steering council with a few mandatory and many optional elements. At the group or divisional level, the improvement process should be more narrowly defined as it relates to the group needs. At the location level, the program becomes specific with set requirements for all functions. At the department level, it becomes a detailed process, utilizing all the pertinent elements available to meet the exact needs of the employees and their customers. In a large organization, an improvement steering council should be formed at every major location to customize the improvement process to the needs of that location.

The improvement steering council members must become thoroughly familiar with all the elements of the improvement process. They must understand how the elements can be used and what impact they will have on the company's operating system. This is necessary because the council members will be responsible for providing guidance in both program strategy and technical applications of the selected elements. This is a critical phase of the total process and requires an understanding of not only the improvement tools but also of the quality needs of the organization.

As soon as the improvement process elements have been selected by the improvement steering council and approved by the executive improvement team, the improvement steering council needs to prepare a time-line implementation plan. At this point, only major activities will be scheduled, but as the program develops it will be expanded to cover the detailed steps in its implementation.

Each major activity should also have a project file assigned to it that will capture details of how it was developed, technical references that were used, authorities that can be contacted for assistance, and results of any pilot programs conducted. This record will be invaluable if it is necessary to change members on the improvement steering council and will also provide the information necessary for individual managers to evaluate each element's impact on their department's activities. In larger corporations, this project file should be used as a basis for a technical report that defines a detailed, recommended procedure for implementing key elements of the improvement process.

Measure Today's Needs and Progress

The key to improvement is measuring the current excellence (quality) level and then establishing a process that will effectively raise that level. This means that quantified data must be available to evaluate the results of each activity implemented. Unfortunately, in most companies the only area that has good quantified performance data is manufacturing and customer service. Supplementing this data with special studies in high-cost areas of the business should provide the improvement steering council with information to start, but eventually excellence indicators (measurements) should be developed for every area of the business. Figure 4.2 provides typical excellence indicators by functional area. The expansion of excellence indicators can best be developed by the functional areas

1. MANUFACTURING
   a. Amount of scrap and rework
   b. Errors in labor claim cards
   c. Percentage of parts scrapped
   d. First-time yield

2. QUALITY ASSURANCE
   a. Percentage of lots rejected in error
   b. Number of engineering changes that should have been detected in design review
   c. Errors in reports
   d. Cycle time to get corrective action

3. ACCOUNTING
   a. Percentage of late payments
   b. Time to respond to customer requests for information
   c. Billing errors
   d. Incorrect accounting entries
   e. Payroll errors

4. INFORMATION SERVICES
   a. Errors per line of code
   b. Percent of reports out on schedule
   c. Number of rewrites
   d. Errors found after program accepted by customer
   e. Number of test-case runs for successful completion

5. PRODUCT ENGINEERING
   a. Number of engineering changes per document
   b. Number of errors found during design review
   c. Number of errors found in design-evaluation test

6. PURCHASING
   a. Premium freight cost
   b. Down-time because of parts shortages
   c. Number of parts off-spec'ed to keep line going
   d. Cycle time from start of purchase request until items in house
   e. Excess inventory

7. MARKETING
   a. Accuracy of forecast assumptions
   b. Number of incorrect order entries
   c. Overstocked field supplies
   d. Contract errors

Figure 4.2   Measures of excellence.

as the improvement process is being integrated into the departmental activities. The importance of measurement cannot be overemphasized. Measurement is the first step that leads to control and eventually to improvement. If you can't measure something, you can't understand it. If you can't understand it, you can't control it. If you can't control it, you can't improve it.

Poor-Quality Costs. All the excellence indicators must be pulled together in a single denominator that top management understands and relates to. This common denominator is dollars and is commonly called "quality cost," but the phrase "poor-quality cost" better defines what it is. Good quality saves you money; it doesn't cost you money. Philip B. Crosby, author of *Quality Is Free*, would be quick to tell you, "All too often, quality and excellence are perceived as goodness." Unfortunately, when goodness is forced to compete with the harsh reality of business, it cannot stand up to the pressure of schedule and cost. Using the poor-quality cost approach to presenting data as the measurement of quality takes it out of the abstract and puts it on a par with its competing business factors, cost and schedule.

Poor-quality cost is defined as all the cost incurred to prevent errors from happening (prevention cost) plus all the costs incurred when output is evaluated to ensure that it is good (appraisal cost) plus all the costs resulting from output that does not meet customer expectations (failure cost).

Poor-quality costs are divided into five major classifications:

1. *Prevention cost.*   The cost to prepare for an activity so that it can be performed error-free. Some examples of prevention costs are
   a. Training
   b. Process capability studies
   c. Vendor surveys (see Chapter 9)

2. *Appraisal cost.*   The cost related to evaluating an output to be sure it is error-free. The following are examples of appraisal cost:
   a. Inspection and test operations
   b. Maintenance of inspection and test equipment
   c. Cost to process and report inspection and test data
   d. Design reviews
   e. Expense account reviews

3. *Internal failure cost.*   The cost that occurs when errors are detected before the product or service is delivered to the external customer. The following are examples of internal failure cost:
   a. Scrap and rework
   b. Charges related to late payment of bills
   c. Inventory costs required because process yields fluctuate
   d. Engineering change costs to correct a design error
   e. Retyping letters
   f. Processing late time cards

4. *External failure cost.*   The cost incurred because an error was not detected before the product or service was delivered to the external customer. Examples of this type of cost are
   a. Warranty cost
   b. Field service personnel training cost
   c. Recall costs
   d. Product liability suits
   e. Complaint handling

5. *Measurement and test equipment.*   The cost of the capital equipment used to perform appraisal activities.

Although many manufacturing companies have fairly well-developed poor-quality cost systems for manufacturing operations, very few have a good measure of poor-quality cost related to the white-collar workers' activities. Numerous studies have been made in this area and they indicate that white-collar workers are spending 20 to 35 percent of their time either checking to ensure that their output is correct or redoing incorrect output. In trying to make a rough estimate of the poor-quality cost in your company, 20 percent of the white-collar effort would probably be conservative.

In addition to the costs that can be directly measured in the company's ledger, an indirect poor-quality cost is also incurred by your customers and by the company. An example of this type of indirect poor-quality cost is the cost to your customer of returning an item for repair while it is still under warranty. If a generator fails while under warranty, the company pays for the new part, while the customer pays in inconvenience, frustration, lost time, installation costs, and travel expenses. Furthermore, there is another indirect cost called "the silent dissatisfied customer." This is an individual who does not complain about being dissatisfied but will never again use your product or service. It has been estimated that in the service industry there are over twenty silent dissatisfied customers for every customer that complains.

To get an idea of how substantial these indirect poor-quality costs can be, look at the computer system at California's Bank of America. It has been estimated that a downtime of 24 hours on the main computer system will affect the bank's financial results. A downtime of 48 hours will affect the economy of California, and a 72-hour downtime will affect the GNP of the United States.

Poor-quality cost reporting is a strong tool to gain management attention and to pinpoint problem areas that will provide maximum financial return when the problems are defined and solved. A poor-quality cost report should be produced by the financial areas in most companies.

Finance provides legitimacy to the report that is never recognized if quality assurance prepares it.

The magnitude of poor-quality cost varies greatly from industry to industry, from new to established products, and depending upon which items are included in the report. Because of this, it is difficult to provide a good guideline related to what your company's poor-quality cost should be. It can vary from 40 to 2 percent of the sales price of a product or service. Anything over 8 percent of the sales price should be considered out of line. Most companies should be able to reduce it to less than 5 percent. Some companies have been able to reduce poor-quality cost to less than 2 percent of sales price through the proper application of improvement and quality principles.

Poor-quality cost can be looked at in two basic classifications: avoidable and unavoidable. We would not want to eliminate *some* poor-quality costs. Most of these are prevention costs, and there is and will always be a need to measure and report the excellence of the products and services we're providing. Because of this, they are considered *unavoidable* quality costs. On the other hand, no real benefits are gained from most appraisal failure costs, so you should strive to minimize them as you strive for error-free performance. Failure cost is money poured down the rat hole, so we should always strive to eliminate it. Failure and appraisal costs are classified as *avoidable* quality costs.

A typical commercial product would have its operating quality cost divided approximately as follows:

Prevention cost	10%
Appraisal cost	35
Internal failure cost	48
External failure cost	7
Total	100

If your company doesn't have a poor-quality cost system in place, make this the top-priority project for the improvement steering council. Your first step to make this happen is to bring together quality assurance people and the controller to discuss poor-quality cost, explaining the benefits of reporting poor-quality cost and obtaining their commitment to implement a poor-quality cost system immediately. (For more information about poor-quality cost, see *Poor-Quality Costs* by Dr. H. J. Harrington, published by the American Society for Quality Control.)

As the improvement process is implemented, poor-quality cost will be reduced. It is reasonable to expect poor-quality cost to be cut 30 percent over a 3-year period after the improvement process is fully implemented.

Develop and Maintain the Awareness Program

The awareness program should start slowly and build as the total improvement process is implemented. It shouldn't be a surge, with banners, posters, and pledge cards, that takes everyone by storm and then dies out. Excellence awareness is part of management's continuing responsibility, and the sharing of success stories is a major part of the awareness, recognition, and learning cycle.

Quality Policy.   The awareness program starts when the company president prepares the company quality policy and presents it to the company along with the new error-free performance standard. This is a very important breakthrough for the company; it sets the direction for the total process.

Management Awareness.   The next phase of the awareness program is directed at management. It is very important that every manager understand and effectively communicate the need to improve. One effective way of accomplishing this is to prepare a series of memos from key executives to provide the management team with data pertinent to how the company is performing in comparison with its competitors—and to explain why it is important for everyone to improve his or her output. A typical example is Douglas D. Danforth's statement, "It's vital for every employee to share a sense of urgency about quality performance. In particular, our management has to demonstrate and communicate that conviction. Then the dedication builds from there."

These memos should also be used to keep the management team informed about the status of the improvement process. People like to talk about things that they feel familiar with and understand. Keeping the management team knowledgeable on the subject ensures a continuing exchange of information to the employees.

The Second Partner, the Employee.   A company really has two partners— the stockholder and the employee. Although most companies provide their stockholders with insight into the business on a quarterly basis, the same companies ignore the other partner. Management has an obligation to keep both partners equally informed and involved. At least once every quarter, the president should report to the employees on the health of the business and the status of important business indicators. During this meeting, quality and improvement items should be highlighted. This is the ideal place to recognize individuals and groups that have made improvements in their output.

Employee Awareness.   When the improvement process reaches the total employee involvement stage, it is time to think about using the company's newsletter to highlight things that are happening in the improvement process and accomplishments related to it. It is also time to start the use of posters to emphasize the importance of improvement and quality. The purpose of this phase of the awareness process is to confirm to the employees that management is earnest about the improvement process and to keep it visible to all employees on a regular basis.

Establish and Maintain the Improvement Educational Process

There is a need for a new brand of education for all managers and employees—one that will show them that errors are avoidable. It must provide everyone with the tools to prevent errors from occurring, with proven techniques that will help determine the true failure cause (when problems do occur) and select a correction method to prevent the problem from recurring.

Thus, the educational system needs to change some of management's basic beliefs, as James E. Preston, president of Avon, explains: "The first thing we had to do was try to overcome four very large misconceptions. The first was that quality improvement is limited to products; second, that quality improvement is just another program; third, that the responsibility for quality resides in the quality department; and fourth, that the process should be implemented by the quality department."

Error-free performance does not start with any new statistical method or problem-solving technique. It starts with each person having a thorough understanding of the job and having the confidence that he or she can do it correctly. This means that management must provide

1. Detailed individual job descriptions
2. Relevant measurements
3. Tools that will allow the job to be performed error-free
4. Training about the job and understanding of its importance
5. Feedback from the customer about the adequacy of the output
6. Time to do the job correctly

The education program should envision prevention methods and techniques. It is always better and less expensive to prevent a problem than to correct one.

It is only when we have failed to perform at the error-free level that we need to understand the problem-solving techniques. Because we are starting the improvement process in an environment in which errors frequently occur, the training program also has to address error-correction techniques as well as prevention methods. This training should cover both the present management team and employees and also new employees and new managers. It must also address the special training needs of all functions.

The improvement steering council, with the assistance of the company's training department, should concentrate on developing common training packages that will have wide application. They should also serve as consultants for special application packages developed within the individual functions.

It is very important that a total database related to improvement training be maintained in a single area. This database should include a description of the materials covered and assessments of their effectiveness. This allows the total company to benefit from the experiences, both good and bad, related to the total improvement training package.

In today's environment, there are numerous programs, books, papers, tapes, movies, videotapes, and consultants available to help with your improvement training program. (Suggested Readings list just a few.) Because of the large amount of information available on the improvement process, the improvement steering council, along with the company's education department, needs to provide a screening function that evaluates the individual materials to ensure their compatibility with the habit patterns the company is trying to cultivate in its managers and employees. This is accomplished by assigning people to sample courses and to read new material and then report their impressions and recommendations to the improvement steering council. The improvement steering council should prepare a list of recommended reading and classes to support the improvement process.

Developing the training strategy for the company requires a great deal of work, resources, and understanding of the subject and the company—for even the gurus in quality do not agree on a correct approach. They all agree on the fundamentals and the need to improve, but they do not agree on the priorities and the means of applying the techniques. For example, Dr. W. E. Deming has become world-famous by preaching the importance of statistics, while Philip Crosby, another well-known consultant, refers to statistics as a recent fad in his book, *Quality Without Tears*.

The subject of training is discussed further in Chapters 5, 6, and 7 and in Appendix A.

Assist Management and Employees in Implementing the Improvement Process

The improvement steering council will develop a body of knowledge that serves as a valuable resource for the company. Every function has a member on the improvement steering council who is deeply involved with developing the basic concepts and implementing them in his or her function. This functional representative does not have to depend solely on his or her own expertise since the full resources of the improvement steering council are available. When a unique problem arises, the full knowledge of the improvement steering council can be focused on it to develop a solution.

Review Each Function's Annual Strategic Improvement Plan

Each function should prepare an annual strategic improvement plan that defines and commits that function to a set list of improvements for the coming year. The annual strategic improvement plan should define the resources required to support the process and the projected savings that will result from the initial expenditures. These plans then become part of the function's and company's annual operating plan (see Chapter 11).

The improvement steering council is responsible for reviewing each function's annual strategic improvement plan to ensure that it is complete, that it reflects the company's strategy, and that the requirements and estimated returns are reasonable. In some cases, there will be a need to implement pilot programs that have wide applications. These pilot programs will be used to evaluate implementation methods and potential paybacks from various techniques. During this planning cycle, pilot areas should be identified and resources set aside to support the activities. As a result of these reviews, the improvement steering council will list suggested changes to the individual function plans and submit a report of each function's plan to the controller and the company president.

Manage the Improvement Fund

The annual operating plan should set aside a special fund that can be utilized to implement productivity and quality improvement projects not defined during the budget cycle. This special fund will be administered by the improvement steering council, which will be held accountable for ensuring that there is a proper return on the investment. Targeted first-year return on investment should be an estimated three-to-one minimum. During the year, when an area has a new improvement project that will require funding, it will present the project to the improvement steering council, and, if approved, funds will be provided from the special improvement fund.

Develop and Implement Improvement Recognition and Awards Plans

Behavioral scientists have long contended that the best way to modify undesirable habits and to reinforce desirable ones is by rewarding individuals when the desirable patterns develop. Providing the proper recognition and rewards for improved employee performance plays an important part in reinforcing the new habit patterns you are trying to develop within your company.

The improvement steering council is responsible for reviewing the company's recognition and awards plans. These plans need to be customized to the individuals and the circumstances. The award does not have to be a large sum of money, although in some cases that may be appropriate. Often a thank you, a pat on the back, an article in the company paper, or a cake at a department meeting may be more appreciated and more appropriate. The important thing is that the individual or group of individuals know that management recognizes that they have accomplished something and that management appreciates their additional effort. (For additional detail, see Chapter 12.)

One of the biggest problems in more extensive use of award systems is the inability of management to recognize people that are doing a good job at preventing problems from occurring. The improvement steering council should endeavor to define ways that management can identify these individuals. They are the new breed that the company is looking for. Although management has the primary responsibility for recognition, the council should take the leadership role in ensuring that individuals and groups that successfully implement improvement activities are brought to management attention and receive appropriate recognition.

Be the Focal Point for Sharing Success Stories

The functional representatives should stay on top of the improvement activities going on within their areas. When a new concept, unique application of an old concept, or a significant idea is developed within a function, the representative should arrange for the group or individual to present it to the improvement steering council so that the entire company can benefit from it. The functional representative should also be alert to significant milestones within the function and arrange for them to be presented to the improvement steering council. This provides recognition for the group or individual, encourages all the members of the improvement steering council, and stimulates increased emphasis in all the functions.

Resolve System Problems that Adversely Affect the Improvement Process

The improvement steering council has a unique overview of the company's interaction that allows them to identify systems and interface-related problems. Because work flows across many functional lines, the total system is rarely evaluated, which results in suboptimization in some areas. Furthermore, systems are developed to accomplish a given task without considering its impact on the interfacing areas. Equally bad is a system that is needlessly complex, with too many reviews and approvals or needlessly complicated documents. The improvement steering council should search out these types of problems and vigorously attack them, getting commitments and target dates for their correction. Then, they should follow up to ensure that the problems are corrected, on schedule, and that the corrections are effective.

Establish and Maintain an Interface with Other Improvement Activities, Both in and out of the Company

The improvement steering council is the focal point for all improvement activities. In large corporations that have facilities at many locations, a number of local improvement steering councils will interface with the corporate council to share experiences, develop new ideas, and eliminate duplication. The corporate council should hold "share meetings" on a regular basis. One representative from each location's improvement steering council should attend each of the share meetings. Normally, this is the improvement czar.

As the process develops, people who make significant or unique contributions to the improvement process will also be invited to share their experiences. This meeting should move from location to location so that the share-meeting members can observe the improvement process in operation under different environments. This also allows the local executive improvement team to observe firsthand what activities are taking place at the other locations.

There is also a need for the improvement steering council to stay abreast of the improvement activities taking place outside the company. This can be accomplished in a number of ways.

The American Society for Quality Control (ASQC) was the first and is the largest society dedicated to quality improvement. They publish a number of journals and hold educational classes and conferences around the world. They also publish book reviews and sell most of the best publications on the subject of quality, reliability, and improvement. They can also help you to make direct contact with other companies that are involved in the improvement process so that you can exchange methods and concepts directly with them. Contrary to what the name may imply, they have hundreds of members located outside of America. They also have affiliation agreements with most major quality societies throughout the world to ensure that their members are informed about what is happening in every corner of the world. ASQC also maintains an extensive list of consultants.

Hitchcock Publishing publishes a trade magazine called *Quality* that is an excellent source of information on quality-related subjects. Many other societies throughout the United States have committees and/or divisions that specialize in quality related to their special discipline (e.g., The Institute of Electrical and Electronics Engineers and American Association of Electronic Manufacturers). Select one or more of these outside sources of information so that you can stay abreast of the latest developments outside of your company. Today, it is truly a worldwide market; all the world is your potential competition as well as your potential customer. To work and prosper in today's marketplace, we need to understand what is going on around us, for no one, no company, and no nation has the exclusive right to good ideas. You need to put yourself in a position in which you will learn about new improvement strategies and concepts so that you can assess their applicability to your own company's environment. There was a time when being good was all that it took; today, you need to be *the best* to succeed in business.

JUST-IN-TIME STOCK MANAGEMENT

Elimination of large stock reserves is part of the natural cycle of the improvement process. In the past, management has created a false sense of security by setting aside large quantities of component and work-in-process assemblies to make up for shabby products provided by suppliers with inadequate production systems. But in truth, this false sense of security increased cost, raised taxes, and created longer cycle times and larger manufacturing plants that were only partly productive. Stock rooms, staging areas, storage areas, and drop areas crowded the productive portion of the company into small corners. Large groups of part movers, expediters, and crib attendants searched frantically through mounds of parts trying to find the ones required yesterday, for until they found those, they couldn't locate the ones needed today. Expensive, complex, first-in/first-out stocking systems were developed and installed to ensure stock rotation, but even that didn't work. Good parts were destroyed in the unpacking-counting-repacking-storage cycle that was repeated time after time.

Many disciples of the just-in-time production plan liken it to a river flowing over a bed of boulders. With large stock reserves, the boulders (quality problems) are deeply submerged and the boat (production) floats over the boulders without damage. Because there is no major interruption in production, the quality problems are never solved, as they are never seen. These disciples claim that by lowering the water level, the boulders are exposed and must be removed before the boat can progress down the river. In theory and in practice this idea will work, but the costs are ridiculously high. Every time a boulder appears the boat is stopped, and even worse, a boulder just below the water level can rip out the bottom of the boat. The theory is right but the sequence is wrong. First the boulders must be removed, then the water level lowered.

The improvement steering council needs to develop a strategy and coordinate implementation for the company's just-in-time system. The manufacturing engineering department needs to be involved to design tooling to minimize setup time. Industrial engineering needs to be an active participant in laying out the manufacturing flow so that products come directly from the receiving dock to the production area and back to the shipping dock. Preparations should be made for the time when improvement process activities start having a positive impact on the suppliers and the company quality levels so that reserve storage areas can be eliminated or at least drastically cut back.

Going from a just-in-case stocking plan to a just-in-time plan should improve your company's performance in many ways. Joe Burger, manufacturing manager for Tektronix, Inc., Portable Instrument Division, knows what just-in-time did for them. He has said about it, "After 1 year inventories dropped 75 percent, floor space was cut from 15,000 to 7000 square feet, work in progress was reduced 50 percent, cycle time cut from 30–40 days to 12 days, and customer delivery time cut from 14–15 weeks to 2 weeks."

This concept, as straighforward and simple as it sounds, is not easily grasped by most American managers because of their dependence on reserve stock. Eliminating these just-in-case stocks can be traumatic for them. They argue, "It can't be done. What will happen if just one vendor goes on strike or just one bad lot of parts reaches the back door?" These are legitimate concerns when you consider the way business was done in the past. It is also the reason surplus stocking levels cannot be reduced until the rest of the improvement process is fully implemented and effective.

5

Management Participation

INTRODUCTION

The most important requirement to make the improvement process part of your management system is to have your full management team participating in the process. This must take place before the nonmanagement employees become involved in the process. And I really mean *participate*. I don't mean that management should be aware of the process or just supportive of the process. Management must be totally dedicated and be an active participant in the improvement process before and after it is presented to the employees. If the process is to work, management must set the standards. Yes, quality is everyone's responsibility, but quality must be led by management if the results are to be long-lasting and meaningful.

THE MANAGER'S ROLE IN THE IMPROVEMENT PROCESS

Managers are individuals who get work done through other people. Their success should not be measured by what they do but by what they can inspire others to do. Managers who treat employees as they are will keep them as they are; but managers who treat them as they could be will cause them to grow and become more than they would have been. As managers we need to let employees know we believe they can do better. We must expect them to do better and help them set goals that stretch and exercise their abilities.

One of the primary responsibilities of every manager is the quality of output from his or her area of responsibility. It is not the quality assurance function's responsibility; the most sophisticated quality assurance function does not have the ability to produce one good product. Management wouldn't go to the controller to ask why a department was over budget and what is being done about it; they'd go to the department manager. Nor would management go to production control when a manufacturing department doesn't meet the shipping schedule. Why is it, then, that management goes to quality assurance to find out why a quality problem occurs and what is going to be done about it?

There is really no such thing as a quality problem; there are workmanship problems, design problems, accounting problems, and the like. There can only be problems with the output of an individual, a group, or a system. Quality is a measure of the usefulness of output. This is true at the department level and at all other levels of management, right up to the president of the company. Management at every level must accept the responsibility and accountability for the output from their own areas.

Setting the Standard

Each manager is also responsible for setting the standards for quality and setting the example for the employees. Each manager must become personally involved and an active participant in the improvement process. James E. Preston, president of Avon, discussing the improvement process, put it this way: "The manager's role is to set an example; to educate; to organize, support, and encourage the quality-improvement teams; and to participate generally in quality-improvement efforts." Managers can speak with honest conviction about the importance of quality and the need to improve, but their actions broadcast a completely different message. First-line managers and their employees want to do a quality job, but frequently they receive conflicting messages from upper and middle management. During three-quarters of the month, management talks about the need for quality, but during the last quarter of the month, the only important thing is meeting the ship schedule. Management's actions count, not management's words. No one is fooled when a department produces 100 parts per hour for 18 days in the month and for the last 3 days of the month produces 200 parts per hour. Something has to be compromised and normally that something is the quality of the product. Employees and subordinate managers will adjust to the quality standards set in the last 3 days of the month and make them standards for the entire next month. Management must place as much or more emphasis on quality as on cost and schedule because when the quality problems are solved, many cost and schedule problems are also corrected. What is the chief reason for missing schedule? A line-down situation, caused by a poor process or by rejected supplier parts. What is the chief reason for cost overruns? Scrap and rework costs. Solve your quality problems and many of your cost and schedule problems will also go away.

Now, step back and take a look at your calendar. Are you spending as much time controlling the quality of your department's output as you are investing in cost and schedules? If not, you should adjust your priorities. If you don't have time for quality and don't value it enough to be interested in it, how can you expect your employees to? This applies to every level of management, as well as to the employees. Plant managers hold production status meetings in which quality, schedules, and costs are reviewed. Normally, schedules are addressed first, then cost and then quality—if there is time. Time after time, a problem with schedules uses up more than its share of the meeting; as a result, quality is not discussed. If quality is really the most important factor, it should be first on every agenda. The order of a meeting agenda is a telltale sign that shows what management is most concerned about.

Employees' Measure of Management

If those in management are going to set the improvement standards, they need to understand how their employees measure them and strive to improve in these areas.

Managers at all levels have employees they are responsible for and to. No matter where you are in management, someone is evaluating your performance to determine if you really mean what you're saying about quality. If you are going to set a standard of error-free output for them, you'd better try even harder than they do to produce error-free work yourself. Errors will occur, but they must not be accepted as the normal way of doing business. You need to get angry when you see the waste that errors cause. You need to be unhappy with the way things are and expect things to get better. You need to communicate, in words and deeds, that good enough is *not* good enough, that we can be better, and will be better, that our ultimate goal is to do it right *every* time.

James Preston, when discussing the problems he had with some of the management team, said, "Their focus had always been on meeting efficiency requirements and quotas. Their crisis-ridden tight schedule discouraged prevention procedures. Many viewed quality and productivity improvement as just another program that would disappear if it was quietly ignored! They also rejected the idea that it could be applied successfully beyond the manufacturing environment."

The Waterfall Effect

The change in quality attitude must start at the top, with the company's top executives and, like a waterfall, wash each level of management clean of its old, bad habits before it touches the next lower level of management or employees. The improvement process must be embraced by each level of management. F. James McDonald, General Motors president, said, "We believe that the whole top management team must be aboard. Even the most inspiring leader can't hope to reach the organization without total commitment from everyone at the top." Middle management makes the difference between success and failure. All too often, the man at the top tries to implement something at the employee level without convincing middle management that there is a need. Although these programs may work for a while, the fad is soon replaced with something else, with the middle manager saying, "I won't fight it. I'll just let it run its course and soon the old man will have another hot button to push."

In trying to improve quality, many companies make this big mistake. They jump on the bandwagon of the day—quality circles, work teams, or whatever—and get it started throughout the plant but it never becomes as really effective as it should. There are two reasons for the failures. First, because first- and second-level managers are not convinced that the time their employees spend away from the job is going to benefit management. They aren't convinced that the payback to them personally is going to offset the cost. The second reason is that the few major problems that account for 85 percent of the total poor-quality costs require management action. Until the major problems have been addressed by management, they serve as a frustration base that detracts from the overall effectiveness of the departmental teams.

The improvement process truly starts with management, and its success is directly proportional to the degree that management participates in the process. This is so because management is responsible for so many of the key factors:

1. Allocation of resources
2. Establishing the organizational structure

3. Selecting the leaders
4. Setting policies
5. Setting performance standards
6. Making job assignments and preparing job descriptions
7. Establishing operating procedures
8. Setting priorities
9. Measuring and rewarding performance
10. Selecting and training employees

Removing Roadblocks

It is by exercising these responsibilities that management removes the roadblocks that keep employees from performing the job correctly every time. Management must provide the following things to allow employees to do their jobs well:

1. Adequate time to perform the job in a superior fashion
2. Appropriate tools and training tools
3. Managers who can explain why it is important to do the job correctly every time, recognize good performance, and remove roadblocks
4. Managers who encourage and recognize improvement

A manager's primary jobs are to understand the activities he or she is accountable for and to know the employees well enough to identify the real roadblocks.

The best way to identify roadblocks is for management to actually do the job. When one plant went on strike and managers ran the production line, they gained a whole new understanding of the line problems. As soon as the strike was over, high priorities were placed on acquiring new equipment, providing better tools, and streamlining work practices. Management started to listen to the employees' problems, rather than treat them as excuses.

For some managers there is no such thing as a problem. They see only opportunities to contribute to the success of the company. Managers must be trained to take advantage of these opportunities, and if they cannot be trained, they should be replaced.

THE IMPROVEMENT STAIRWAY

The three levels of knowledge in the improvement process are called the "improvement stairway" (see Figure 5.1). The first step is to make the management team aware of the need to improve, what the new standards are, who is responsible, and what the improvement process

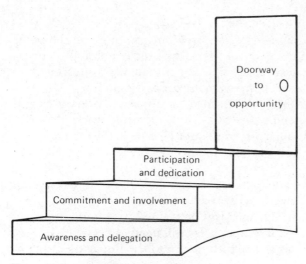

Figure 5.1 **The improvement stairway.**

is. Managers who reach the first step are aware of the need for quality improvement but are usually too quick to delegate authority to someone else—often quality assurance.

The next step is to obtain management commitment to support for the process. This means they are convinced that improvement is necessary and that they are willing to invest some of their resources.

This is still not good enough. Managers cannot just be "aware" or even just "supportive" of the improvement process. Habit patterns are only changed when management stands on the top step and actively participates in the improvement process.

INTRODUCTORY MANAGEMENT MEETING

It is now time for the company president to bring the management team together and review the improvement process and their involvement in it. This meeting is designed to put all managers on the first step of the improvement attitude stairway. Certain points should be made during this meeting.

1. Make everyone understand that the performance standard is "error-free."

2. Announce that the company is going to prevent problems from occurring rather than react to them.

3. Review the seven basic rules for excellence (Chapter 4).

4. Review poor-quality costs for the company.

5. Point out that 85 percent of the problems can only be solved by management and make it clear that the president is holding management, not quality assurance, responsible for the quality of output.

6. Review the company's improvement process plan.

7. Point out that the improvement process applies to every area and every department in the company, not just to manufacturing.

8. Explain that this is not a program but a change in the management system that will become part of the company's personality and the management style.

9. Point out that for the process to succeed, it needs more than management support; it needs active participation.

10. Tell them that each manager will be trained to use the improvement tools and that the first-line managers will need to become efficient enough at using these tools to teach their use to the department members.

11. Explain that at the present time the process is management-oriented but that it will be expanded to cover all employees as soon as the management team understands the process and becomes personally dedicated to it.

12. Introduce the improvement steering committee and the improvement czar to the management team.

PARTICIPATIVE MANAGEMENT

Managers realize success is more dependent upon their employees than on their own efforts. Participative management is a style of management that actively seeks employee inputs, allowing the employee to contribute to improving work-related issues.

Participative management does not mean copying the Japanese. Frank Cary, when he was IBM's chairman of the board, wrote in the November 1981 issue of *Think* magazine: "Wholesale imitation of the Japanese won't travel well, but we can and should emulate their success in making people productive and bringing out the best that's in them."

A number of currently popular programs are built upon this concept. They include quality circles, work teams, process control teams, improvement teams, task groups, and semiautonomous work teams. This concept has been very effective in many companies, but in other companies it has failed miserably. The difference is the way management implemented the process.

The challenge to the manager in a participative management environment is to learn how to manage groups effectively so that eventually the group itself, without the manager, can identify and make business decisions related to its activities. At that level, responsibility and involvement are maximized.

James Harbour, a well-known consultant to the automobile industry, stated: "The Japanese don't manufacture a car with any better technology than we do, but they are stomping us into the ground because of absolutely superior management." Participation must be a managed process. It will not occur by itself, nor can it be forced into the system.

John Young, president of Hewlett-Packard, talking about what makes teams succeed, noted that responsibility and involvement are keys. "Successful quality teams were fully integrated into their group's business strategy. They weren't just viewed as ancillary employee development exercises. Instead, they were considered as vehicles to pursue major strategic objectives."

One word of caution about getting employees involved. When you ask employees what they think is wrong, they tell you. First-line managers are going to be deluged with problems and ideas. This pressure on the first-line managers is passed on up the organization, and if the total system is not prepared, it can come apart. Never ask an employee for a suggestion or an opinion unless you are ready to use it or to explain why you can't.

What Makes It Work?

If participative management is to work effectively

   1. Managers must be willing to share some powers and responsibilities.
   2. Managers must trust employees.
   3. Problem solving and prevention training is paramount.
   4. Work must be viewed as a cooperative effort between management and employees. Workers must accept majority decisions, and management must have the courage to reject suggested solutions that are not beneficial to the company.
   5. Management must be willing to accept a system that decentralizes decision making. We like to be able to point at a single individual who made the decision. With participative management, this is impossible. Upper management must resist the tendency to hold the department manager responsible for any decision that is made by the group. We need to get out of the finger-pointing mode of operation and on to something that is more productive.
   6. Management must believe that everyone has good ideas and that combining individual ideas will produce the best possible solution.

7. Management must be willing to implement employees' suggestions when feasible.

8. Management must provide an environment conducive to developing employee loyalty.

9. Management must recognize the group's accomplishments.

10. Organized labor must become an active partner in developing the participative system.

11. Managers must accept participative management as a long-term effort and not expect immediate results. Westinghouse estimated it would take 2 years for any significant results and 10 years before the full benefits of participative management would be realized.

Benefits to the Business

If participative management is effectively implemented, the following benefits will be realized by the company:

1. Quality and productivity, both inside and outside the company, will be greatly improved.

2. The business will be developed and improved.

3. Communication, both upward and downward, will improve.

4. Employee morale will improve as a stronger management-employee relationship develops.

5. Problems will be solved that would otherwise never get high enough priority to get attention.

6. The employees will help things run smoothly as the goals of the informal leader of the department and those of the formal leader and of the company become aligned.

Benefits to the Employees

As much as the company stands to gain from participative management, employees have even more to gain:

1. All employees find opportunities to grow.

2. The employees get the feeling they are part of the action and are making things happen.

3. Employees gain increased job satisfaction as monotony is eliminated and job stature improved.

4. Individuals are given new training and provided with opportunities to demonstrate their abilities, and new doors for recognition and promotion are opened.

5. Job security is enhanced because the profitability of the company is improved.

6. Employee intellectual stature is heightened.

Management Roadblocks

Given all these advantages, why have we been so slow to implement a participative management system?

When a company's leaders decide to implement participative management, they anticipate that the employees and the unions will be the roadblocks. The truth of the matter is that the employees take to it like ducks take to water, but the first-line and middle managers are the ones who don't want to get their feet wet. Lockheed in Sunnyvale, California, was one of the first companies in the United States to put quality circles into operation, but the program collapsed when its main mover, W. S. Rieker, left to become a consultant in 1976. Why weren't the circles continued? Because first-line and middle managers were not convinced that the results were worth the expenditure, and they saw little benefit to themselves in continuing the program.

First-line and middle managers resist participative management because they're not familiar with it, and they feel uncomfortable facing the uncertainty. They have, over the years, developed a management style that is uniquely theirs. It's one that works for them. It is natural and not put on. To change at this point in their careers is perceived as high-risk activity. They admit that participative management is good for the employee and good for the company, but they don't view it as being beneficial to themselves. In fact, they see it as a threat, taking away some of their authority. A survey of first-line managers, conducted by M. S. Janice Klein, an assistant professor at Harvard Business School, reported that "nearly three-quarters (72 percent) of the first-line managers surveyed viewed employee involvement as being good for the company, and more than half (60 percent) felt it was good for the employees, but less than one-third (31 percent) viewed it as being good for themselves."

In most companies, participative management processes have been dictated down to management from the top and very carefully sold to the employees. The first-line managers have been told that the company was changing to a participative management system and if they could not adjust they would have to find someplace else to work. As a result, they have implemented the program half-heartedly. This attitude is quickly recognized by employees, who begin to wonder if they are not being "used" by management.

Klein's survey indicates that a high level of concern is shared by most first-line and middle managers, regardless of their age, leadership style, or background. Their concerns usually can be divided into the following categories:

1. Loss of job security
2. Loss of authority
3. Increased workload
4. Loss of responsibility and measurements
5. Erosion of one-on-one relationship between the manager and employee
6. Loss of power
7. Doubt about upper-management commitment
8. Fear of failure

The fear and concern about the loss of power, prestige, and control must be dealt with in a very serious manner. Over the years, middle and first-line managers developed and refined the techniques required to survive and prosper in a hierarchical organization. It is unrealistic to expect them to discard this successful experience to try some new fad without devoting a great deal of time to help them develop a new set of management skills.

Before participative management is introduced, a plan must be carefully developed and implemented to train and prepare the total management team to change management style. Then participative management should be practiced within the management ranks before it is used at the employee level.

Organized Labor

History has led American management to believe that organized labor wants nothing to do with the participative management system. That was some time ago, however. Today things are changing. At first there was a fear that cooperation between organized labor and management would erode labor's position at the bargaining table. Experience has proven this not to be true. Both sides can play two roles—a role of cooperation and team spirit when solving problems and a role of fierce competitors when bargaining for benefits and wage increases. Old suspicions die slowly, and organized labor is proceeding cautiously in their support of a participative management system.

As Glenn Watts of Communication Workers of America points out, cooperation with management may seem a high-risk activity for unions but is essential if both parties are to survive in the long run. He said, "The only real risk is if the union does not participate." How do the union members feel about participation? They are for it. Labor leaders who support the program find themselves in a stronger political position than ever before. Based on comments made by United Auto Workers leaders, officers who campaign with a quality-of-work-life theme are almost sure of winning elections.

Organized labor should be involved early in the planning cycle and take an active role in defining how the participative management system will work. This is necessary because the success of the program rests in labor's hands.

How to Make Participative Management Work for You

The following actions can be taken to minimize the problems that occur when the participative management process is implemented:

1. *Training.* All managers need the same tools that will be used by subordinates in the problem-solving and decision-making processes. They need to become familiar with group dynamics. In short, they need to understand the process before the process will work for them.

2. *Job definition.* All managers of managers or supervisors must define what is expected of their subordinates in the participative management environment and how they will be measured. Then, this information needs to be clearly presented to their subordinates and they must agree with it. Each manager's job description should be rewritten to reflect participative management.

3. *Modified reward and penalty systems.* Management cannot reward the group and punish the manager. In the participative management process, it may take a longer time to identify poor managers, but this disadvantage is offset because fewer errors are made. On the other hand, it highlights the good manager, since he no longer needs to be the major technical leader of the department. Top management must make a very careful review of the company's reward and punishment systems to ensure that they reflect management's new roles and then modify the systems to enforce desirable behavior patterns.

4. *Early involvement.* It is important to involve all levels of management in the design and implementation of the participative management process. Although it may not be practical to have all the first-line managers participate in designing the participative management process for your company, it is essential to have at least a representative group review the proposed design and help with the implementation.

5. *Peer networks.* The best way to convince managers that something is good for them is for them to be told by peers that it worked for them. Establishing peer networks that encourage peer managers to get together to review and interchange ideas about participative management and

the improvement process is an effective way to convince managers of the benefits they will receive.

6. *Visits to other plants.*   The textbook is good at presenting theory, but nothing beats seeing the theory put to use under real manufacturing conditions. A visit to another company or another plant within your company—one that has effectively implemented participative management—will do more in 1 day to convince the skeptics than will a week-long class.

7. *Role models.*   The best way for higher-level managers to convince subordinates that they believe in the participative management process is to become participative managers themselves.

8. *Enhance decision making and authority.*   As work-related decision making is shifted to the employees, middle managers must transfer some of their decision making to the first-level managers to strengthen their prestige. It follows that the same delegation of decision making needs to be followed all the way up through the management process.

The key to implementing a successful participative management process is to convince the first-line and middle managers that it will be beneficial to them, for they are the ones that make it work—the employees do the work. Although the employee is the hub of the process, management is the axle that makes it turn. Without management's personal commitment to the process and quick response to the employees' suggestions, the process will quickly come to a halt. Passive support from management is not enough and in the long run will undermine the process.

A word of caution. Don't confuse participation with permissiveness. Even in a participative management system, managers must assert their authority. The workers must realize management will not approve implementation of any solution that does not improve quality, productivity, and/or costs.

MANAGEMENT EDUCATION

Quality education for all levels of management and employees is critical to the success of every company today. Just as a manager needs financial training to meet his area's financial goals, he also needs quality training to meet the quality goals. When discussing Avon's quality training and improvement process, the operations manager in personnel said, "It really made us refocus our attention as to what the requirements are and what we want to get out of a job. Requirements are the same as expectations—so we can more clearly define what our expectations are to our employees." The goals of the quality education program should be to

- Develop an understanding of the fundamentals of quality
- Create awareness and perspective of the national and international quality issues as they apply to any company's growth strategy
- Provide tools to help management build and use quality systems as a major lever to achieve business objectives
- Influence management to integrate quality as a primary company goal in the decision-making process

The education process must present a realistic picture of where you are and what can be done to improve your quality posture. It should contain real case studies that directly apply to the audience's job. For example, you would not want to use a manufacturing case study when the audience is made up of financial and sales people. It should be obvious that a quality education program must consist of two parts. First, establishing the quality personality for the company and, second, teaching the quality science that is needed to implement and support that personality. The educational cycle should be

1. *Awareness.*   Establish that the audience needs to improve the quality of their activities.

2. *Quality truths.*   As long as quality is a nebulous thing without bounds, it can never be measured. Motherhood-type terms get everyone's support, but few people's action. No one is against quality. Everyone supports quality, but you will never get real improvement until it's quantified in terms that your audience understands and that will be used to measure their progress.

3. *Attitude change.*   The first two steps set the stage for an attitude change in the attendees. Now is the time to present the audience with data that will help them make their personal decisions. A good way of accomplishing this is through the use of successful case studies. These will provide the needed stimuli to change attitudes, either by willingness to accept a new challenge or through fear that if they don't accept the challenge, someone else will, leaving them out in the cold.

4. *Quality science.*   Provide the audience with the specific tools and methodology they need to know and use to implement an improvement process.

5. *Implementation.*   Now, as the attendees return to their working environment, they need to integrate their quality training into their daily work activities. The students are now well-prepared and have the confidence to accept this new challenge since they have the knowledge that if they run into problems of implementation, they can discuss their

problems with the improvement steering councils and get competent advice and support.

The quality educational process must be directed at the audience and customized to their needs and interests. To accomplish this, it should be divided into three levels:

1. Quality education for third-level managers and above
2. Quality education for second-level managers
3. Quality education for first-level managers and supervisors

Quality Education for Third Level and Above (Upper Management)

The higher you go in the company, the more you must understand the relationships between interfacing functions. Because of this need, the quality education program for upper management is developed along a common theme. It could be called "executive improvement focus." There should be mixed disciplines in the same class so that a broad company view is presented and discussed. The class should present a body of quality-oriented concepts, tools, and management techniques that will develop awareness and skills to manage the company's improvement objectives. It also should provide an understanding of the improvement activities in the interfacing functions. Figure 5.2 shows a content for a typical course at this level.

The course material can be presented in a number of ways, depending on the personality of the company. Some companies prefer to hold a number of 1- or 2-day classes every week, while other companies hold a 1-week, full-time class to cover everything at one time. It is often preferable to have an initial 2-day class located off the company grounds, far enough away that although the participants can drive to the class, they cannot easily return to work to do a few important things at the end of the class day. The participants should live, breathe, and feel quality during their 2 days and 2 nights at the class, without outside interruptions and distractions. The evening interchange and discussion related to the company's improvement strategy is an important part of the educational cycle, and its results can be as valuable as the classroom sessions. The class could start the night before with a social dinner, followed by a force-field analysis session directed at developing a list of bottlenecks that prevent the company from being as good as it could be.

As a follow-up to the first class, a number of 2-hour classes can provide the details related to the process. How many hours should be devoted to quality education for managers? The answer varies, depending on the sophistication of each company. Table 5.1 shows the time devoted

1. Quality awareness
   a. Fundamentals of quality
   b. Worldwide quality challenge
   c. Quality's impact on productivity
   d. White-collar and blue-collar quality
   e. Moving from a reactive to a preventive style of management
2. Assessment of the company's quality status
   a. Company long-range quality goals
   b. Customer performance
   c. Review of competition
   d. Company quality direction
   e. Company quality assurance role
3. Life-cycle poor-quality costs
4. Manager's role in improvement
   a. Behavioral and personality change
   b. Defining customer expectations
   c. Measuring quality performance
   d. Setting quality goals
   e. Establishing an error-free performance standard
   f. Department activity analysis
5. Overview of improvement processes
   a. Manufacturing
   b. Marketing
   c. Service
   d. Finance
   e. Administration
   f. Product and development engineering
6. Quality tools (for more detail, see Appendix A)
   a. Systems controls (basic statistical applications)
      $\overline{X}$ and R charts
      Median charts
      P charts—percentage nonconforming
      NP charts—number nonconforming
      c charts
   b. Data collection and analysis
      Histograms
      Run charts
      Pareto diagrams
      Fishbone diagrams
      Scatter diagrams
      Pie charts
      Stratification
      Frequency distributions
      Sampling
      Process capability analysis
   c. Experimental design

Figure 5.2   Executive improvement focus.

(Continued)

Figure 5.2 *(Continued)*

7. Participative management
   a. Types of team involvement
   Department improvement teams
   Quality circles
   System improvement teams
   Task forces
8. System control (business process)
9. Going from just-in-case to just-in-time stock management
10. How to manage the improvement process
11. Improvement success stories

to each subject at a typical top-level management class on quality conducted by the Japanese Union of Scientists and Engineers (JUSE). This class is followed up by frequent refresher courses.

Quality Education for Second-Level Management (Middle Management)

The second-level quality education process should be separated from the higher-level process because the second-level managers have a unique role to play since they are responsible for training the first-line managers. This means they need to have the very best understanding of how to use the quality tools, participative management, and the improvement process. A unique program should be developed for the second-level managers in each function. Normally disciplines are not mixed in the same introductory class. The format of the introductory class can be

TABLE 5.1 Quality Training Course of Japanese Top Management

Topic	Hours
Role of Top Management	1.5
Statistical Methods	3.5
Quality Control Management	3.5
Quality Control in Manufacturing	3.5
Quality Control in Purchasing and Sales	3.5
Quality Assurance	3.5
New Product Development	2.0
Quality Control in Japan and the World	3.5
Group Discussion	3.0
Report on Group Discussion	3.0
Total	30.5

similar to that of the executive class, but it should emphasize the detailed use of problem-solving methods, process control techniques, participative management, changing from a reactive management style to a preventive style, and the use of error-free performance standards. It should include a number of case studies and role-playing exercises. One output that should be generated from this class is a documented quality education plan for first-line managers that the second-level manager is responsible for implementing. You will find that you have a very different level of interest and participation in some managers when you start the class by telling them that they are responsible for developing and conducting the quality education program for their first-line managers.

A form similar to the one shown in Figure 5.3 should be filled out by the attendees at the beginning of the introductory class. At the end of the class, each question should be reviewed and discussed. This procedure shows the students how their beliefs changed as a result of the introductory class. Figure 5.4 provides the correct answer to each question and the reasons behind it.

Quality Education for First-Level Management (Supervisor)

It is the first-level manager who has the biggest impact on the individual employee's morale, attitude, work habits, and quality standards. The first-level manager is the one who portrays the ultimate company personality to the employee. Therefore, it is essential that the first-line manager have a complete understanding of the company's quality principles, its performance standards, and how to effectively implement the improvement process. Upper management can only set the stage and prepare the backdrops, the first-line manager directs the actors.

The basic educational process for the first-line manager is developed by the second-level manager, but many elements of that training have already been developed during the second-level and executive training processes. Often, the first-level manager's educational process will exactly parallel the second-level process. The important thing is that the second-level managers develop a process that is customized to the needs of the managers that report to them, keeping in mind that the first-line managers have the ultimate responsibility for communicating the improvement process to the employees. The educational process should contain short sessions to review such items as participative management, problem-solving methods, statistical tools, and department activity analysis. The program must emphasize that it is the employee doing the job every day who has the most to contribute to defining problems and correcting them.

Please complete the following questions based on your present knowledge. This questionnaire will not be collected; it is intended to provide you with an assessment of how your views coincide with the improvement process.

1. Quality assurance is responsible for the quality of the product and/or services provided by the company. _____ True _____ False
2. Everyone makes errors, so the standard should take this into consideration. _____ True _____ False
3. It is better to get the work out on time with some errors in it than to be late with a perfect output. _____ True _____ False
4. The employees are the cause of most of the errors and mistakes. _____ True _____ False
5. Management must motivate the workers to do a good job. _____ True _____ False
6. Lack of knowledge and attention cause most errors. _____ True _____ False
7. Quality is conformance to requirements. _____ True _____ False
8. In our plant, quality comes before cost. _____ True _____ False
9. Quality comes before schedule. _____ True _____ False
10. In our plant, we have a poor-quality cost reporting system. _____ True _____ False
11. The best measure of overall improvement is reduced error levels. _____ True _____ False
12. The quality of the output from my area can be measured. _____ True _____ False
13. The best management system is an error-prevention system. _____ True _____ False
14. The improvement process is a program to motivate the employees and management to make fewer errors. _____ True _____ False
15. Participative management will benefit the first-line manager. _____ True _____ False
16. What percentage of your area's time is lost due to poor quality and/or checking to ensure that output is good? _____%

Figure 5.3 Improvement concepts questionnaire.

Quality Education for All Levels

Each introductory session of the quality educational process should be hosted by the highest-possible-level manager and kicked off by a videotape from the president.

All classes should provide the attendees with written material that can be later reviewed. In addition, upon completion of the introductory educational process, the attendees should receive a framed diploma, plaque, or some other small recognition item that can be displayed in their offices. This provides recognition to the individual and also publicizes management participation in the improvement process.

The educational program must be well-balanced. Many companies have put all their eggs in one improvement basket such as quality circles, participative management, or statistical quality control. Taking a single-minded approach to improvement limits the potential improvements that can be made and unnecessarily handcuffs the management team. Even Dr. W. Edwards Deming, who today is one of the world's leading disciples of statistical quality control, has stated, "Anyone who supposes that quality, productivity, and competitive position can be achieved by massive immediate use of control charts and other statistical techniques by hourly workers will doom his own career and carry his company along with him." Clark Mozer, production manager for Hewlett-Packard, has said, "The usefulness of statistical methods was secondary to the commitment to improvement, clear designation of responsibility, good data gathering, and customer feedback." Statistical methods are an important improvement tool but only one of the many tools available to us. Success stems from knowledgeably applying a combination of the available tools to the needs of each individual condition. Improvement does not result from one major change; it occurs as a result of permanently correcting many small problems and changing the company's system so that the problems do not repeat themselves.

Quality education must be an ongoing process to keep each manager up to the state-of-the-art. Training programs are also needed for new managers and for managers that are promoted to higher levels of responsibility.

MANAGEMENT IMPROVEMENT TEAMS

Between 70 and 85 percent of all errors can only be corrected by management. How can you expect an operator to make good parts with equipment that is poorly maintained? How can you expect a maid to make up a hotel room correctly when she hasn't been trained and doesn't know what is expected of her?

With the quality education process, we have started to move the management team up the quality attitude stairway. We have made them aware of their quality problems and the amount of waste that is going on around them, and hope we have their support in correcting the problems. Now is the time to get them involved and to make them active participants in the improvement process. Each manager will become a

Figure 5.4 Answers for improvement concepts questionnaire.

1. Quality assurance is responsible for the quality of the product and/or services provided by the company.   FALSE

   Although the chief operating officer has ultimate accountability for the delivered product and services, the responsibility for quality has been delegated to the individual performing the task. Quality assurance's job is to measure the degree of conformance of output and report this to management and those who can take action to correct the problems.

2. Everyone makes errors, so the standard should take this into consideration.   FALSE

   The company's standard should be error-free performance. A standard of 1, 2, or 3 percent errors will produce 1, 2, or 3 percent errors. Does that mean that every job can be done error-free? No. In many cases, the process that has been provided to the employee is incapable of producing error-free work. These cases must be identified and corrected by management.

3. It is better to get the work out on time with some errors in it than to be late with a perfect output.   FALSE

   It is always better to do the job right every time than to do it a second time later in the process—even on Friday.

4. The employees are the cause of most errors and mistakes.   FALSE

   Only 15 percent of the problems in most companies can be attributed to the employees. The other 85 percent are directly related to management.

5. Management must motivate the workers to do a good job.   FALSE

   Most workers come to work on their first day motivated and enthusiastic. Management's job is to keep from demotivating them.

6. Lack of knowledge and attention cause most errors.   TRUE

   Most problems boil down to these two main sources.

7. Quality is conformance to requirements.   FALSE

   Quality is meeting customers' expectations at a price they can afford and having it there when they need it. Requirements take the form of specifications, procedures, and other documentation that may or may not truly reflect the expectations of today's customers. Many critical problems occur because employees believe that the specifications reflect what the customer wants and do not challenge them. Many companies have gone out of business making products and providing services that meet every specification and documented requirement but do not conform to the customers' expectations. Conformance to requirements is not enough.

8. In our plant, quality comes before cost.   TRUE

   In the long run, you will have the best-priced product if first priority is placed on quality. The best way to improve productivity and reduce cost is through elimination of waste. Not only will you produce more products at less cost, but your customers will be willing to pay more for your products because they can rely on them.

9. In our plant, quality comes before schedule.   TRUE

It always takes more time, effort, and money to do the job over than it would have taken to do the job right the first time.

10. In our plant, we have a poor-quality cost reporting system.   TRUE

If they are not in use they should be. Often, surprisingly few people know about the poor-quality cost system and how to use it effectively. This educational process should provide them with the information needed to use this concept.

11. The best measure of overall improvement is reduced error levels.
                                                                 FALSE

Error levels are good indicators, but the real measure of improvement is reduced poor-quality cost.

12. The quality of the output from my area can be measured.   TRUE

The output of every department and every person in the department can be measured. Measurement in manufacturing is commonplace, but white-collar and support areas can and should be measured. To measure an activity, define what the value-added content of the job is and then measure how effectively that content is being added.

13. The best management system is an error-prevention system.   TRUE

Return on prevention can be as high as 500 to 1. The most important change in any company takes place when management stops reacting to problems and starts preventing them.

14. The improvement process is a program to motivate the employees and management to make fewer errors.   FALSE

The improvement process is not a motivational tool; it is a new company personality. Programs tend to last for 1, 2, or even 3 years and then fade away, but the improvement process is designed to become part of the management system and to have a permanent effect on every decision made in the company.

15. Participative management will benefit the first-line manager.   TRUE

Allowing the employees to make more decisions about their work and to accept more responsibility for it will free the first-line manager to do more meaningful jobs and to accept additional responsibilities that have an impact on the company's larger goals.

16. What percentage of your area's time is lost due to poor quality and/or checking to ensure that output is good?   2 TO 40 PERCENT

There is no one right answer. Your poor-quality cost will vary based on product line, product sophistication, and management style. Commonly, the cost of poor quality accounts for 20 to 30 percent of the effort expended in white-collar and service departments that have not implemented an effective improvement process. In the manufacturing environment, a poor-quality cost of 30 to 40 percent of value added is not uncommon. Whatever your poor-quality cost is, the improvement process should help to reduce it.

member of one improvement team and a leader of another improvement team. First-line managers will not become team leaders until their own employees become involved in the improvement process.

The improvement network starts with the executive improvement team, then each vice president forms an improvement team with the functional managers that report directly to him or her. The functional managers then chair improvement teams that consist of the second-level managers that report to them, and so on.

The improvement teams meet on a regularly scheduled basis, weekly at first, but after a while meetings can be cut back to once a month. Minutes should be published from all meetings.

The purposes of the management improvement teams for each area are to

1. Define appropriate, management-agreed-to department missions
2. Develop ways of measuring the quality of output
3. Define the improvement educational needs
4. Solve problems that cannot be solved at a lower level
5. Develop short- and long-range improvement strategies and tactics
6. Develop ways to move from a reactive management style to a preventive style
7. Identify individuals who should be rewarded for their improvement activities and their abilities to prevent problems from occurring
8. Provide two-way communication up and down the management ladder
9. Share experiences related to the improvement process
10. Evaluate interrelated systems to improve their effectiveness

Of all the activities listed, the one that seems to be the most difficult for nonproduction areas is how to measure the output from the area. Many managers will claim that there is no way to measure the quality of a manager's output, but if that is true, how would you know who to promote and who to fire? The quality of every job, every individual, and every department is measurable. It may mean that new systems must be developed to provide the required data, but all activities can and should be measured.

James Preston stated, "Even our creative groups now realize that the quality improvement process has a positive effect on creative output. By spending more time 'up front' and asking probing questions necessary to establish mutually agreed upon design requirements, they can eliminate the need for going back to the drawing board because of misunderstandings."

When you realize that 85 percent of the errors that occur within a company can only be corrected by management, it is easy to see that these management improvement teams will have some very full agendas.

TWO TYPES OF PROBLEMS

Management must handle two types of problems: Problems of today and problems of tomorrow. Too often, managers get involved in today's problems (firefighting) and don't have time to prevent the same problems from rearing their ugly heads tomorrow. They are letting the business manage them rather than managing the business. Management as a whole spends far too much time fighting today's fires and too little time preventing tomorrow's fires from occurring. The only way to produce error-free output is by preventing problems from occurring rather than correcting them after a failure.

CUSTOMER CONTACT

At General Motors, management provided the employees who worked on the Fiero assembly line with the opportunity to call customers who had purchased Fieros to find out how they liked them and if they were having any problems. The employees volunteered to call on their own time and the company paid for the calls. The employees reported the information they gathered to management and the other workers. This close customer contact had a positive effect on both the customers and the employees. It also provided rapid feedback that identified some major problems.

Top management must keep in close contact with customers and understand their desires. Management must understand that customer desires are continuously changing and that the product or service that was outstanding yesterday just meets requirements today and will probably be inadequate tomorrow. A well-designed customer survey at least once a year, and preferably every 6 months, can supply much of the needed information related to changing customer desires. Another effective approach to understanding customers is to assign each vice president to a major customer, making him or her responsible for understanding the customer and reacting to any complaint the customer has. This is a good way of keeping key executives close to the most important part of the process, the customer, and at the same time providing major customers with the feeling that their business is valuable.

JOB DESCRIPTIONS AND EMPLOYEE TRAINING

All too often, we bring people into the work environment after the time that they were really needed. As a result, we are forced to put them right to work without the proper training, justifying it in our own minds by saying that any level of output is better than no output. Nothing could be farther from the truth. What we have done is to take highly motivated new employees and break their enthusiasm the very first day by placing them in an unfamiliar situation with inadequate information to succeed. Far too many companies spend millions of dollars on trying to motivate their workers when they really don't need to. No one hires a worker that isn't motivated; in today's job market, there are many people who will accept the job enthusiastically. When a worker reports to work on the first day, you don't need a motivation program. What you need is a change in the management system so that your managers don't demotivate the employee. One sure way to demotivate the employee is to place him or her in a situation that causes uneasiness about what is required to accomplish the assigned tasks and uncertainty about what management expects. Although obviously true of the employee just walking in off the street, it is equally true of the employee who has been with the company for 25 years and is given a new assignment. It makes no difference. Too often employees are placed in new assignments where they are untrained, unmotivated, unsure of themselves, and undereducated. Management has the responsibility to prepare the employee for the job so that the activity and the expectations are truly understood. Without the required preparation, management is taking away from the employee the right to perform the assigned task in a superior fashion. I am just waiting for the first human rights suit levied against a company because of an unfair training practice.

At Walt Disney World, all employees (the street sweeper, the dishwasher, the ticket taker—everyone) start their employment with a 3-day training school at Disney University. Management trains their 14,000-plus "cast" (not employees) to provide friendly service to their "guests" (not customers). Disney requires "people who fulfill an expectation of wholesomeness, always smiling, always warm, forever positive in their approach."

One of the fundamental parts of the improvement process is to develop job descriptions for every position. This activity must be supported with a training plan that will totally familiarize the employees or managers with their new assignments. The training process should also have some method of evaluating the trainee's ability to meet the requirements of the job. This provides a two-way protection: It protects the employee from inadequate training and long-term frustration, and it protects the company from an onslaught of errors.

Management should review each job description for accuracy and completeness. The job description should also state how the employee is to be measured in each job. Many large companies use general job descriptions for pay purposes. In most cases, these are not adequate to truly define the exact job that is being performed. In these cases, the employee's manager has the responsibility for generating a specific description that will serve as the basis for a work contract between the manager and the employee.

The employee must be totally familiar with and thoroughly understand the job description. Training requirements should not be left up to the discretion of the manager, allowing the training process to be easily modified because of the pressures of the day. Minimum training requirements for every job must be well-documented, and each manager should be required to keep records that prove to an audit function and upper management that the required training has been properly conducted. In addition, upper management should not place first-line managers in the undesirable position in which they must make the trade-off between training and output.

SELF-ASSESSMENT

No one is in a better position to know if the job is being done correctly than the employee who is doing it. The next person who is best prepared to evaluate an area's output is not quality assurance, but the department manager. We normally think of the department managers as working so closely with the employees that they always know what is going on, so without any research they can provide an accurate assessment of the department's quality level. The truth of the matter is that often the manager becomes part of the problem. What the manager needs is a systematic and objective way of assessing the department's activities, allowing undesirable situations to be corrected before they become problems. One way of accomplishing this is for the first-line manager to conduct a quarterly self-assessment.

Department Self-Assessment Checklist

The first-line manager has the primary responsibility of ensuring that all the department's activities are managed in accordance with the company's practices, procedures, and good business judgment. Each first-line manager must understand the company control documents, the intent behind each of them, and how to implement them. Each manager must also periodically review with all employees the control aspects of their jobs and ensure that they clearly understand them. The control aspects of each job should be part of the training package for that job, and the first-line manager should conduct systematic audits to ensure that employees are in compliance with these requirements.

A self-assessment checklist can be used to evaluate how effectively the department is adhering to control requirements and to identify requirements that are needlessly complex, restrictive, time-consuming, burdensome, or demotivating.

The self-assessment checklist should identify key control items related to the department's activity. It should specify how the item can be evaluated, the size of the sample that will be audited, and what constitutes acceptable performance. The first-line manager's draft of the self-assessment checklist should be submitted to the second-level manager to be sure it is comprehensive and that the performance standards are reasonable. Items that might be found on an accounting department manager's self-assessment checklist can be found in Figure 5.5.

Self-Assessment Procedure

Each first-line manager should personally conduct a self-assessment at least once every 3 months. Adequate data should be maintained to ensure that an audit can verify that the self-assessment was conducted. All items that fail the self-assessment performance standard must have corrective actions planned for them.

When the self-assessment form and corrective action plans have been completed, the first-line manager should meet with the second-level manager to review the self-assessment. The second-level manager will verify that the assessment was conducted, that the results are valid, that problems are classified correctly, and that the corrective action plans are adequate, and then sign off on the form.

The second-level manager will summarize, on a quarterly basis, all the unsatisfactory items in the area and present the action plans at a functional-level improvement team meeting. Each significant problem and action plan will then be presented at a vice president's improvement team meeting by the appropriate functional manager.

It is very important that the self-assessment system be presented to the first-line managers as a tool to help them identify problems and develop plans to correct them, not as an axe to be held over the manager's head. Each first-line manager should also be told that failure to record the true findings of the self-assessment could lead to dismissal from the company. The self-assessment system helps to develop and maintain an

Figure 5.5   Sample self-assessment checklist.

	TARGET
PASS FAIL	DATE

1. Review twelve travel expense accounts that have already been processed by the department to ensure they are filled out correctly and the calculations are accurate.

   PERFORMANCE STANDARD: One error is marginal if another error has not been recorded in the last three audits. Unacceptable performance is two errors.

   ASSESSMENT DATA: Numbers of the travel expense accounts checked

1 _____	5 _____	9 _____
2 _____	6 _____	10 _____
3 _____	7 _____	11 _____
4 _____	8 _____	12 _____

   Number of errors: _____

2. Check eight employees in the department to see what jobs they are performing. Ask them if they thought their training was adequate. Check the training log to verify that each person was trained for the job actually being performed.

   PERFORMANCE STANDARD: Zero errors is acceptable. One error is marginal if no errors were recorded in the previous three assessments. Two errors is unsatisfactory.

   ASSESSMENT DATA: Names of employees evaluated

1 _____	5 _____
2 _____	6 _____
3 _____	7 _____
4 _____	8 _____

   Number of jobs evaluated: _____
   Number of employees not trained for the jobs they were doing: _____
   Number of employees not satisfied with training or not trained: _____
   Number of errors in records: _____

3. Security
   (a) Check your records to see if a security awareness meeting has been held in the last six months. Record the date of the last meeting.
   (b) Check 5 combination locks to be sure they have been changed in the last 12 months.

(Continued)

Figure 5.5 (*Continued*)

> (c) After working hours, check 8 office cubi-
> cles to be sure the desks and files are locked
> and that no confidential material has been
> left out.
>
> Performance Standard: Zero errors is accept-
> able. One error in the last four assessments just
> meets requirements. Two errors in the last four
> assessments is unsatisfactory.
>
> ASSESSMENT DATA:
> (a) Date of the last meeting: _____
> (b) Numbers of the 5 combination locks that
> were checked, and dates the locks were
> changed.
> 1 _____
> 2 _____
> 3 _____
> 4 _____
> 5 _____
> Numbers of the cubicles that were audited.
> 1 _____   5 _____
> 2 _____   6 _____
> 3 _____   7 _____
> 4 _____   8 _____

effective preventive system of management controls. It brings the exceptions to the attention of management, where the problems can be
resolved, allowing company procedures to be modified as business and
customer needs change.

No auditor can do a more effective job of assessing an area's operation
than its immediate manager. No one knows more about its people, its
customers, its strengths, its weaknesses, its pressures, and its compromises than the manager directly responsible for the area.

STAYING WITH IT

The most difficult part of the process is during the early phase, when
management is spending a lot of time, effort, and money but seeing
little or no results. As William J. Weisz, president of Motorola, said,
"There was a lot of frustration and concern by managers that with all
this effort going on, they really were not yet able to measure the definitive
results. Then we crossed that hurdle and began to definitely measure
substantive improvement. It was like a snowball. The enthusiasm is higher
today than it was in the beginning."

6

Team
Participation

INTRODUCTION

The old dictatorial methods of management had their place in history. They were effective at the turn of the century, when during the start of the era mass production hand tools gave way to large relatively sophisticated equipment. The main part of the labor force was uneducated and, as a result, jobs were designed to suit the needs of the machine instead of people. Jobs were reduced to the most simple repetitive tasks possible requiring a very minimal level of specialization and training, removing from the employee the freedom of action and even, in some cases, the freedom of thought. The educational level of our labor force has changed, and we need to provide employees with much more challenging jobs to keep their active minds fully utilized. We need to make effective use of all the talents that our labor force has to offer, both mental and physical. The employees want to participate in the decision-making processes that affect them. They want to help solve the problems.

STRUCTURING TEAM BUILDING INTO THE
PRESENT MANAGEMENT TEAM

Managers around the world are beginning to recognize that they have a vast untapped potential in their employees' minds. This talent and knowledge can be effectively used to improve both products and services and also efficiency. Northrop Corporation's Aircraft Division near Los Angeles has been using teams for years, and this approach has had a major impact on cost and profit. Bev T. Moser, vice president for commercial operations, said, "During the 2 years we've emphasized that it is *us* rather than *thee* and *me*, the cost of the 747 unit we're delivering to our customer went down 50 percent." It is wrong to use team activities just to solve problems. We must also give the team increased decision-making powers. Many companies such as IBM, TRW, Dana, and Hewlett-Packard have been using team participation and quality of work-life processes very effectively for years.

F. James McDonald, president of General Motors, when talking about the use of teams, made the statement, "As far as I'm concerned, it's the only way to operate the business—there isn't any other way in today's world." Tom Peters, coauthor of *In Search of Excellence*, has said, "The major failure of American business is seeing the employee as a part of the problem instead of part of the solution."

Dr. Ishikawa, Japan's leading quality professional, said of team involvement, "A people-building philosophy will make the program successful; a people-using philosophy will cause the program to fail." Team participation is built on providing opportunities for people to make decisions and correct problems. Team building means that upper management places more trust and responsibility in the hands of the first-level managers and employees. Likewise, team building means that first-level managers and employees must realize that along with the increased responsibility comes increased accountability to the company for improving quality, effectiveness, and profit.

There is no need for an organization change to increase team participation in the improvement process. In most cases, it is best to structure the team participation process around your present management system and as the employees' capabilities increase, expand the first-line manager's span of control to offset the decreased work load that has resulted from the additional decisions being made by the employees. John Young, president of Hewlett-Packard, said, "Where quality teams at HP have been successful, managers have been closely involved. They used quality teams as a resource for accomplishing their business objectives. And they practiced what they preached."

The other factor that must be present is the employees' belief that they can trust management. Without a strong feeling of mutual trust and respect, it is difficult if not impossible to get the employees to identify problems and solve them.

MANAGEMENT FIRST

Team participation should never occur until the management team is totally participating in the improvement process, if you don't want the employees to believe they are being manipulated. Management must provide visible evidence of the company's thorough commitment to a policy of preventing problems rather than reacting to them. Don't rush into this phase of the process until the new management personality is solidly in place.

One word of caution. Just because a decision is made by a group does not necessarily mean it is the best one, for these reasons:

1. Group decisions are often gained by compromise. Remember the old saying, "A camel is a horse designed by a committee."

2. The group may be misled by a flashy member who expresses himself well, while the one with the best solution may need help in organizing and expressing his or her thoughts.

3. People tend to lose accountability for group decisions.

Management needs to be aware of these potential problems so they can be involved with the process and have final approval. Success requires a great deal of management and employee participation. Without an up-front investment in management and employee training, the process will drift aimlessly. Without good guidance, employees will spend fruitless hours deciding what problems should have emphasis and what role they should play in solving them. This leads to discouragement of the employees and management, and the process is discarded.

WHAT ARE TEAMS?

A team exists when two or more similar entities cooperate to accomplish a specific task. Four different types of teams are used extensively around the world today:

1. Improvement teams
2. Quality circles

3. Process improvement teams
4. Task forces

Table 6.1 compares the primary characteristics of the four types of teams. By reviewing Table 6.1, you can see that there is only one constant element in all four types of teams. It is that the team identifies the solution to the problem. Although all four of the team concepts have their place in a company, the improvement team is the best way to implement the improvement process. Toyota started its worker participation plan in the early 1950s. Today they receive 500,000 employee proposals per year, which results in a reported $230 million in savings. Later on, the process improvement teams will become a critical element of the improvement formula (discussed in Chapter 8).

Walter A. Fallon, chairman of Eastman-Kodak, said, "You can't drive a good work force 30 percent harder, but we've found that we could often work 30 or 50 or even 150 percent smarter."

DEPARTMENT IMPROVEMENT TEAMS

As you can see from Table 6.1, department improvement teams (DIT) are comprised of all the members of a department. Their purpose is to provide a focus and a means for all employees to contribute to an ongoing

TABLE 6.1   Team Characteristics

Characteristics	Department improvement teams	Quality circles	Process improvement teams	Task forces
Membership	Department members	Department members	Selected members of work-related departments	Selected members based on experience
Participation	Mandatory	Voluntary	Mandatory	Mandatory
Management direction	Moderate	Minimal	Moderate	High
Problem selection	By group	By group	By group	By management
Solution urgency	Moderate	Low	Moderate	High
Scope of activity	Within department	Within department	Interdepartment	Interdepartment
Identification of solution	By members	By members	By members	By members
Schedule pressure	Moderate	Minimal	Moderate	High
Activity time	Short meetings, long period	Short meetings, long period	Short meetings, long period	Long meetings, short period, no other assignment
Process facilitator	Optional	Encouraged	None	None
Implementation	By members	By members	By members	By others

activity aimed at improving the quality level and productivity of the department. The manager is usually the chairperson of the team, but in time, the chairperson may also be a trained and capable nonmanagement employee. The team identifies problems that cause errors and/or items that decrease the department's productivity. It then develops and implements corrective actions to eliminate these roadblocks to high productivity and/or error-free performance.

The team's efforts are directed at activities within the department or that have a direct impact on the department's activities. Problems are defined and priorities are set by the team. The team is responsible for setting improvement targets for the department and defining activities that will allow the team to meet or exceed these goals.

The department manager is responsible for forming the department improvement team. All members of the department are required to be active participants in the team's activity.

Ground Rules for the Department Improvement Meeting

The entire department should meet close to the work area so that the department members can study specific problems or get sample items without delay. A short meeting should be held on a regular basis. Under no circumstance should the meeting ever be canceled because of production schedules. For this reason, it may be best to schedule the meeting early in the week.

Here are some of the ground rules that apply to the department improvement team meetings:

1. An agenda should be prepared and distributed beforehand.
2. The meeting should start at the scheduled time by reviewing the agenda and modifying it as appropriate. Once the agenda has been agreed to, it should be followed. New noncritical items should be set aside for another meeting. The manager is responsible for ensuring that the meeting progresses efficiently, according to the agenda.
3. The manager should conduct the meeting in a manner that encourages participation from all the members of the department. This means that he or she may have to ask shy individuals for their opinions on some issues. The manager should serve as the catalyst and should not hold the floor for more than 25 percent of the meeting time.
4. The responsiblity for taking minutes should be rotated among the members. Some managers may feel it is easier and faster to prepare the minutes themselves, but this impulse should be resisted. This plan ensures that no one person is burdened with documenting all the meetings,

and it provides a learning opportunity for employees who are not effective at business writing.

The minutes should track corrective action status, employee suggestions, and team progress as it relates to team goals. Department members and higher-level managers should receive copies of the minutes.

5. The manager should avoid having the group vote on an issue. Instead, consensus decision-making techniques should be used to set directions, or priority-setting techniques used to give priority to the problems or to rank alternatives. Sometimes an informal show of hands may be helpful. It is very important that the department support the decisions that are made and that all individuals have adequate opportunity to influence the entire department before a firm decision is made. In most cases, the problems that the department improvement team is working on will not keep the department from functioning and, as a result, there is no real pressure to obtain an instantaneous solution. Problems that have the department split can be assigned to subgroups who can report to the entire department with recommendations.

6. The meeting agenda and problems discussed should be restricted to items that are controlled by the department and that affect the department's output. If the department's problems are caused by inputs, the manager should quickly feed this information to the other area.

7. The meeting should define the inputs that the department is dependent upon, what the department value-added content is, who the department's customers are, and how the quality of the department's output should be measured.

8. The department manager should make it clear that all employees are required to attend the meetings and that reasons for absence should be reviewed in advance.

How to Start Department Improvement Teams

The initial activities of the department improvement team must be thoroughly thought out. The employees should be trained to accept their increased responsibility. To accomplish this, the department improvement team evolves through the following three phases:

1. Awareness and education
2. Understanding
3. Problem solving and decision making

Awareness and Education Phase.   The following items should be covered during the awareness and education phase of the department improvement team activities:

1. Understanding the company's goals
2. Understanding the improvement process
3. Reasoning behind an error-free performance standard
4. Data collection and arrangement methods
5. Ways to identify problems (brainstorming, checklists, etc.)
6. Ways to analyze problems (Pareto and cause-and-effect diagrams, force-field analysis, histograms, etc.)
7. Documenting improvement (graphs, charts, management presentations, etc.)
8. Measuring results
9. Control charts and sampling

Understanding Phase.   "Department Activity Analysis" (DAA) is a tool that helps employees understand how they fit into the improvement process. DAA provides a technique to assist the department in defining its work flow. It starts by looking at the overall function of the department, defining major activities, and then detailing each of them. It focuses on customer-supplier relations and the internal workings of the department. The analysis (DAA) results in a document that is prepared for each department by the department improvement team. As illustrated in Figure 6.1, DAA is based on the premise that all departments and individuals get inputs from sources (suppliers); take these inputs and process them, adding value to the inputs they receive; and provide their customers with a product or service. This concept recognizes that each employee is a customer for output from another employee and, in turn, has a customer to whom he or she provides output. With this concept as a base, quality becomes an individual responsibility.

To start the process in motion, a form is filled out, listing the department mission and the major activities performed within the de-

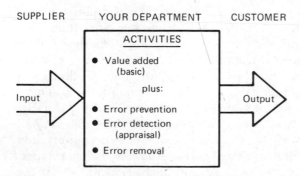

Figure 6.1   The customer-supplier relationship.

partment. The manager should present the department's mission as it has been established by upper management and should lead an open discussion of the mission. This discussion often results in the generation of a new mission statement that is submitted to upper management for consideration.

A list of major activities performed within the department is then prepared. It could include such things as

- Conduct market surveys
- Prepare cost estimates
- Interview potential employees
- Arrange for employee physicals
- Develop forecast assumptions
- Write installation manuals
- Answer customer complaints
- Design test equipment
- Maintain security records

The list should contain no more than ten major activities. When the list is complete, each activity is looked at in detail, one at a time. First, a list is prepared of inputs, where they come from, and the form in which they are received. The department should study each required input to determine if it is adequately specified, how feedback is provided to the supplier, and how well the supplier is performing. Systems then should be established to provide specifications and supplier feedback when they do not exist. It is the department's responsibility to ensure that the supplier understands how the output is being used and what the department expectations are.

The department should then define, in very specific terms, what value-added content their activity has to the input. Then they are in a position to define what the department output for that activity is, what form they deliver the output to their customer in, and who their customers are.

The next thing to do is prepare a customer specification for each department output. This is accomplished when the department improvement team meets with their customers and has them define their expectations for that activity. During this meeting, output requirements should be given priorities, and appropriate performance feedback systems should be evaluated and established. The customer is the real measure of performance, not the supplier. There must be a strong working relationship between customers and suppliers *within* the company. If you cannot define and satisfy your *internal* customer expectations, how can you ever hope to define and satisfy your *external* customer expectations? When the output specifications and measurement criteria are completed, both the supplier and the customer should sign the document indicating that it was developed as a joint effort and that they both agree with its content. The last part of the activity analysis is to answer the following questions:

1. Is this activity measurable? Yes _____ No _____
   If no, explain why not. If yes, list the measurements: _____
   _____

2. Is there a need to improve? Yes _____ No _____
   If yes, indicate the target date for an improvement plan _____

3. Estimate how many hours per week are spent on this activity in your department by answering the following questions:
   a. How many total hours are spent on this activity? _____
   b. What percent of total time is spent on prevention activities? _____
   c. What percent of total time is spent on appraisal activities? _____
   d. What percent of total time is wasted due to error? _____

This may seem like a lot of work for the department, and it is, but the results will be well worth it, as it provides an excellent understanding between the departments. This exercise should be reviewed every 6 months and repeated at least every 2 years or whenever the department scope changes drastically.

TIC Indicators (Team Improvement Charts).   As a result of the DAA cycle, a list of department performance measurements can be prepared. The team should select three to five of the most important measurements for posting in the department. These department measurements are called "TIC indicators." Keep the TIC indicators simple and large enough so that they can be read from a distance. Each chart should show at least 6 months of data and should have a targeted performance level on it. Each indicator that has met the target for 3 consecutive months should have its targets reset. Remember, there is no shame associated with not meeting targets; the real objective is to constantly improve.

As shown in Figure 6.2, two types of targets are used—first, the performance levels that the customer expects and then tighter targets called "challenge targets." The challenge targets provide the team with interim goals between the customer-expected performance level and the ultimate standard of error-free performance. This scheme eliminates the tendency of most companies to stop all efforts to improve an activity just because the target has been met. It also means that management must look at targets in a new way. Management should expect all customer targets to be met 100 percent of the time, but they should not expect the challenge targets to be met.

For best results, TIC indicators should look professional, as they can have a major impact on improving performance, increasing awareness,

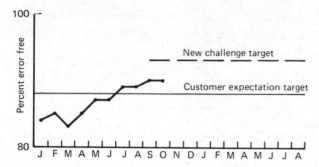

Figure 6.2 **Team improvement chart (TIC indicators).**

and increasing productivity of the employees and managers alike. TIC indicators should be updated and reviewed at department improvement team meetings.

Problem-Solving and Decision-Making Phase. Now the employees are ready to start into the most productive phase of the department improvement team's activities. The team selects challenge targets for a group of department measurement indicators. Probably the items that should be worked on first are the items that were selected to be shown on the TIC indicators. The team will then use problem-solving techniques to develop a time-line plan designed to allow the department to meet and/or exceed the new challenge targets. The team then implements the plan, adjusting it as necessary to meet the established targets. When the targets have been reached, the team receives proper recognition from management for the efforts. Then, the team sets new improvement targets and the cycle starts all over again. The quality ring (Figure 6.3) portrays the departmental improvement activities.

Each time a change is implemented or a problem is solved, the team should prepare a documented estimate of the quality impact and/or net cost savings that resulted from their activities. This estimate should be submitted to the improvement steering council.

Why Does the Department Improvement Team Work?

The department improvement team works because it provides the department members with an understanding of how they fit into the big picture and proves to them that management is truly committed to the

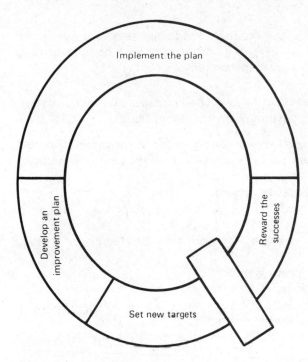

Implement the plan

Develop an
improvement plan

Reward the
successes

Set new targets

Figure 6.3 The quality ring.

improvement process, not only by words that have been said but also by actions that have been taken and priorities that have been set. It also allows the people who know the most about the activity to modify the system they are using, thereby providing them with a say about their work.

Another factor more subtle but possibly more important is the effect of peer pressure on individual performance. When the department is being measured as a team, people begin to help and police those who detract from the total performance, thus increasing quality and output. "I remember how hard I worked in the paint shop," recalls a former automotive worker. "We had a pool-type work concept and our pay was based on how well the team did. One poor performer dragged everyone down, and as a result everyone was on his back. This caused all of us to try a little harder." In addition, the department improvement team allows informal group leaders to influence management in setting targets, performance standards, and activity planning. In the past, the informal leader may have resisted change and created an atmosphere of hostility to improvement because it frequently jeopardized some of his or her previous authority. In making the informal leader part of the improvement process, management obtains a very strong ally who in some cases has a significant influence over the employees.

Benefits and Advantages.   The following advantages and benefits result from implementing a department improvement team:

1. All employees are actively involved in the improvement process.
2. Employees that contribute to the success of the improvement process can be rewarded by management.
3. Leadership traits are developed.
4. Problem-solving methods and skills are developed, and real problems are solved.
5. The department manager still maintains the role as department leader.
6. Employees' self-esteem is improved.
7. Employees start to self-police the activities of the department.
8. The system provides realistic customer-satisfaction specifications that have been agreed to by the customers and the suppliers.
9. A measurement system for key activities within the department is provided.
10. The employees are helped in aligning their goals with those of the department and company.
11. An effective escalation cycle is provided for problems that cannot be solved at the department level.
12. Employee-manager relationships improve as employees see that management is interested in their problems and helping to solve them.
13. This all supports the "people-building" philosophy.

The team approach works for Motorola. Before the improvement team tackled the problem of lost gold, only 9.6 ounces of every pound reached the final product. Within 4 months employees had improved the gold yield, resulting in a savings of $3 million in the first year. At Hewlett-Packard, teams and their total quality control (TQC) program were applied to order processing. Customers now pay more promptly. The average days outstanding dropped from 62 to 54 days. This improvement represents more than a $150 million savings per year.

Teams do work in all functions. For example, Ed Kane, director of quality for IBM, reports, "To improve large customer accounts receivable delinquencies, a process focus external and internal was employed. As a result, there was a tenfold improvement in delinquency, 85 percent reduction in customer's time (monthly) on invoices, $18,000 administration savings, and $100,000 per year cash flow improvement."

Too often, in talking about employee involvement or participation, we think about the manufacturing employees and forget about the support areas. In most companies, white-collar and clerical costs are more than double the manufacturing direct labor cost. In Westinghouse, for example, managers and white-collar workers account for half the work force and 70 percent of the payroll. Studies indicate that better than 80 percent of written documentation contains errors that should have been detected by the originator. This waste is costing the average company more than 25 percent of the service areas' productivity. Teams are a very good way of improving quality and productivity in the service areas.

Disadvantages.   The primary disadvantage to the department improvement team is that it requires that the total department stop doing its assigned task while the meetings are being held. However, most departments quickly adjust to this system and within 2 months, weekly output exceeds previous levels.

QUALITY CIRCLES

The quality circle is a small group of employees (6 to 12) who meet voluntarily on a regular basis to solve problems related to their work environment. In most cases, the group is not chaired by the department manager.

Quality circles work on problems that directly affect the employees' output. The group is formed with management approval to attack a specific bottleneck or problem that the employees have identified. The quality circle is terminated when the problem has been solved to the satisfaction of the participants.

The employees are responsible for defining the problem to be solved, selecting their own chairperson, establishing the meeting schedule, and obtaining management approval of the project. They are then responsible for collecting pertinent data, analyzing the problem, evaluating viable alternatives, recommending solutions to management, and implementing those solutions approved by management when they are within their sphere of control.

The key ingredients of the quality circle program are

1. Circles meet frequently.
2. Membership is voluntary.
3. Problems are work-related.
4. Problems are identified, evaluated, and corrected, and the results are measured.

5. The quality circle is terminated when the problem is solved.

The quality circle movement in Japan was a bottom-up movement. It started with the foremen and employees, not top management. This meant slow growth, but it had the full support of the work force, which is one of the reasons it has weathered the test of time so well.

Quality Circle Facilitator

A facilitator is generally chosen to coordinate the quality circle program for the company. Except in a very small company, the duties of the facilitator should be full time. Among the duties of the facilitator are to

1. Direct the total program
2. Prepare material to explain to management and employees the advantages of the program
3. Prepare and conduct quality circle training programs
4. Interest employees in forming quality circles
5. Help quality circle teams solve problems
6. Make arrangements for specialists to advise quality circles as necessary
7. Provide special training for quality circle leaders
8. Lead the initial quality circle meetings until the chosen leader is comfortable in the role

Labor Involvement

Particular attention should be paid to involvement of the labor union in the quality circle program. Most labor unions today are very familiar with quality circles and have generally become very supportive of the activity. You need to have full labor union support before you go to the department members.

The Department Meeting

At department meetings, the facilitator should explain, in detail, how the quality circle program works, the education that will be provided, and the advantages offered by the program. He or she should also explain that meetings will be held on company time and that employees will not charge their time to production while attending the meetings. The manager should tell the employees to think about the program and decide if they personally are interested in working with a group to solve some of the department's problems. The manager should emphasize that participation in the program is absolutely voluntary.

Quality Circle Leader

The department manager or the employees of departments that have sufficient volunteers to start a quality circle should select someone to be trained as a quality circle leader. The training includes such items as

1. Quality circle operations
2. Quality circle organization
3. Small-group behavior training
4. Problem-solving methods and techniques
5. Participative management methods
6. Interpersonal relations

The quality circle leader is responsible for

1. Encouraging participation in quality circle activities
2. Making arrangements and preparing agendas for future meetings
3. Helping the facilitator train the quality circle members
4. Chairing the quality circle meetings
5. Documentation related to meetings and activities

Quality Circle Meetings

Quality circle meetings should be scheduled for a maximum of 1 hour in a place that is free from noise and distraction. The first seven or eight meetings will be training sessions. Subjects are (see Appendix A for more detail)

1. Introduction to quality circles
2. Brainstorming, cause and effect, and fishbone diagrams
3. Histograms, graphs, check sheets
4. Management presentations

Following this initial phase, the meeting agenda should emphasize new concepts and problem analysis. The problem analysis activity should reinforce training provided earlier in the cycle. In this later stage, the following subjects should be taught:

1. Data collection, analysis, and presentation methods (scatter diagrams, design of experiments, stratification)
2. Process controls (control charts and sampling)
3. Force-field analysis, mind maps

In a methodical way, all the problem-solving techniques will be covered and, eventually, 100 percent of the meeting time will be occupied in problem analysis and solution. After every meeting, the leader prepares minutes that are distributed to the quality circle members and the department manager. At the completion of the project, the results are presented to upper management.

Recognition

A system of support by management must be put in place to recognize successful quality circles. The system most frequently used provides the quality circles' members with an opportunity to present their success story to upper management. The more important the contribution, the higher the level of manager the story should be presented to. The presentation should answer the following questions:

1. What was the problem?
2. What methods were used to analyze the problem?
3. What was the solution?
4. How effective was the solution?
5. What are the savings that resulted from the effort?

The company newsletter should feature a quality circle success story about once a month. Once a year, a quality circle recognition event should be held by the company to honor quality circle teams that have completed highly successful projects.

Quality circles can supplement the department improvement team activities. For example, the quality circle program is effective when a problem comes up in the department improvement team meeting that only affects a small part of the department, its potential saving does not make it a priority problem, and employees volunteer to work on the problem. Normally, the department improvement teams are not named, but nicknames are given to most quality circles.

Benefits and Advantages

1. Only employees who want to be involved become members of the quality circle; as a result, they are highly motivated to participate.
2. The training broadens the individual members.
3. Employees are solving the problems that are personally meaningful to them.
4. The members are committed to making the solutions work.
5. The program helps overcome resistance to change.

Disadvantages

1. The total department is not involved.
2. Employees who are not quality circle members may be reluctant to accept quality circle suggestions.

PROCESS IMPROVEMENT TEAMS

A process improvement team is created to qualify the process, improve quality, decrease waste, and improve productivity related to a process that crosses many department lines. The process improvement team is made up of experienced, trained professionals and problem solvers from each department affected by the process and supporting areas. The members are appointed by management and the activities are a prime assignment. The chairperson is appointed by management.

Activities are limited to a specific mission predetermined by management. The members represent their department and must be able to commit resources for the department to meet the assigned objectives. Usually, the assignment is for a long period of time.

Ideally, the team is assigned before the process is designed and implemented. This allows the process improvement team to focus its combined knowledge and experience to prevent problems from occurring. Basically, the team is responsible for optimizing profit from the assigned process and ensuring that schedules are met and that the product is as error-free as possible. Salaries and future growth in the company are affected by how well members perform in the team environment.

The team takes whatever action is necessary to bring the process under control and optimize its overall effectiveness. A more detailed description of the process improvement team's activity can be found in Chapter 8.

Benefits and Advantages

1. Because of combined disciplines, the scheme ensures that a total cause and effect analysis can be made.
2. As expert professionals, team members require no education and training to become effective.
3. Since the team understands the total process and its interaction, team decisions can optimize total efficiency and minimize suboptimization.
4. Links between functions are provided and are united by common goals.
5. Waste and cost can be effectively reduced.

6. If implemented before the process design is complete, the process improvement team is an effective way of preventing problems from occurring.

7. The team members become acquainted with the total business concept.

Through the use of process improvement teams one IBM distribution center reduced inventory errors from 30 to 0.08 percent, a 300-fold improvement.

Disadvantages

1. A major time commitment by experienced employees is required, which often has an impact on other company activities.

2. The employee's time may not be used effectively when another discipline is discussing a problem that does not involve all the team members.

TASK FORCES

A task force is formed by upper management when a major problem occurs that must be solved immediately, such as one that shuts down the plant or a major product line. It is made up of highly skilled professionals selected to study and solve the specific problem. These employees are normally temporarily removed from their permanent assignments to work full time as task force members.

The activity of the task force is limited to a single problem that must be solved immediately, after which time the individuals return to their original assignments. The task force is responsible for quickly putting a temporary solution in place and also for developing a plan that will permanently solve the problem. Usually the permanent solution is implemented by the normal work force. The problem-solving techniques used by the task force are similar to the ones that have been discussed in the other problem-solving techniques. Task forces are not considered a useful tool in the improvement process because of their short-range activities.

Problems assigned to task forces receive a great deal of upper management attention. Task force activities must have top priority throughout the plant and cooperation must be excellent. Normally, daily reports about progress are given to top management and potential solutions are discussed openly with top management before they are completely evaluated.

Benefits and Advantages

1. Very skilled people focus on a specific problem.
2. There is complete dedication of the people who are assigned to the task force with no conflicting assignments.
3. The problem is solved very rapidly.
4. A great deal of cooperation exists with the task force activity.

Disadvantages

1. It is a very high-stressed working environment.
2. The final solution is normally not implemented by the task force.

MEASUREMENTS

One of the team's most important activities is the development of a measurement system for setting priorities and gauging progress. Quality is defined as meeting customer expectations. The real job is to quantify these expectations and document them so employees know when they are conforming to expectations.

Many departments and individuals feel their jobs do not lend themselves to measurement. This is not true. And any job that cannot be measured is probably not worth doing and should be eliminated. The problem many people have is they don't understand the difference between activities and output. When you ask your data processing organization what they do, they talk about filling out forms, loading programs, and inputting data. What they do is generate organized consolidated reports. At IBM when the data processing group determined that their measure of excellence was the percentage of acceptable reports delivered on time, things immediately began to get better. In just under 24 months, the percentage of good reports delivered increased from 86 to 97.4 percent. Any job that begins with an input, adds value to it, and passes it on to a customer can be measured. To quote one of the closing and dock supervisors at Avon, "I have learned how to measure so we could see how we are performing in the first place. I have not only established requirements, but I now have a measurement system in place."

Most activities have two key measurements—a productivity measure and a quality measure. Productivity is normally measured by dividing total output by total input. Quality, on the other hand, is measured in terms of percentage of good output. Real improvement occurs when both the productivity and quality measurements get better or when one of the measurements improves while the other remains unchanged. For example, an accountant could be processing 25,000 vouchers per month at a 0.5 percent error rate. She then decides to work harder on productivity and processes 35,000 vouchers that are 5 percent defective. The apparent result is improved productivity, but the overall result suffers.

The ideal improvement measure is the sum of all inputs divided into the quantity of output that met customer expectations. Unfortunately these types of indicators are often difficult to calculate. As a result, separate quality and productivity measurements need to be compared simultaneously so the true degree of improvement can be assessed.

At General Dynamics (GD) measurement is at the heart of their quality improvement process (QIP). Oliver C. Boileau, president of GD, reported, "There are as many as 60 QIP parameters and hundreds of projects in productivity improvement projects (PIP). Each general manager is measured on productivity/quality improvement process (P/QIP) results, and he, in turn, measures his staff on P/QIP accomplishments." Table 6-2 shows some of GD's measurement goals.

EDUCATION FOR TEAMS

As stated earlier, a team is a group of individuals working together in a cooperative fashion to accomplish a common result or objective. In athletics, there are good players and there are good team players, but

TABLE 6-2   Typical General Dynamics Measurement and Goals

GD organizational measures and goals (corporate: common elements)	
Organization	Measurement parameter
Engineering	Avoidable changes per month, %
Program office	Deviation/waivers
Materials	On-time deliveries to production, %
	Accepted purchased items, %
Production	Scrap (labor)
	Scrap (material)
	Rework and repair
	First-time yield
Data systems center	Software change requests
Quality assurance	Inspection escapes
	Number of MRB QARs per 1000 direct labor hours
Logistics	Service report response time
General manager	Overtime

the two are very different and have a totally different effect on reaching the objectives.

Traits of Good Team Members

Before discussing the training of the team members, let's look at the traits of good team members that should be developed and encouraged:

1. They want to understand the workings of the total team and the activities going on around them so they can help others.
2. They want to know what the total team is expected to accomplish, not just what is expected of them, and to understand where they fit in the big picture.
3. They want to take part in setting the goals for the group and in developing the plan for accomplishing those goals.
4. They share mutual respect for and trust in other team members.
5. They take part in decision making.
6. They are willing to share the rewards and the spotlight with the team. Since team members work together, no one individual can take credit for the team's ideas.

As we train people to function in the team environment, the importance of team interaction and overall respect cannot be overemphasized. We can provide the team members with the most sophisticated problem-solving and process-control tools, but if we haven't taught them to cooperate and respect one another, it is all to no avail.

There is not much difference among the techniques and methods used in group dynamics and problem solving in any of the four types of teams we have discussed. There are differences in the difficulty of the problems and the sophistication of the techniques used, but basically the approach is the same. Because of the similarities, the education and training requirements for all teams will be described together here.

Team education and training (see Appendices A and B) can be divided into the following general categories:

1. Team interaction and member responsibilities (group dynamics and team building)
2. Decision making
3. Quantitative measurement
4. Data collection and analysis
5. Process control
6. Problem solving
7. Design of experiments

The individual members need to understand their roles in the team environment. Normally, a 1-hour session is devoted to this topic and the specific ground rules that will apply. The group leader needs to have had about 8 hours of class training in group dynamics and team building that combines theory with case studies and role playing.

Industrial education does not detract from profit—it enhances it. In the long run, it is ignorance that costs money. James E. Preston, president of Avon, has said, "Last year we spent about $300,000 on education and the implementation of the quality and productivity improvement process (QPIP), but we recorded savings totaling more than $10 million, all directly attributable to the quality and productivity improvement process. Two headquarters' departments together achieved savings of $2.5 million." F. James McDonald said, "We've trained more than 30,000 GM workers in statistical quality control (SQC) techniques. And I must say, to see their tools put to work right on the line is one of the most rewarding experiences I've had at General Motors."

The United States and Japan are not the only nations that are training their people in quality methods. Zhao Ziyang, Premier of the Peoples Republic of China, reported in October 1985,

> According to incomplete statistics, since 1978, we have conducted over 29,000 lecture tours on total quality control, with an audience of more than 4,100,000. We have run 250,000 study courses in total quality control, attended by more than 16,000,000 participants. Total quality control has been carried out among 38,000 enterprises. We have established more than 590,000 quality control circles, which have directly increased income and reduced expenditure of enterprises by over 89,000,000,000 (89 billion) yuan. We have produced high quality products and set up high quality projects, and have acquired remarkable economic benefits.

PROBLEM SOLVING

Roadblocks to Successful Problem Solving

Whenever you discover a problem, a defect, or a nonproductive situation, you can look at it in three different ways. You can think of it as a burden that has been put upon your shoulders; you can ignore it, hoping that it will go away; or you can look at it as an opportunity to contribute to the success of your company. In truth, it is an opportunity to make things better and to make a meaningful contribution to the company. Unfortunately, many people—management and employees alike—put up roadblocks in their own paths to success. Some of the more common roadblocks are

1. *Lack of time.*   "I don't have the time now." The reason we don't have the time to fix it today is that we didn't take the time to do it right yesterday.

2. *Lack of problem ownership.*   "It's not my problem—Joe did it wrong, let him fix it." The lack of problem ownership causes many problems to stay with us when they could have been solved in a very simple way.

3. *Lack of recognition.*   "Sure, I could tell Joe that he is doing it wrong and show him how to do it right, but that doesn't give me any points with my boss. All it does is put me behind schedule and make Joe look better." Management needs to find ways to recognize people who go out of their way to help correct problems, who take the time to do the job right every time.

4. *Errors as a way of life.*   "Mistakes are bound to happen—we're only human." This type of attitude is the beginning of the end for a company.

5. *Ignorance of the importance of the problem.*   "It is just a little burr, it will fall off sometime." But what if that sometime occurs in a precision servo system that is used to navigate a plane and it jams the gears? Every job is important; if it wasn't, it wouldn't be done. An error that is repeated is unforgivable.

6. *Belief that no one can do anything about some problems.*   "You can't do anything about it" is no answer to a real problem. It may cost too much to prevent it from recurring, but don't stop short of finding out what it would cost.

7. *Poor balance by upper management between schedule, cost, and quality.*   If management places priority on quality, schedules and cost will take care of themselves. Remember, the bitterness of shipping poor quality lingers long after the sweetness of meeting schedules.

8. *People who try to protect themselves.*   All too often, people are more interested in proving that the problem was not caused by them than in solving the problem. When such people realize that a problem is coming close to their front porch, they put it on a detour route so that it takes much longer to solve than it should have.

9. *Head hunting by management.*   If management is more interested in placing blame than eliminating the problem, the error-prevention program is doomed.

The success of your error-prevention program rests in knocking down these roadblocks and creating a belief that preventing errors will benefit the individual, the company, and the customer.

Ingredients Required to Correct Problems

Six critical ingredients are required in any long-range plan to permanently eliminate problems:

1. *Awareness.*   The employees and management must be made aware of the importance of eliminating errors and the cost of errors to the business. In many companies, eliminating errors could reduce costs by over 30 percent.

2. *Desire.*   A desire to eliminate errors must be created. No one wants to be wrong; just give them a chance to do it right.

3. *Training in problem solving.*   The individuals working to eliminate the problems need to be confident problem solvers. They need to do more than just present problems; they need to collect cost and supporting data. They need to assemble a number of alternative solutions and then select the very best one.

4. *Failure analysis.*   A system is needed to translate symptoms into a precise understanding of what caused the problem (failure mode). Without this type of data, many problems can only be solved by very expensive trial-and-error methods that take too much time and cost too much.

5. *Follow-up system.*   A system to track problems and action commitments is an essential part of the total preventive system. It should also provide a means to evaluate the effectiveness of the preventive action.

6. *Liberal credit.*   Credit and recognition should be liberally given to all who participate.

Opportunity Cycle

Each problem that is investigated should go through the five distinct phases indicated in Figure 6.4.

Problem-Selection Phase.   The first phase of the opportunity cycle is to select the problem (or opportunity) that represents a bottleneck or a waste in the area. To get the cycle started, the team should make a list of problems that are potential candidates. They should then collect data that will measure the magnitude of each problem. The most important step in solving a problem is recognizing that you have a problem. The Pareto principle can help you determine which problems should be worked on first. This principle holds that the "few major errors" account for the greatest part of the problem (70 to 80 percent). The Pareto diagram helps you to quantify and identify problems and then also to prioritize your activities. Figure 6.5 shows a typical Pareto analysis diagram.

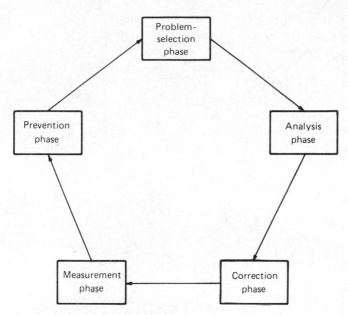

Figure 6.4   The opportunity cycle.

The Pareto diagram uses vertical bars to present a graphic picture of all the problems related to an area, product, or situation. Problem classifications are arranged in descending order of importance from left to right. The cumulative curve traces the sum of the bars as they are added together.

You will note that 90 percent of the errors (few major errors) are caused by only three error sources (contamination, chips, and cracks). The other 10 percent (many minor errors) should be given low priority until the few major errors are brought under control.

In this case, we used the number of times the problem occurred in a given period to make up the Pareto diagram. In many cases, however, the quantity of errors can be misleading, and cost should be used. For example, the contamination may be easy to wipe off at a cost of 1¢ per part, but the crack may cause a $100 part to be thrown away. If you completely solve the contamination problem, you would only save $.40 per hundred units processed, but if you only cut the crack problem in half, you would save $750 per hundred units.

Analysis Phase.   The next step is to perform a detailed analysis to gain as much information as possible about the problem. First, double-check the collected data for accuracy. This is a critical step because often mis-

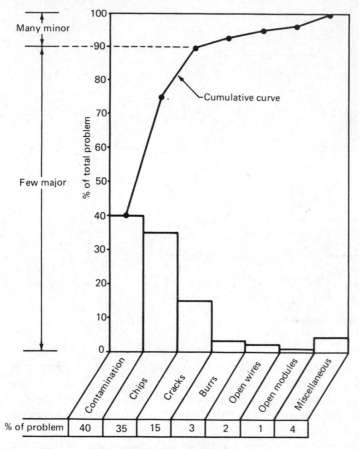

Figure 6.5 A typical Pareto analysis diagram.

leading data can cause a great deal of effort to be wasted. Once you are sure that the basic data is valid, determine the failure mechanism. This may involve having detailed failure analysis performed on the defective item or conducting controlled experiments designed to pinpoint the source of the problem.

The analysis phase is an exciting phase of the opportunity cycle. It's a lot like detective work for a modern Sherlock Holmes. There is no standard procedure to find the criminal (the root cause of the problem). It just takes a lot of hard work, a careful collection and understanding of all the clues. The team simply must be smart enough to put all the data together to provide a clear picture of the real failure mechanism.

Correction Phase. Once the root cause of the error has been found, the team is ready to develop a plan that will permanently prevent the problem from recurring or at least reduce it to a level compatible with the team's goals. The correction phase consists of six steps:

1. Determine if a temporary fix should be implemented. Sometimes a "Band-Aid" fix is appropriate to protect the customer on a temporary basis until a permanent fix can be implemented. Normally, however, a temporary fix results in an increase in appraisal (inspection) activity. A problem eliminated by appraisal must be re-eliminated each time it occurs, a process which can be very expensive.

2. Develop alternative solutions. At this stage, there are no bad ideas, and one should resist the temptation to accept the first solution that is proposed. The less acceptable ones will fall out quickly later on in the process, but they may stimulate another thought that will build into the best solution.

3. Select the best possible solution. The team should narrow down the proposed solutions using one of the priority-setting methods learned previously. When two or three are chosen, a detailed effect analysis should be conducted to select the best. The effect analysis evaluates the potential solutions from the following standpoints:
   a. Cost of implementation
   b. Effectiveness of solution
   c. Negative side effects (if any)
   d. Ease of implementation

Of course, at this point, each of the effects can only be estimated, but that is good enough for the selection.

4. Establish a plan to implement the solution, which should include a time schedule for implementation. If other groups are involved with the solution, they should be consulted and should approve the plan. The implementation plan should answer the following questions:
   a. What needs to be done?
   b. Who will do it?
   c. When and how will it be done?
   d. What is the measure of success?

Many plans should also include a pilot run to prove out their feasibility.

5. Gain management approval. The proposed solution should be presented to management.

6. Implement the plan. As soon as the plan is approved by management, the team should implement it. The team is responsible for en-

suring that the proposed schedule is followed. If unable to take the necessary action, the team should request assistance from management.

Measurement Phase. The impact of the corrective action plan should be measured in order to be certain that the solution has really solved the problem. If the solution does not solve the problem or the level of correction is unsatisfactory, the team should then go back to the beginning of the correction phase to develop an alternative approach. If the plan is successful, the team should prepare a summary report that describes the problem, the methods used to correct it, and the quality-cost-productivity gains. They should also remove the temporary protective action.

Prevention Phase. After the problem has been solved, the team members, with the aid of the improvement steering council, enter into the prevention phase of the opportunity cycle. During this stage, they review the knowledge gained about the problem and then apply it to the rest of the product lines and/or company activities with similar conditions. This final phase of the opportunity cycle allows the experience gained on a single problem to be applied to a global solution. The object of this phase is to alter the systems so that the problem can be permanently eliminated from future activities. This probably will be the most difficult phase of the cycle, but it is the phase that could have the most important consequences. Figure 6.6 illustrates the opportunity cycle.

PROBLEM PHASE: A small wire breaks at a printed circuit board connection, causing an open circuit.

ANALYSIS PHASE: The heat required to melt the solder caused embrittlement to take place in the wire in some cases, depending on how long the soldering iron is left on the connection or if the solder joint is reworked.

CORRECTIVE ACTION PHASE: The solder pad size was increased to allow the heat to be more evenly dissipated.

MEASUREMENT PHASE: Broken wire failure rates in the manufacturing cycle decreased from .01 to .005 percent. In the customer's application wire failure rates decreased from 100 parts per million to .5 parts per million per 10,000 hours of use.

PREVENTION ACTIVITIES PHASE: The team found four other printed circuit boards in two other product lines that had the potential for the same problem, so the design was changed on all four part numbers. In addition, the engineering standards manual was changed to define the minimum solder pad versus wire size.

Figure 6.6   Illustration of the opportunity cycle.

The first phase of the prevention activities should be focused on the procedures that control the problem (engineering specs, manufacturing operating procedures, management procedures, etc.). These procedures should be modified to reflect the solution as appropriate.

Frequently, the team does not have a good overview of the company's activities so that they cannot define all other potential applications for their solution. For this reason, management should identify solutions that could have further applications. These solutions should be published regularly in an "opportunity newsletter" that is sent to all managers. This provides management with a list of new ideas.

The opportunity cycle provides a systematic way to solve problems and prevent them from recurring. All too often, people will select a problem, analyze its root cause, implement action to correct it, and then go on to the next problem, failing to measure how effective the action was and never applying the knowledge they have gained to other situations. Prevention occurs through the application of knowledge learned, not by solving individual problems.

Sunciti Manufacturing Ltd. in Hong Kong provides an excellent example of white-collar team corrective action. In June 1983, a team from the personnel department set out to reduce errors in wage computation. Error rates were running at about 6 percent when they could be below 5 percent. The team established a data system and developed a Pareto diagram that showed

Cause of errors	Percentage
Carelessness	52.4
Insufficient rechecking	23.8
Time clock	15.8
Supervisor's remarks	8.0

Once the problem was understood, correction came quickly. By September, wage error rates dropped to 0.4 percent and have not gone up.

At IBM, information system support had a significant number of reruns each month in support of a major design area. By systematically analyzing the problem, new process requirements were prepared and a feedback system established. As a result, reruns dropped 50 percent at a savings of $70,000 per year. CPU time was decreased 30 percent, and one man-year effort was saved annually.

DEPARTMENT QUEST-FOR-EXCELLENCE LEVELS

A department's quest for excellence has two levels:

1. Meeting customer expectations

2. Excelling at the job the department is doing

Meeting Customer Expectations (Level 1)

Before a department can begin its quest for excellence, it needs to concentrate on fulfilling customer expectations. Until this is accomplished, the department is not meeting minimum requirements. This is a phase in the improvement process that is driven by feedback from the customer.

1. The department meets with the customer to document the expectations and to agree on how to measure the department to ensure that these expectations are being met.
2. The department meets with the suppliers to ensure that they understand the department's expectations and agree on how to measure the quality of the supplier's output.
3. The department performs its basic value-added activities.
4. The department establishes measurements that evaluate the quality of the supplier's output and the department's value-added activities.
5. If department-related errors are detected, the department removes the source of errors.
6. If supplier-related errors are detected, the department provides the supplier with the necessary data with which to take action to remove the source of the errors.
7. The customer evaluates the department's output. If errors are detected, the customer provides the department with the necessary data to allow the department to take action to remove the sources of the errors.
8. The department implements action to remove the source of the errors; it also upgrades its in-process measurements to detect the errors before the output is delivered to the customer.

Note: Steps 4, 5, and 6 are repeated until the measurements indicate that the process is under control and will provide output that meets customer expectations. Steps 7 and 8 are repeated until the customer expectation level is met. Periodically, steps 1 and 2 should be repeated to ensure that there is a good understanding between the department and its suppliers and customers.

Excelling at the Job (Level 2)

After the minimal acceptable level has been reached, the department is ready to embark on its quest for excellence (level 2). Level 2 activities are driven by the department and are directed at the excellence of the activities being performed.

We are now ready to start down the long road to error-free performance. In most cases, the department will never have to go back to level 1 because the quality of output will stay ahead of customer expectations—but that does not mean that level 1 activities can stop. Quite the contrary, it is very important that they continue so that the department understands where it stands related to customer expectations.

In level 2, the department strives to be better today than it was yesterday, and better tomorrow than it is today. The quality ring (Figure 6.3) is used to accomplish this goal.

TEAM COMMUNICATIONS

Communication is the key to making the team feel part of the total company's activities and to motivating the team to want to improve.

Daily Team Meetings

The first 10 minutes of each shift should be devoted to a short department meeting between the manager and the employees. At this meeting, the manager should review the work that needs to be accomplished and the current or potential quality problems. The manager will also provide information about changes inside and outside the company that affect or interest the employee. It is also the right time to make personal announcements. The manager should also ask if anyone had any work-related problems yesterday that they had not already told him about. He might also have someone report on how well the department performed yesterday relative to the current challenge targets.

Business Strategy and Status Meetings

Business strategy and status meetings should be held every 3 months or when a significant new product or management change is announced by the company. The purpose of these meetings is to keep the employees informed about the business. The meetings should provide the employees with information on how well the company is doing and some of the challenges the company will be facing in the future. The business status meeting should be kept simple and should use terms that every employee understands.

Team Progress Meetings

When the department improvement team meets the challenge targets, it should prepare a report that will be presented at the functional managers' improvement team meeting. The report should cover the method used to improve the activity, the results that were obtained, and an estimate of the savings that resulted from the improvement. The entire department should be invited to attend the presentation.

The success of Avon's literature estimating and trending team, headed by Alvor Brown, is the type of information that should be reported at the functional managers' improvement team meeting. Alvor's team reduced excess brochures from 1.3 million in 1983 to 4000 in 1984 at a savings of $2.4 million over the 2-year period.

Individual Involvement

INTRODUCTION

In every culture around the world the individual desires to succeed and be recognized for accomplishment. People are individuals, and, when it gets right down to it, they want to be treated as individuals. They want to be called by name, not "hey you." They want to possess their own things. They want their own families. They want to be noticed for what they do. They want to be successful. Group participation is satisfying and rewarding, but let's not forget what has made the world move forward—the individual. Almost every great breakthrough has been the result of an individual's efforts, not group activities. When management loses sight of individuals, they lose sight of reality.

Even in Japan, where they have had a most interactive and supportive society for many years, people are beginning to demand recognition as individuals. Since World War II, the individual competition in schools has been escalating rapidly. Despite the social group molding, each Japanese child is subjected to academic competition that is almost savage in intensity.

This keen scholastic competition between Japanese students has created unrest in the younger generation because there is just no way an individual can compete so feverishly through the formative years and not be expected to carry this strong competitive spirit into the work environment. This has resulted in a great deal of dissatisfaction in the Japanese labor force. Workers are beginning to take exception to a system in which pay is based on age rather than on individual contribution.

Even in mainland China, the system is changing to provide more incentive to the individual workers. The success of an individual incentive project that was undertaken in the agricultural areas has spawned a massive program to put all Chinese workers on an incentive program by the end of the 1980s. The Chinese government now has realized that individual recognition is the best way to get improved productivity and quality.

RESPECT FOR THE INDIVIDUAL

One of the basics of a manager's job is to respect the human dignity and thoughts of his or her employees and associates. Only by respecting the individual will management earn his or her true and full participation in the improvement process. Management must remember that an idea is central to the ego. Each time people share their innermost thoughts, they take the chance of being stripped bare of dignity. Managers need to understand the importance of listening and helping employees develop their thoughts.

Lewis Lehr, CEO of 3M, has helped make his company a leader in its field by showing respect for the individual, creating a working situation in which employees are not afraid to fail. He points out, "Vision is not the exclusive province of top management. We must sponsor change by supporting people who have new ideas and ways of doing things. And these people must know that they will not be crucified if a project fails." At 3M, 5000 scientists are encouraged to spend up to 15 percent of their time working on special unapproved projects.

The autocratic manager is giving way to the managing helper, more a servant than a master. In this role, leadership comes from showing respect for the individual and listening and reacting to employees' needs.

TRAINING THE INDIVIDUAL

Management's primary responsibility to the individual is to provide the right tools for the job, an environment conducive to doing the job right every time, and the job-related training appropriate for the many variations that will be encountered on the job.

Training cannot be left to chance or to another employee who may be doing the job but is not trained to instruct a newcomer. The training requirements for each activity should be well-thought-out and documented.

Major corporations have found that training pays off and so have made enormous investments in the area. At IBM, for example, there is an education and training staff of more than 3000 people. "Worldwide, we spend hundreds of millions of dollars annually on our education program," says Ray AbuZayyad, president of the General Products Division. "Every year IBM employees spend the equivalent of 4 million student days in class. That's like having a student body of 40,000 students."

Polaroid's system is a good example of an advanced improvement training class. Harold Page, corporate vice president of Polaroid, when talking about their quality education program, said, "You talk about management commitment. This course is 176 hours; that's 8 hours 1 day a week for 22 weeks that we're taking people off their jobs."

When you invest in educating your employees, you invest in the future of your company.

PERSONAL GOAL SETTING AND MEASUREMENT

William J. Weisz, chief operating officer for Motorola, Inc., has said, "Our experience to date underscores again the precept that if you set high expectations and give people the support and opportunity they need, they can achieve."

People like to be told that they are doing a good job, but how can they perform at a superior level if management does not tell them what is expected of them? The basis of any good employee-manager relationship is a clear understanding of what management expects from the employee and what the employee expects from the company. This understanding requires that

1. A performance plan is agreed to between management and the employee.
2. A development plan is prepared to direct the employee's future growth.

Performance Planning

Each year a personal performance contract, called a "performance plan," should be developed between the manager and each employee. The performance plan should be task-oriented and should define what is expected of the employee to meet the requirements of the job. The key to developing a good performance plan is establishing and clearly communicating organizational objectives to the employee. These organizational objectives are converted into a set of tasks agreed to by the manager and the employee in an open and timely manner. In all cases the individual performance plan must support the overall organizational objectives.

The process of clarifying organizational objectives is usually a long, challenging, and difficult job, but managers will find it worthwhile for several reasons:

1. They are better able to delegate work.
2. They develop a better understanding of what they are doing.
3. They are able to develop more meaningful plans for the future.
4. They are able to align employee performance plans with department and company goals.
5. They are better able to justify actions of their employees and upper management.
6. They experience greater comfort in conducting performance evaluations of their employees.

The employee should always contribute to the setting of requirements for his or her job and defining the company's support required for successful completion of the job. This is a very important step in the process because it ensures that the employee understands his or her responsibilities. Each task should be defined in terms that are measurable in one or more of the following categories:

- Quality of the end result
- Cost versus value of end result
- Adherence to committed schedules

Ask yourself and the employee, "How will we know that this particular objective has been accomplished and how well it was accomplished?" This questioning forces the manager and the employee to think in terms of results. Then establish with the employee an understanding of what *meets* the requirements for the task and what would be needed to *exceed* requirements.

A typical factory worker would have 40 percent of the performance plan based on the quantity of work produced, 40 percent on the quality of output, and the remaining 20 percent on attitude toward the job. Security, attendance, safety, and similar items should never be part of the performance evaluation because these are behaviors that are governed by rules and regulations. Violation of these rules can lead to termination, and acceptable adherence does not usually influence the overall performance evaluation.

Most personal traits have only an indirect influence on an objective and should not be formally evaluated. Evaluating them is redundant because the objectives are being evaluated already since they are contained in the basic tasks. However, personal traits are important to take into account when objectives are *not* accomplished because they may point to employee weaknesses that need to be corrected. For example, a manager may determine that an individual is preparing memos that the recipients do not understand, causing the employee not to complete the assignment on schedule or at the correct quality level.

The performance plan should be customized to the individual and the job. It might simply consist of three columns with the following headings at the top and the rest of the form left blank to be filled in by the manager and the employee.

1. Task name
2. Task description
3. Task priority

The performance plan should be generated jointly by the employee and the manager, but it must be based upon the employee's job description. The performance plan should always be written so as to define the requirements of the job. Living up to the contract with no additional contributions or improvements means the employee *met* the requirements of the job and nothing more. The agreed-to performance plan should be signed by the manager and the employee and both should be provided a copy for ready reference. A yearly performance plan should be prepared for each employee and should be supplemented with shorter-range plans consisting of specific activities that will be accomplished during quarterly periods. The yearly plan may be general in nature, but the quarterly plans can be very specific.

After agreed-to yearly and quarterly performance plans are completed, the manager has the responsibility to continuously monitor and feed back performance information to the employee—not once every 3 months but every day, reinforcing the desired performance and helping the employee to change undesirable performance. It's an ongoing process that ensures that there are no surprises during the quarterly or yearly reviews.

Quarterly Performance Reviews

Once every 3 months, the manager and employee sit down in a quiet confidential area to review progress compared to the quarterly and yearly plans. Both the manager and the employee should spend some time preparing for the quarterly reviews by filling out a simple performance evaluation form similar to the one shown in Figure 7.1.

Each of the quarterly tasks or objectives named will be recorded, along with its priority. Both the employee and the manager then determine, independently, how well the job was performed by classifying it in one of the six performance levels shown in Figure 7.1.

The performance review focuses on tasks for which the employee rated himself or herself as performing at a higher level than the manager rated the employee. The objective of these discussions is to have the manager and employee agree on each of the individual ratings. When they cannot agree on an item, they should jointly establish a more detailed performance plan for that item, which will be used during the next 3 months with the objective of providing data to resolve the differing opinions. If the employee's own ratings are lower than those of the manager, the manager's rating will prevail.

As soon as the manager and employee have agreed on the individual task ratings and an overall rating for the previous 3 months, they will generate a performance plan to cover the next 3 months.

The quarterly sessions are informal reviews, so there is no official report to personnel. However, the quarterly reviews form the basis for the formal yearly review, which is simply the average of the quarterly review ratings.

One of the biggest problems with performance evaluations is management's not being honest with employees and rating them higher than they are actually performing—because it is the easiest way out of an uncomfortable situation. This practice is unfair to both the company and the employee, for three reasons:

1. It is unfair to the employees because it misleads them and does not provide them with the information they need to improve.

2. It is unfair to the company because the employee really is not doing the job as well as the manager indicates it is being done.

3. It is unfair to the other employees that are performing their jobs better and receiving similar ratings.

A good performance evaluation system, given a large population, should show a distribution similar to the one in Figure 7.2. Performance populations that are skewed to the high side should be questioned by upper management.

QUARTERLY PERFORMANCE EVALUATION FORM

Employee's name _____ Date _____

I. Employee's performance rating for the past three months

Task	Priority	Far exceeds requirements	Consistently exceeds requirements	Exceeds requirements at times	Meets requirements	Meets minimum requirements	Unsatisfactory
1.							
2.							
3.							
4.							
5.							
6.							
Total (performance level)							

II. Employee's major accomplishments since the last review

_____

_____

_____

_____

III. Employee's major goals for the coming three months

_____

_____

_____

_____

Prepared by: _____

Figure 7.1 Quarterly performance evaluation form.

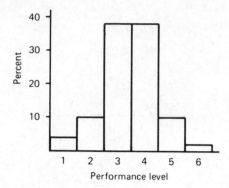

Figure 7.2 Performance distribution.

PAY FOR PERFORMANCE

Salaries should be directly related to both the level of job the employees have and how well they are performing their responsibilities. All job assignments can be performed at different levels of effectiveness, productivity, and quality, so it is only logical that each job should have a salary range associated with it. The employee that puts out large quantities of work at high quality levels should be paid more than the employee that just meets standards and frequently makes errors. The yearly performance evaluation provides an ideal way to relate the employees' salaries to their performance (see Figure 7.3).

By relating the individual's performance evaluation to the quality of output and then by relating performance level directly to salary, you have provided a financial incentive to the individual. This provides the individual with strong motivation to improve. The same reasoning applies to employees and managers alike: Why shouldn't a manager be held accountable for the quality of his or her department's output and get credit when it improves?

CAREER DEVELOPMENT AND PLANNING

Effective human-resource management is critical to conducting a successful business. Management has the responsibility not only to enhance the effectiveness of people on the job today, but also to plan for their utilization and growth as a resource of the future. Employee career planning is a significant part of such human-resource management. Essentially, it is a process of

- Identifying individual strengths, preferences, and development needs

$525	$550	$575	$600	$625	$650
Unsatisfactory	Meets minimum requirements	Meets requirements	Exceeds requirements at times	Consistently exceeds requirements	Outstanding performance

Figure 7.3   Pay for performance. Note: People who meet the requirements for the job would be paid between $550 and $575 per week.

▪ Implementing action to build on these strengths and meet these needs

Career planning does not create new job opportunities, nor does it guarantee either promotion or reassignment. It does, however, help the employee develop and grow both personally and professionally, enhancing his or her value to the company and qualifications for whatever new opportunities arise in the future.

There is a distinct difference between career planning and performance planning. Performance planning addresses the immediate job and its responsibilities. Career planning deals with the individual's skills and preferences for the future, as well as for today. Although career planning is a shared responsibility, the basic responsibility rests with the individual employee. The manager's role is one of giving the employee encouragement, information, and support.

What Is Career Planning?

A career plan can be defined as a plan of activities for an individual in pursuit of a personal occupational goal. A manager might ask a new employee what job he or she wants to have at retirement and then help to develop a plan that will provide the opportunities to meet the objective. The first hurdle that must be overcome in career planning is to look beyond the employee's immediate goal of being promoted to the next most obvious assignment. The most obvious move may in reality put that person on a detour or even a dead-end road as it relates to the true objectives. Management is responsible for providing the time and motivation to develop a career plan, but they cannot do it for the employee. It is the employee that must define goals, define willingness to sacrifice, and define action by determining personal needs and family needs. The employee must establish priorities because nothing comes free, not even failure. The cost of failure is success itself. The career plan provides a road map and a schedule that will lead the employee to the desired objectives.

Why Do Career Planning?

Career planning helps align individual growth plans with company goals. The object is to have employees and managers have careers with the company, not just jobs. When an individual's career is directly aligned with the company, that person will become part of the company and will want to know about it and help it to grow and improve because the company's growth will directly relate to the individual's growth. Furthermore, career planning strengthens the employee-manager relationship by placing the manager in a helping role.

The objectives of career planning are to

1. Help fulfill employees' desires to develop their potential and grow in their jobs
2. Ensure a continuous supply of qualified people as a resource for the future
3. Make the best use of employees' abilities now and in the future
4. Enhance employees' feelings of personal value
5. Provide resources that allow for promotion from within
6. Show that the company has respect for individuals

Career Planning Procedure

In the total career planning development team, three partners cooperate in making the career plan a success:

- The company has the responsibility to establish an environment for personal growth, education, and training for employees, both on company time and after working hours. This allows the employees to obtain the needed skills to develop their true potential, allows employees to obtain information about careers in other disciplines within the company, and last but not least important, it provides greater opportunity for promotion from within. Most new hires should enter the work force at the lowest entry level.
- The manager is the catalyst that encourages serious planning for the future. Furthermore, the manager understands the company's operation, procedures, and programs. The manager can guide and explain background needs that must be developed to be competitive in a new career opportunity. The manager also knows the employees' abilities, allowing for reality testing of the employees' aspirations. Finally, the manager also maintains continuous communication with the employees so that they are aware of the changing company needs and their impact upon career plans. The manager provides encouragement, recognition, and advice as the employees work to prepare themselves to move along the steps of their career plans.

- The employee obviously has the largest role to play. The employee must make hard choices about goals, willingness to sacrifice, and personal and family needs. The employee must identify strengths and weaknesses and determine how and why he or she got to the present position. Finally, the employee must determine the next career development action, how progress will be measured, and contingency plans.

Dr. Walter D. Sporey, author of *Career Action Planning*, states, "The greater the difficulty one has in charting his own career, the more one has to learn, not the more he needs to be directed or controlled." Many exercises and books are available to help an individual determine career interests and set long-range goals. Three exercises commonly used are the following:

1. *Values clarification exercise.* This exercise helps clarify what is important in life and on the job. Such factors as prestige, location, variety, stress, intellectual stimulation, and power are considered and ranked according to their value to the person.
2. *Satisfying job experience exercise.* This exercise asks the individual to describe several satisfying job experiences and answer probing questions as to why they were satisfying. After carefully analyzing jobs that produced satisfaction to the individual, usually a pattern emerges of the type of job the employee finds most rewarding.
3. *Personal growth and vitality.* This is a series of exercises that a person can use to assess the important elements of a job. Factors such as growth, utilization, challenge, opportunity, sense of contribution, and the like are considered in these experiments.

Many self-assessment workbooks are available at local bookstores or from publishers. Two examples are *Voyage: A Chart Book for Career/Life Planning* by Margaret Anstim (Kendall/Hunt Publishing Company) and *Coming Alive from Nine to Five* by Betty Neville Michelozzi (Mayfield Publishing Company).

Managers must realize that some employees are perfectly happy where they are and with what they are doing. These individuals should never be forced along a career path. At the same time, management must make them aware of what else might be available to them.

Development Plan

Once a year a development plan should be prepared by each employee and the appropriate manager. This plan focuses the primary attention of the employee on developing the most critical next step in a career cycle, as opposed to ultimate goals. The yearly development plan contains

- The employee's career aspirations (long-range goals) and the next step in the career plan (short-range goal)
- The most critical needs for improvement to reach the next career step
- What the employee will do over the next year to become more competitive for the next career step and the long-range goal (examples: correspondence school, preparation of technical papers, formal education after work, professional society, community leadership)
- What the company will do to help the employee prepare for the next career step (examples: in-house education, paid-for outside education, conferences, job rotation, special job assignments, loaning the employee to other departments)

When the development plan is complete, both the manager and employee should sign it and each of them should keep a copy. Periodically, throughout the year, the manager and employee should meet to review progress in carrying out the development plan.

The career planning process is a useful tool to help the company develop its people to their full potential and to make the individuals feel that they are part of the company. The career planning process helps the employee think about work assignments as a career with the company, not just a job. This attitude stimulates improvements in all areas and reduces labor turnover rates significantly.

SUGGESTION PROGRAM

The suggestion program is an American institution started in 1896 by National Cash Register Company. The suggestion plan offers the person closest to the work activity the opportunity to suggest improvements. This results in more efficient utilization of assets, increased productivity, waste reduction, lower product costs, and improved quality. For the employee, the suggestion plan offers, in addition to extra income, a means for self-expression, a path toward achievement, recognition, and a feeling of contributing. Paul Petermann, manager of field suggestions at the IBM Corporation, has stated, "Ideas are the lifeblood of the company and the suggestion plan is a way to get these ideas marketed."

Suggestion programs save companies around the world billions of dollars each year and allow the companies to share these savings with the employees who contribute to the savings. The National Association of Suggestion Systems reported that its member companies in the U.S. recorded savings of $800 million in 1984 and paid out $98 million in awards to their employees. The average savings per employee was $12,657. From 1975 to 1984 the IBM Corporation alone paid out $60,000,000 for suggestions made by employees—a bargain when you consider that these ideas meant $300,000,000 in savings to IBM.

How Does the Suggestion Program Work?

Normally, all employees document their ideas for improvement and submit them to a central suggestion department. The suggestion department chooses the area within the company that is best suited to evaluate and implement the suggestion. If the suggestion is accepted by the evaluation area, the evaluator will determine what tangible savings will result from implementing the idea. In some cases, suggestions will be accepted even though the savings are intangible; these ideas have benefit to the company, but the savings cannot be measured or estimated in precise dollars-and-cents terms.

Both the accepted and rejected suggestions are then returned to the suggestion department where the evaluations are reviewed for completeness and accuracy. Then a letter is sent to the employee's manager, describing the action taken on the suggestion. For accepted suggestions, a check usually accompanies the letter. Each suggestion is then reviewed with the employee by his manager. When major cash awards are received, the manager will usually call a department meeting to present the award to the employee. This provides recognition for the employee and incentive for the other members of the department to participate in the suggestion program.

Cash Awards

Although all employees may submit suggestions, some employees are not normally eligible to receive cash awards:

1. Suggestion department personnel and managers with people responsibility are not usually eligible for awards.

2. Nonmanagerial exempt employees cannot receive awards for suggestions that are part of their normal job responsibilities or related to their area of responsibility.

3. Nonexempt employees cannot receive awards for suggestions that are part of their duties and responsibilities as outlined in their job descriptions or performance plans. (For example: An analyst who writes procedures would not receive an award for suggesting a change to a document he or she wrote, but the assembly operator could receive an award for making the same suggestion.)

Cash awards should be calculated according to a standard company procedure. In some companies, all suggestions receive the same cash award, but in many leading companies the award is a percentage of the net savings to the company over a specific time period. For example, IBM currently awards the employee 25 percent of the net savings for the first 2 years after the suggestion is implemented, with a minimum award of $50 and a maximum award of $100,000. Eli Lilly also awards the employee 25 percent of the total net savings, but the national average for all companies is 17 percent.

Japanese Suggestion Activities

The Japanese, in the 1950s, imported the suggestion program concept from the United States and expanded its application and use in much the same way they did statistical quality control and total quality control. Today, it is the most effective employee involvement tool used in Japan, surpassing even the quality circle movement. In a recent study the Japanese Suggestion Association reported, "As viewed from the relationship with small group activities, which is the nucleus of suggestion activities, 50 times as many suggestions are made for every solution of one problem by one circle; as to the patent and the utility model, one application is made for every 2500 suggestions."

Today the number of suggestions per eligible employee in Japan is 100 times larger than in the United States, and the amount of economic return per eligible employee is estimated to be quadruple that in the United States. The Japanese suggestion system is not a passive system that waits for suggestions from the employees, but an active system that educates, promotes, and gives targets for suggestions. The suggestion system in Japan started by building in the Japanese worker the habit of making sugggestions. This included training people to become accomplished at making suggestions. Employees are trained on how to collect data and write suggestions so they can readily be adopted. Targets are established for the number of suggestions per employee, and lists of participants and nonparticipants are published. The object is to encourage every person to become an active participant in the suggestion program. Employees that do not participate are requested by their managers to take part in the program, and major companies throughout Japan try to create an environment in which every person in the company is participating in the suggestion system.

The results have been significant. In 1983, 2,410,000 people contributed 40,980,000 suggestions—an average of 17 suggestions per participating employee. This was an increase of two suggestions per eligible employee over the 1982 figures. This average is much higher than the American average. Sanyo's suggestion program is typical of the Japanese method. Sanyo started their program in 1965. The first year they received 12,389 suggestions; in 1983 they received 356,104. The average suggestions per qualified employee increased from 6 to 37.7 per year over the same time period. The quality level of suggestions also greatly improved, as only 21.6 percent were adopted in 1965 compared to 92.9 percent in 1983. Over the years participation doubled to 67.2 percent.

Initially, the Japanese program aimed at getting 100 percent participation of all eligible employees, pressing quantity, not quality, of the suggestions. They believed that quantity would naturally lead to quality, but they found this to be a false assumption. Today's Japanese suggestion system is moving in the direction of increased quality of suggestions through employee education. This has resulted in a decrease in the number of suggestions in companies such as Hitachi, Fuji Electric, Toyota, Fuji Heavy Industry, and Sumitomo Metals Industries.

The total savings realized as a direct benefit from the suggestion system in Japan for 1983 came to $1952 million, a significant increase over 1982 when the savings were $1305 million (yen was converted to dollars at a rate of 200 yen per dollar).

The cash award system in Japan is not nearly so generous as it is in the United States. Of the total savings realized in 1983, cash awards paid to Japanese employees equalled $59 million, an average of $1.44 per suggestion and about $24.48 per participant per year. In spite of this, the suggestion program in Japan is moving ahead at a very fast pace.

JOB IMPROVEMENT PROGRAM

The job improvement program provides a way that employees can document and receive recognition for accomplishments that they implement within their regular job responsibilities—accomplishments that are not eligible for suggestion awards. A job improvement program

- Provides a recognition system for employee job-related ideas
- Creates an environment that encourages change
- Increases the level of quality and productivity

Job Improvement Procedures

Each time an employee has an idea related to the business, the idea should be evaluated to determine if it is eligible for the suggestion program. If it is not, it will probably be eligible for the job improvement program. All items that are candidates for the job improvement program should be implemented before a job improvement form is submitted. This form will answer the following questions:

1. How was the task done before the change?
2. How is the task being done now?
3. What is the estimated impact of the change on quality, performance, manpower, and/or cost?
4. What is the estimated cost of implementation?
5. What will be the job improvement savings?

The form should be completed and signed by the employee. It is then turned in to the department manager who verifies the information, signs the form, and forwards it to the job improvement coordinator. The job improvement coordinator checks the form, then inputs the data into the job improvement database.

Job improvement changes that have general and/or multiple applications will also be noted at this point. These multiple-use changes are then documented in a quarterly report that is circulated to management. This report provides the stimuli for many spin-off job improvement activities. The job improvement coordinator will also set up educational programs on subjects such as work simplification or value engineering to help the employees develop new skills to improve their abilities to develop new creative ideas.

Job Improvement Commitments

Because job improvement is the responsibility of all employees, the department manager should be required to submit a job improvement commitment for the coming year and measure himself or herself and the department against this goal. A typical commitment would be "record a $100,000 savings over the next 12 months and have 100 percent of the employees participating by submitting a minimum of one job improvement idea." This could be used as the basis for one of the department TIC charts. It can also be a line item in the performance plans of all the employees because it is directly related to the jobs they are performing.

This same process is repeated by each level of management until a companywide job improvement commitment has been established for the coming year. Management should take these commitments very seriously and include the committed savings in the business plan.

Job Improvement Recognition

There are as many recognition systems for the job improvement program as there are companies involved in such programs. A typical recognition system would involve monthly and quarterly competitions, small prizes (ranging up to about $100), luncheons with company officers, certificates, and so forth. Of course, the job improvement program can also provide management with information that leads to the employee's receiving one of the major company awards at a later date.

REQUEST FOR CORRECTIVE ACTION

Many times an employee has a problem and doesn't know how to solve it. When this condition occurs, the employee should be encouraged to discuss the situation with his or her manager, but sometimes this is ineffective or the employee may be reluctant to do this. Experience has proven that many of the problems reported to the first-line manager are not corrected because he or she has not been given the time or the resources to correct them or doesn't know how to get them corrected.

A very effective way of identifying problems before they become serious is through the use of a request for corrective action form (RCA). Any employee who is having a problem or knows of a problem can fill out an RCA form and send it to the quality assurance control center. The writer has the option of signing or not signing the RCA, with the stipulation that he or she will remain anonymous unless the employee indicates a desire to discuss the situation with the investigator. The RCA is assigned by the quality assurance control center to the area that is most likely to be able to solve the problem. When a plan of action is developed, this information is sent to the person who identified the problem (assuming she or he signed the RCA).

Companies that have implemented this type of program indicate that over 90 percent of the items submitted can be acted upon and brought to a successful conclusion.

BACK TO BASICS

The basics of people management are the foundation of the improvement process. A simple letter of appreciation for a job well done will do more than wallpapering the area with posters and slogans will.

Too often, managers look for new programs, new methods, new gimmicks that will turn the company around, but in reality the company is made up of individuals, and individuals all want about the same things:

- Being appreciated
- Accomplishing something worthwhile
- Growing with the company and feeling they're part of it
- Having a manager that levels with them
- Being a person, not just a number

8

System Improvement

INTRODUCTION

The only way improvement gains can be effectively and permanently embedded in the fiber of a company is through changing the systems that control the company's operations. It is not the employees who cause the majority of errors; they are just unwilling pawns who operate in the environment often controlled by obsolete and cumbersome operating systems. It is not the managers who cause the errors; their only error is allowing the company to operate with systems that have not been fine-tuned to today's needs. As we try to eliminate errors, we must not attack people. They are not the problem. What needs to be attacked and re-structured are the operating systems that govern and control the company's performance. We then need to install procedures to ensure that these critical systems are regularly updated and followed.

In a survey conducted by the Institute of Industrial Engineers, almost 45 percent of the responding companies said that over the past 5 years they had invested in altering the systems that controlled their operations; 70 percent of those companies reported improvements in quality and productivity resulting from changes in systems.

PROCESS MANAGEMENT

To get economy of scale, most companies have organized themselves in vertical functioning groups with experts of similar background grouped together to provide a pool of knowledge and skill capable of completing any task in that discipline. This provides an effective, strong, confident organization that functions well as a team, eager to support its own mission. Unfortunately, most work activities do not flow vertically; they flow horizontally.

The horizontal work flow and vertical organization result in many voids and overlaps that have a negative impact on the efficiency and quality of the operation. Consider a hypothetical order processing department that decides to stop comparing the item order number to the written description, even though they have been finding 3.3 percent errors. They reason that it is the salesman's responsibility to be sure that the order is filled out correctly, not theirs, and they could use the 40 hours per week that they are investing in checking out the order to process the growing backlog of orders they have. This has a very positive effect on their primary measurement. The number of hours before an average order is processed drops from 38 hours to 12 hours.

Unfortunately, the end results are disastrous. Two percent of the customers begin to receive the wrong product. Suboptimization is exactly what you want to avoid. In effect you have a group of individuals being measured on goals that are not in tune to the total needs of the business. Despite cases like these, a functional organization has many benefits, and there is a strategy available that takes maximum advantage of the effectiveness of the functional organization and drives the process to ensure that all activities provide maximum benefit to the company. That strategy is process management.

What Is Process Management?

Most repetitive activities (both white- and blue-collar) can be considered processes and controlled much the same way as manufacturing processes are controlled. We manage many white-collar processes that are equally as complex as manufacturing processes—such activities as engineering, distribution, personnel, data processing, and others. In the past, most of our attention has been directed at process controls for the manufacturing areas only. Today, the real payoff comes from applying the proven manufacturing control and feedback techniques to all key activities in the business and treating the entire company as a complex process that contains many subprocesses, only one of which is the process that produces the products sold to the customer.

To help bring this concept into focus, "process" is defined as

> A series of activities that takes an input, adds value to it, and produces an output (application of skills adding value to an input)

The definition just given is simple; most processes are not. Edward J. Kane, IBM Corporation's director of quality, who has been very active in applying this concept in the white-collar areas of IBM, has stated:

> Just taking a customer order and moving it through the plant and distributing these requirements out to the manufacturing floor—that activity alone has thirty-one subprocess steps to it. Accounts receivable has over twenty process steps. Information processing is a whole discipline in itself with many challenging processes integrated into a single total activity. So we do manage some very complex processes separate from the manufacturing floor itself.

Role of the Process Manager

Vertical organizations in most companies studied tend to defuse the process and proliferate suboptimization. To offset this negative situation, you need to identify a process manager. For each major process, this individual is given full responsibility for the process and is held accountable for cutting across organizational lines. The process manager's duties are to ensure that proper focus is placed on the entire process across all organizational structures, to drive process improvement, and to ensure that all changes to the process have a positive effect on the total process.

In most cases this does not turn out to be a full-time job. In fact, after the process gets started, the individual who assumes ownership for it will probably have more time than before because less time will be spent chasing problems. The person selected to be the process manager should be the one who has the most to gain or lose from the success of the process. That is the person to make responsible for the process.

Why have a process manager? Most processes either have no owner or several people that think they own it, which is the same as no one owning it. If no one owns the process, the process will never be improved.

The first duty of the process manager is to define the boundaries of the process. The boundaries should include everything from the point at which the first supplier provides input into the process to the point at which the customer is supplied with the output. For example, the hiring process starts when a manager realizes he or she has a need for another employee and ends after the new employee has completed the introductory company training sessions, including all the steps between. Once the boundaries are defined, the members of the process improvement team can be identified.

PROCESS IMPROVEMENT TEAMS

The process manager is responsible for organizing a process improvement team made up of representatives from each function involved in the process. Each member of the team will be assigned by the department manager and will be representing and making commitments for the entire department. The team is responsible for developing and implementing the improvement activities for the assigned process. Their major activities will be

1. Developing a flow diagram of the process
2. Establishing measurement points and feedback loops
3. Qualifying the process
4. Developing and implementing improvement plans
5. Reporting quality, productivity, and change status
6. Developing and implementing the just-in-time stocking system

This is a radical departure from the way we have done business in the past in the support areas, but it will be very familiar to those who come from the manufacturing process areas, where it has been a proven way of doing business since the early 1950s.

Flow-Diagramming the Process

The first job that the process improvement team undertakes is to flow-diagram the process. This diagram should identify each time a person comes in contact with the process. Here are the first five steps in the process of hiring:

1. Manager fills out rough draft of the employee requisition form.
2. Secretary types form.
3. Manager checks and signs form.
4. Secretary sends form to second-level manager for review and signature.
5. Second-level manager signs completed form, verifying that it is filled out correctly and that the requesting manager has authorization for the additional headcount.

The rest of the process can be broken down the same way.

The next activity is for the process improvement team to define what procedures apply to each operation. They would also define what documented training requirements exist for each operation.

To ensure that the flow diagram is complete and accurate, members of the improvement process team should make a trial run through the process. Typical questions that the process improvement team should ask at each operation are

1. What document controls this activity?
2. How were you trained?
3. Was the training adequate?
4. Where do you get the inputs you need to do your activity?
5. How do you know you are doing the activity correctly?
6. What types of errors do you see coming in to you?
7. Do you have any problems related to this activity?
8. Do you have any suggestions that would improve your activity?
9. What makes the job difficult?

This walk-through provides the process improvement team with new insight into the process and a list of problems as viewed from the workplace, a list of improvements that can be made to the process, an assessment of the adequacy of the training, and an overview of the process and its weaknesses and strengths. A walk-through such as this could point out that the car door inhibits the installation of interior components. American car manufacturers put the door on once and customize it to fit. Japanese auto companies build the door to fit without customizing so it can be easily removed to install the interior. As a result, the interior work is of higher quality and the total time cycle is reduced. In General Motors and Toyota's joint venture to build the Nova in Fremont, California, the doors are installed twice.

Measurement Points and Feedback Loops

The process improvement team must first define potential sources of errors, then define measurement points to evaluate the output as close as practical to the source of the errors, and finally establish a feedback loop that will allow the individuals to correct the errors that are within their control. This data system will also provide the process improvement team with the information needed to allow management to invest in equipment and training and/or to change procedures to prevent the error from recurring.

Often, in the white-collar areas, few measurement points exist, and where they do exist, there is little or no feedback. But there are exceptions. American Airlines constantly measures the time it takes the reservations people to answer the phone (the average is 20 seconds). They also measure departure and arrival times. They shoot for 85 percent of the flights to take off within 5 minutes of the scheduled departure time and arrive within 15 minutes of scheduled arrival time. They also measure to see if 85 percent of the people in line get their tickets within 5 minutes. The time it takes to get bags off the plane is also gauged, as are many more items of customer satisfaction.

Managers and employees alike often rely on "gut feel" to solve problems. At times this method works, but more often it fails. It is essential to have an objective understanding of the problem before you try to solve it. Thus, measurement is absolutely essential to progress. Quantitative measurements are better than qualitative ones, but sometimes error-related measurements are not available and you have to rely on your customer's judgment. There is nothing wrong with asking someone what they think about your people, your operation, or your output.

It is essential that measurement points be placed close to the activity being performed. Ideally the measurement point should be part of the activity. Reducing the feedback cycle saves money in two ways. First, the employee does not continue to make errors, and second, additional resources are not added to an already defective item. Studies at Hewlett-Packard revealed that a defective resistor costs 2¢ if thrown away before use. It costs $10 if they find it at the board-assembly level, and hundreds of dollars if it is not detected until it reaches the customer. IBM studies indicate there is a 50 to 1 leverage in finding a defective circuit card in the subassembly test area over finding the same defect in the customer's office. The leverage for software errors is 80 to 1.

An essential part of any measurement and feedback system is an independent audit system that will ensure compliance to the procedures. It is nonsense to blindly accept data that are generated without proper checks and balances, not because people will falsify data—most people won't—but most employees have a strong desire to satisfy management and tell them what they want to hear.

The process improvement team should also ensure that the product specifications are documented and truly reflect customer expectations and that customer feedback loops are in place to ensure that the degree of customer satisfaction is being measured and changes in expectation levels can be recognized.

STATISTICAL PROCESS CONTROL

Once the measurement characteristics are defined and the measurement system is in place, the process improvement team should make a thorough analysis of the total process to identify characteristics that lend themselves to statistical process control methods. (See Appendices A and B.)

Statistical process control requires a radical change in thinking for most companies. But the technical aspects of statistical process control are quite well-developed. The mathematical aspects are very rigorous and well-documented. Instruments for measuring process and output characteristics are becoming increasingly accurate and economical, to the point that real-time fully automated in-process measurement and control charting tools are now widely available.

THE PROCESS CYCLE

The objective of the early-entry activities is to bring the process under control, then implement improvement activities. A typical process evolves through four different phases during its life cycle:

Phase A: Out of control
Phase B: Stable
Phase C: Step-by-step improvement
Phase D: Customer ship (continuous improvement)

Phase A: Out of Control

During this phase of its evolution, the process frequently goes out of control, indicated by small circles in Figure 8.1. The first priority of the

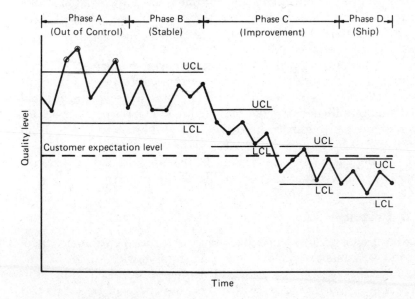

Figure 8.1 **The process cycle**

process improvement team is to understand the true cause of each of these spikes and to implement control over the process elements that cause them. By understanding and controlling these elements, the process improvement team begins to understand the process and soon it will stabilize and enter into phase B, where the chronic problems can be addressed. The process should always be brought under control before the chronic problems are attacked.

Phase B: Stable

During this phase, the process performance is statistically stable, but it is not producing output that meets customer expectations. It is a major breakthrough to bring the process to a stable state, but it is not an answer in itself. Stabilizing the process is only the starting point at which the process improvement team should begin to direct its attention to the chronic problems in a systematic way, defining a plan of action to improve the process output so that it meets customer expectations.

Phase C: Step-by-Step Improvement

Once the process is under control, we need to carefully analyze and give priorities to the potential improvements, based on cost, ease of implementation, and estimated impact. Then a plan should be developed that allows the potential improvements to be implemented and evaluated one at a time (see Figure 8.2). In this example, four different actions were taken, one at a time, to improve stock inventory integrity to a level acceptable to the customer.

After each action, the process is given time to stabilize so that the action's impact on the total process can be evaluated. It is very important to evaluate each action's impact on the total process, not on the individual step that was modified. For example, action 3 (standard storage containers) had a negative impact on the process and increased costs. If all four actions had gone into the process at the same time, the process would have met customer expectations, but you would be trapped into the more expensive containers for the life of the process.

Phase D: Customer Ship

We now have statistical evidence that the output meets customer expectations, and we can start delivery to our customers with a high degree of confidence that they will be satisfied with the output. Remember, the customer who is satisfied today with an output may not be satisfied 6 months from now with an output that has the same quality level because

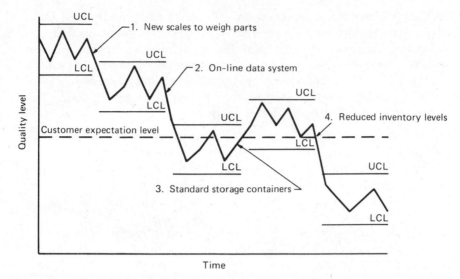

Figure 8.2 Step-by-step actions for inventory integrity.

the customer's expectations are continuously getting more difficult to meet, and as a result, the process output must continue to improve. It is for this reason this phase is sometimes called the continuous improvement phase.

SYSTEMS ENGINEERING

Often the process that is being used evolved over a number of years. Its first concept may have been sound, but over the years, quick patches to correct organizational, equipment, personnel, and product changes may have made the total system cumbersome, slow, unreliable, and unnecessarily complex. If this occurs, it is time to use a systems engineering approach to streamline the process.

Systems engineering involves reasoning backward (top down) to find the best means of achieving a desired goal. The key is to give the goal itself primary importance and the means of achieving it secondary importance.

Using systems engineering methods, the process improvement team can design the most effective system that will meet the primary goal, placing secondary emphasis on the various subgoals, whose only function should be to support the primary goal. The primary goal might be "to provide a continuously high return on the stockholders' investments."

The goal of a major subprocess oriented toward the primary goal could be "to assure that a customer-acceptable product is shipped at minimum cost" (the quality process goal). Activities such as design review, process capability studies, in-process inspections, and test equipment certification are all interrelated subprocesses of the major quality process.

A four-step approach is used by the systems engineering concept to develop an effective process. These steps are

1. *Develop process specification.* The specification defines objectives that the process must meet.

2. *Process network analysis.* During this phase, the various possible process organizations and their interconnected process structures are analyzed to determine what compromises must be made to develop the most desirable total process.

3. *Develop data channels.* Since most processes have interdependent processes, feedback—up, down, and sideways—must be designed into the subprocesses.

4. *Process documentation.* This phase details the documentation of the process operation, data flow, and maintenance activities required to support the process. It also includes a trial run of the process to ensure that it meshes smoothly with interrelated processes. Some of the means of documenting the process are flow diagrams, procedures, and decision tables.

The systems engineering approach concentrates on the whole process rather than the individual subprocesses, thereby giving the overall goal maximum priority.

Practical Applications of Systems Engineering Concepts

Let's apply the systems engineering approach to the process of building a new piece of test equipment. The overall goal is to provide the manufacturing process with the ability to evaluate an output to ensure that nonconforming products do not continue through the process.

A subprocess of this major process is the quality assurance test equipment certification process. The goal of this certification subprocess is to ensure that the test engineering design objective meets the process needs and to verify that the test equipment functions to the design objectives.

Many processes can be formed to meet the certification objective, but two are obvious:

1. Quality assurance is responsible for the total certification activities.

2. Test engineering performs specific certification activities and submits the plan and resulting data to quality assurance for concurrence.

Table 8.1 illustrates the activities that must be performed to certify a piece of test equipment and the times required to conduct each of these activities. The figure outlines a typical 100-hour certification program when quality assurance is totally responsible for the certification effort.

Now, let's look at the advantages of test engineering performing part of the certification activity:

- Manpower required to complete the certification effort is reduced by 67.3 percent.
- The test engineer has total responsibility and accountability for the test equipment. (When quality assurance performs a certification, the only person who has total accountability is the plant general manager.)

A disadvantage is that there are fewer checks and balances built into this process. However, this exposure is minimized since quality assurance still reviews test engineering design activity, the test engineering evaluation plan, and the results of the evaluation. In addition, a data and failed-parts return program is established during the early phases of the program. This activity ensures that all parts that failed after they were tested are recycled through the test equipment to verify that the test equipment can detect the errors.

This is a classic example of process improvement used to offset bureaucracy, but the same type of problems exist everywhere you look to a larger or smaller degree. Intel Corporation reported that it took them ninety-five administrative steps and twelve pieces of paper to purchase a ballpoint pen. By systematically analyzing the procurement process, they were able to reduce it to one form and eight administrative steps. Intel estimates that they can get a 30 percent productivity improvement

TABLE 8.1 Equipment Certification Activities

Program events	Subsystem 1: quality assurance certification	Subsystem 2: test engineering certification
1. Problem definition	15 hours	0 hours
a. Test system philosophy and objectives		
b. Test equipment build and test schedule		
2. Design review	20	1.7
3. Evaluation planning	40	14.0
4. Evaluation	20	10.0
5. Analysis and report writing	5	7.0
Total time required for subsystem	100	32.7

from systems improvements like these—a $60 million a year savings. This $60 million savings in operating costs is equivalent to a $277 million increase in Intel sales volume. The leverage factor is tremendous. The real dollar payback comes from directing the improvement process at the process, not at the people who use the process. See Appendix A for other process analysis tools.

PROCESS QUALIFICATION

A qualified process is one that has demonstrated that all the necessary procedures, training, documentation, measurements, controls, and checks and balances are in place to ensure that the process can produce high-quality output even under stress and extreme conditions. When this level of performance is demonstrated, the product and process design are complete and the program can go into a maintenance and improvement mode.

This does not mean that the process has reached its optimum performance or error levels; quite the contrary, it is the start of the improvement process and the beginning of the voyage to error-free performance. One of the best ways to help a company move from an appraisal-type philosophy into a preventive-type philosophy is by implementing a systematic process qualification activity.

The complexity of a qualification activity varies based upon the complexity of the process itself. To provide as thorough a picture as possible, let's review what is required to qualify a complex thin-film, electronic-component process. A typical component manufacturing cycle will evolve through three stages:

1. Development laboratories produce crude models, using complex laboratory equipment, to prove out a theory or concept.

2. A model pilot line is prepared to manufacture larger quantities of product for internal evaluation.

3. The production line is established to produce finished product for the customer.

Qualification Plan

We must begin our discussion by looking at two definitions:

1. *Certification* applies to a single operation or piece of equipment. When an acceptable level of confidence has been developed that proves that the operation and/or equipment is producing products to specification when the documentation is followed, that item is then certified.

2. *Qualification* is acceptable performance of a complete process consisting of many operations that have already been individually certified. For a process to be qualified, each of the operations and all of the equipment used in the process must be certified. In addition, the process must have demonstrated that it can repeatedly produce high-quality products or services that meet customer expectations.

In the manufacturing process areas, quality assurance normally is responsible for process qualification. In the nonmanufacturing areas, process qualification is the responsibility of the process improvement team and probably will not go through all the stages indicated in this example, which involves four separate qualification levels. Level 1 qualification evaluates the acceptability of the development process. At this stage, it is important to establish basic controls, collect pertinent data, and study manufacturability without interfering with the creative nature of the work environment.

Level 2 qualification is directed at the pilot process that is used to produce product for internal evaluation and specification preparation. The purposes of the level 2 qualification are to

1. Characterize hardware and processes used to submit products to engineering evaluations
2. Provide a controlled environment for assessment of process and performance parameters
3. Establish a database for the manufacturing process
4. Ensure that the process is ready to be transferred from development engineering to manufacturing
5. Provide management with a risk assessment of manufacturability and schedule integrity

Now that we have a controlled development pilot line, the next step in the process is to design and build a manufacturing production facility. Level 3 qualification evaluates this new process to ensure that it meets both customer and company expectations.

In most cases, level 3 qualification applies to a single-stream product line that has limited ability to produce the customer-shippable products. Once this line is established, the process continues to expand, adding equipment to the manufacturing facilities. Hard tooling replaces soft tooling and automation moves into the manufacturing process. During this growth period, sufficient quantities of products are being made to allow extremes of specified test-equipment settings and vendor-material variations to be evaluated through process capability studies. This is the environment that we find ourselves in as we start to perform level 4 qualification.

Up to this point, the process qualification activities have been directed at bringing the process under control before we start shipping products to our customers. The purpose of level 4 is to characterize the process to ensure that it is under control and has the ability to consistently produce output that meets customer expectations.

Qualification Activities

To get a better understanding of process qualification at each of the four levels, let's take a look at the three major activities that go on during a typical qualification study:

1. Certifying each operation in the process
2. Processing qualification lots
3. Independent process audit

Operation Certification.   The first of these, qualification activities, looks at four facets of each operation:

1. *Documentation.*   Documentation allows the experience and knowledge of previous activities to be transmitted to the individual currently performing the job. Frequently, companies build up a bureaucracy around paperwork; the intent is good, but the implementation is poor. Good documentation is short, to the point, and reflects optimum methods of performing the job. Most important of all, it must be easy to understand.

2. *Test and process equipment.*   Test equipment and process equipment can have a major impact on the quality and productivity of the area. Certification of the equipment determines if it is capable of doing the assigned job and being maintained properly.

3. *Operational requirements.*   At this point in the certification activities the support systems of each operation are evaluated to determine its adequacy.

4. *Output acceptability.*   The first three facets of the certification activity have all been building up to the point that we can ensure output acceptability on a continuous basis. Now the output from the activity is evaluated.

Qualification Lots.   Once each activity in the process has been certified, qualification lots are processed to measure the effectiveness of the process design. The purpose of a qualification lot is to evaluate the continuity of the total process, measure process yields, and identify process volume limitations under controlled conditions. A typical level 3 process qualification design experiment would be conducted over a 5-week period; one of the 5 weeks would be used to measure equipment capacity and throughput volumes. A minimum of five separate lots would be processed through the manufacturing operations.

Independent Process Audit.   The next step in the qualification process is a detailed process audit. The audit team is headed by the process improvement team chairman and consists of an independent group not assigned to the process. For example, you might have representatives from product engineering, development engineering, manufacturing engineering, product assurance, and sales. This audit team would evaluate the process status in the following areas:

1. Have product and process manufacturability been proven?
2. Is the complete process documented and understood?
3. Has the design considered and corrected problems existing in similar products?
4. Does the performance specification represent an improvement in reliability and quality performance compared to products that it will replace?
5. Is the program schedule reasonable and does it have committed headcount and equipment funding from all supporting areas?
6. Are there any major technical exposures to the program or the supporting technologies?
7. Have the certification and qualification activities been implemented as required and have all major exposures been highlighted?
8. Is the measurement and feedback system in place and working effectively?
9. Does the end product meet customer expectations?

As soon as the audit team members have completed their assessment, they will meet with the process improvement team and report their findings. These findings will be subsequently documented in an audit team report. The process improvement team will generate corrective actions to solve each of the problems described in this report.

JUST-IN-TIME STOCKING

As the process gets statistically under control and the supplier quality level improves, the large quantities of just-in-case stock can be slowly reduced, bringing the system from just-in-case to just-in-time (JIT). The benefits from just-in-time are many since the company can reduce or eliminate

- Receiving inspection

- Inventory costs
- Inventory space
- Inventory cycle time

Many large and small U.S. companies are now using just-in-time, including IBM, Ford, GM, Chrysler, Hewlett-Packard, Motorola, and Westinghouse. It requires a focused team effort to make JIT work for you. Before starting, the following must be addressed:

1. Set-up times must be minimal.
2. A measurement in-process system must be established that identifies defective incoming parts close to the point they enter the line.
3. The manufacturing floor must have a layout that minimizes stock movement between operations.
4. Operation work times must be designed to keep a continuous flow of work moving through the process.
5. Parts suppliers should be able to deliver high-quality components on schedule.
6. New contracts that define delivery schedules and the maximum turnaround time required to supply good parts if bad parts are received need to be negotiated with the suppliers.

The process improvement team should select a small number of their best parts to get the system started and then expand as the process and supplier quality improve. No supplier part without a 100 percent yield for the past twenty lots should be considered for JIT.

CONTINUOUS IMPROVEMENT PHASE

The process improvement team and department improvement teams are both active during the continuous improvement phase of the activity cycle. The process improvement team's responsibility spans many functions and departments. As a result, they are directly driven by a cost and performance analysis of the total process and only address the critical few problems, concentrating on problems that involve more than one department. Frequently, a problem that cannot be resolved by a department improvement team will be submitted to the process improvement team because its solution involves a number of functions or departments.

The process improvement team is different in another very important way from the department improvement team. The process improvement team manages problems rather than creating solutions to them. Seldom, if ever, are such techniques as brainstorming or force-field analysis used during a process improvement team meeting. Normally, a problem is identified and assigned to an appropriate party to investigate it and report findings to the process improvement team. This allows the process improvement team to work efficiently on a number of significant problems at the same time without wasting individual members' time. The process improvement team will track each problem and ensure that someone has accepted ownership for the problem and is making steady progress in solving it. Frequently, as more data is accumulated, the problem will be reassigned to another individual from a different area because that person now has the best potential for solving the problem.

The process improvement team must provide the driving force that assures that each problem—manufacturing or service—completes the opportunity cycle (described in Chapter 6). Joseph M. Juran, one of today's leading quality consultants, calls this approach project-by-project quality improvement. He believes the best way to improve quality is by identifying a problem project and assigning clear responsiblities for its solution. He provides many examples of how this concept has worked for companies such as Bethlehem Steel, Owatonna Tool Co., Tektronix Inc., Motorola Inc., Union Carbide Corp., and others. In a paper presented in June 1985, in Lisbon, he stated, "The projects resulted in large savings and remarkable return on the investment in the improvement process. The estimates ranged from millions of dollars per project to less than $100,000 each. My best estimate is that they averaged about $100,000 per project." Dr. Juran pointed out that if a company's poor-quality costs were $1 billion (sales of $5 billion and a cost of poor quality equal to 20 percent of sales), it would take 5000 projects to cut the cost of poor quality in half.

Another very important part of the process improvement team's activity is to ensure that all changes made to the process have a positive total effect on the process without introducing suboptimization. All process changes should be submitted to the process improvement team along with supporting data proving that the results of the change provide an overall improvement to quality and/or productivity. This often requires conducting a controlled experiment to obtain the required data.

The process improvement team should approve the content of the experiment that will be used to prove that the change will have a positive effect on the total process. This review eliminates the possibility of completing the designed experiment and having the results rejected because the sample size was too small or an essential consideration was missed.

The process improvement team provides an excellent operating team of process-knowledgeable experienced professionals ready to react to any emergency that may arise within the process.

PROCESS ENGINEERING

The object of all these activities is to get management and key support personnel to think and use process engineering methods as a tool to improve the systems they deal with on an everyday basis. To accomplish this they must

1. Define customer expectations
2. Define input sources and user expectations
3. Document activities and work flow
4. Establish measurements and feedback methods
5. Qualify the process
6. Optimize the process

An IBM process improvement team used these approaches to improve a troublesome process: the generation of special bids to customers. The process was typically taking 90 days, and that was too long. The sales force felt that their ability to make the sale would be greatly improved if the cycle time could be reduced to 30 days. Ed Kane, director of quality, reported,

> Many actions were taken such as redefining and reducing the number of decision points, delegating greater authority to the field organization, and eliminating delay by automating the data collection and approval process.
>
> The results over a 24-month period show clear improvement, reducing the approval cycle to an average of 15 days. Even more significant, the bid closing rate improved from 20 percent to 65 percent over the same period.

REPORTING

Because of the magnitude and complexity of the problems addressed by the process improvement team, their progress should be recorded in the problem-tracking log. Companies that have not been closely following the problem-correction cycle will be amazed at how long it takes to solve many of the problems. A formal system that tracks critical problems and includes the name of the individual responsible for the corrective action frequently decreases the corrective action cycle by 50 percent. Information that should be included in the database is

1. Definition of the problem, where and how it was detected.
2. Root cause of the problem.
3. Time schedule activity plan.
4. Who is responsible for taking action and when?
5. Estimated effect of the action to be taken.
6. Measured effectiveness of the action taken.
7. What control procedures were changed?

8. Estimated savings that resulted from the corrective action.

9. Other areas where the corrective action was applied.

The process improvement team is the ideal group to report to management on the performance of the process as well as the process output. Reporting needs vary, as the complexity of the process varies, from the very simple to the extremely complex. For purposes of this text, let's examine the reporting procedure that should be used in a product that is delivered to an external customer. The following reports and meetings should be used in this situation:

1. Minutes should be prepared for all process improvement team meetings.

2. A problem-tracking log should be maintained.

3. Short weekly status meetings should be held with the plant manager, highlighting major new issues and actions scheduled to be completed during the week.

4. Weekly yield reports should be generated to help define new problems and evaluate the effectiveness of previously taken corrective actions.

5. Monthly management reports should be generated and the highlights discussed with top management during a formal improvement meeting involving the entire process improvement team.

6. Job improvement forms should be used to document the results of the process improvement team's activities.

Process improvement reports and meetings keep the company focused on the priority problems, but they should be used with care or they can be repetitious and a waste of time and paper. This means that the major part of the reports and meetings should be devoted to the exceptions or problem areas that are not progressing on schedule. It also needs to be clearly shown that the other areas are performing well. Use about 25 percent of a meeting agenda's time reporting performance and 75 percent of the meeting's time reporting problem highlights and missed target dates.

The monthly management report presents a different challenge. The reporting structure must be carefully designed, keeping the reader's viewpoint in mind. With this as an objective, the following reporting structure was developed:

1. Overview
   a. Major problems and what action has been taken to correct them
   b. Areas within the process that are out of control and need management action
   c. Comparison of overall poor-quality cost to the most recent 6-month average

2. Customer performance measurements
3. Process yield summary, reporting first-time and throughput yields
4. Process improvement trend charts
5. Input quality measurements
6. Process poor-quality cost

The overview (item 1) should refer to the body of the report by page number, where more detailed information is available on the subject. A corrective action plan should be reported for each graph that has a negative trend and/or is below customer expectation level.

Supplier
Involvement

INTRODUCTION

The success of many advanced manufacturing techniques, such as the use of robotics, reduction in inventories, increases in inventory turnover, and the computerization and sophistication of manufacturing tracking and control systems, often depends on extremely high quality levels of incoming parts and materials. For example, because very complex computer control programs must be written to enable robots to make allowances for variations in parts and materials that human operators make very readily, it is frequently more economical to make parts more uniform rather than to make the robots more adaptable, even for very simple operations such as screw insertion.

Reduction of inventories also demands high quality. In the past, one of the components of overall inventory was "safety stock," which was meant to provide insurance against a number of calamities, including

This chapter and part of the previous chapter were specially written for this book by Patrick J. McMahon, Manager of Procurement Quality Engineering, IBM General Products Division, San Jose, California.

the discovery of defective or unusable material on the manufacturing line. Unfortunately, at just that time when the safety stock was supposed to provide its payoff, all too often it was found to be just as defective as the material on the line. And to make matters even worse, often the defective material found on the line and in the warehouse turned out to be just the first evidence of a completely contaminated material pipeline, stretching all the way back to the original supplier's process. The safety stock usually provided a false sense of security and actually inhibited manufacturing companies from developing truly effective defect-prevention practices.

One powerful instinctive reaction to all of this is that the role of inspection is becoming much more important, and we're going to have to do a lot more of it to be sure that very few defects get into our manufacturing processes. Final inspection of finished parts, however, requires skilled technicians and expensive equipment, is usually performed in a special "laboratory" environment remote from the manufacturing line, interrupts the flow of parts to the line, and is often error prone. Inspection has the even more fundamental limitation that it cannot make the parts good—only manufacturing processes can make the parts to print. A parts quality strategy that relies heavily on receiving inspection will quickly become prohibitively expensive and cannot produce the continuous flow of defect-free parts required by modern high-volume low-inventory manufacturing processes.

Clearly, if companies are ever to operate smooth-running manufacturing lines with sharply reduced inventories, they must first find ways to assure that incoming shipments of parts and materials are functionally acceptable every time. The remainder of this chapter describes techniques to accomplish this difficult task.

FEWER SUPPLIERS

Conventional wisdom has long held that the more suppliers a company has, short of a truly unmanageable number, the better. Advantages of this philosophy are obvious. A large number of suppliers provides an opportunity for very vigorous negotiations regarding price, delivery, or other contract terms. Multiple suppliers for a given part or commodity provide good recovery options if one supplier experiences delivery, quality, financial, or other problems. And a large supplier base provides a great deal of flexibility in the face of sudden increases in production schedules.

These advantages, however, are obtained at a hefty price. The administrative work load, the size of the work force required to place and track orders, the opportunities for error—all these are directly proportional to the number of active suppliers.

There is a more important motive, however, for companies to reduce their supplier bases: As a company works with suppliers to achieve unprecedented levels of incoming parts quality, the demands on the company's supplier technical support staff will be so great that most companies will be forced to limit the number of suppliers their scarce manufacturing engineers and quality engineers are required to support. This is especially true of high-technology companies procuring complex components from outside suppliers. In some market environments it may increase legal risks, both contractually and from an antitrust viewpoint, to limit the number of suppliers. Therefore, legal counsel should be included in the decision to limit the number of suppliers.

Just what will these engineers be doing in this new world of extremely high quality, and how does it differ from what they did in the past? The fundamental change will be that companies will no longer be able to rely on rigorous incoming inspection as their primary means of assuring that purchased parts are acceptable. In any high-volume manufacturing environment, receiving inspection necessarily makes heavy use of sampling plans, simply because it is economically impossible to inspect every incoming part. (Even if it was economically possible, 100 percent inspection does not assure 100 percent acceptable parts because of such factors as operator fatigue.) And with today's increasingly high standards of quality, the levels of quality that can be assured by sampling plans are just not good enough. High-volume high-productivity manufacturing processes require defect rates to be less than a few parts per million, not a few percentage points.

The abandonment of heavy incoming inspection creates a tremendous challenge for procurement manufacturing and quality engineers. In the past, these people relied very heavily on preproduction survey and process setup work for their confidence that suppliers would make acceptable parts. After establishing initial confidence, these engineers gave the supplier the authorization to go into volume production. Ongoing confidence that the process continued to produce good parts was then obtained through continuing *inspection* of incoming parts.

The high-efficiency environment of the future, however, requires that supplier *processes*, once proven capable of producing acceptable parts, be continually monitored and adjusted so they never produce unacceptable parts—even for a few hours. This means that engineers will have to develop far more sophisticated tooling, process monitoring, and control concepts. This will also mean that the intensive technical partnership between supplier and customer will often last for the entire life of the program on critical processes. This technical effort will be so extensive that companies will only want to replicate it to the minimum extent necessary to assure continuity of supply.

LONG-TERM CONTRACTS

In an environment in which consistently high quality is required over an extended period, both the supplier and the customer have strong motivations to enter into long-term contracts. Of the two, the supplier's need for a long-term contract is somewhat easier to understand. To assure very high quality throughout the entire life cycle of a program, some very substantial investments are required by the supplier. These include manufacturing tooling, altogether new process-monitoring equipment, and process-automation equipment, such as automatic transfer line equipment and robotics. In some cases, suppliers will have to invest in new physical facilities, such as clean rooms, or even completely new plants.

The list of major supplier investments, however, goes well beyond these capital items. Suppliers must make an even more difficult investment in educating people—starting with the management team. The most important lesson to be learned by the management team is that the company's commitment to top quality is not in conflict with its cost and schedule objectives, but is, in fact, a prerequisite to minimizing costs and dependably meeting schedules. Any quality improvement efforts made in the absence of such a deep-seated belief will only be transitory and will soon disappear in the face of pressures to reduce costs or increase output.

The management team must also invest in their indirect professional support staff. Everyone from design engineers to maintenance technicians must understand the quality objectives of the company and must have a very detailed understanding of his or her specific role. The engineering and manufacturing support staff develops the specific concepts and programs to implement the improvement process. These include designing for quality and manufacturability, new process-monitoring technologies, modern methods of predictive maintenance, and so forth. Many companies, once grasping the extent of what must be done to achieve quality objectives, will likely find that they lack sufficient numbers of skilled manufacturing support personnel, such as manufacturing engineers and quality engineers, and will have to invest time and money to educate and even recruit such people.

Finally, companies making a commitment to the improvement process will find that the management commitment and technical training count for nothing if the people who are actually making the product fail to understand and support the concept. Therefore an extensive training program is also required to help these manufacturing operators understand the program and why it is good for them as well as the company. They must also be well-trained in the specific new responsibilities they will have, such as collecting measurement data, posting control charts, or participating in improvement teams.

Obviously, before committing the time, money, and people to make all of these things happen, a supplier will want to have a great deal of confidence that a particular production program will last quite some time. Many suppliers have worked with a customer to develop an initial manufacturing process, only to see themselves later underbid by a competitor who hadn't expended these substantial initial development costs. Carefully developed long-term contracts, protecting the interests of both the supplier and the customer, answer these concerns. Once again, legal counsel should be involved in shaping these contracts. In some competitive environments long-term contracts may be inappropriate.

It might first appear that long-term contracts favor only the supplier and, in fact, actually inhibit the customer. Long-term contracts certainly prohibit free-wheeling continuous negotiation, but there are a number of advantages to the customer, too. Sophisticated purchasing departments have developed terms that provide for automatic price reductions or renegotiations within the framework of long-term contracts. Modern contracts even have clauses that motivate suppliers to continually search for cost reduction opportunities, and they provide for both the supplier and customer to benefit from actual cost reductions.

Long-term contracts allow a customer to spend far less for renegotiation, retooling, re-education, and so forth. Long-term contracts also raise the possibility of the customer entering into development contracts with selected suppliers during the initial design phases of a new product. This arrangement gives the customer access to the expertise of key suppliers while it is still economical to alter the design. It gives the supplier an early insight into ultimate process requirements, as well as a chance to begin work early on long-lead-time items—thus shortening lead time from new product inception to availability.

In summary, the long-term contract cements a partnership that is essential to achieve extremely high levels of quality.

DESIGN REVIEW

Huge cost advantages, lasting the life of a new product program, and even beyond, can accrue to customers who are willing to involve their suppliers in early product design reviews. These huge savings, though, do not usually come from a brief brain-picking session in which the customer's design engineer takes a few drawings out to a supplier for a day or two of informal discussion. Instead, they result from a sustained technical partnership, usually lasting a minimum of several months, during which many ideas are considered. In the more extreme cases, some limited tooling is built and prototype processes are developed, involving considerable expense to the supplier. In these cases, it is appropriate to have a development contract. Many suppliers are willing to participate in such a development process without charge, in the hope of landing a long-term production contract, but pursuing such a course only invites ill feelings.

There are other good reasons for covering early involvement of the supplier by a formal contract. One major concern is confidentiality. It is important that carefully worded nondisclosure agreements be executed before the reviews begin. The customer needs to sign similar agreements protecting the supplier's proprietary processes. It is also important to establish contractually that the results of the review become the property of the customer so that it is clearly understood at the outset that the customer will not complete the review only to find that a critical component is now single-sourced for the life of the product because of the proprietary content of the production process. The same contract should make it clear that successful completion of the design review, and even a prototype development contract, is not a guarantee that the supplier will obtain the long-term production contract. The customer retains the right to obtain competitive bidding for the production contract, while the supplier has the advantage of a design based on processes in which their expertise is greatest, as well as having a superior understanding of the customer's requirements and greater familiarity with the customer's key people.

SUPPLIER SEMINARS

No one can be expected to "conform to requirements" without clearly understanding what those requirements are. This is probably the most important motive for a major new trend in customer-supplier communications—the supplier seminar.

Customer requirements are not just limited to characteristics of the parts to be supplied. They include parts cost, delivery expectations, packaging, problem-resolution procedures, and a host of other details.

Supplier seminars complement the information provided to the supplier through two primary written sources: all technical information contained in the engineering prints and specifications and all business requirements contained in the contracts and purchase orders. Although it would be difficult to overstate the importance of these documents, it is now realized that these documents alone are not enough. Supplier seminars bring key customer and supplier personnel together on a regular basis. Seminars involving groups of suppliers are also useful. Questions or problems raised by many different suppliers and discussed in an open forum are usually better understood and more thoroughly explored than they would be in the one-on-one situation.

The content of the seminars should include all of that important business and technical information not clearly covered by contracts and engineering drawings. Changes in business conditions or product plans, new specifications, advances in measurement techniques, changes in inspection philosophy, major new procedures related to incoming material or inventory policy, new concepts in process control, and supplier success stories are all good candidates for the agenda. Every one of these (and other similar topics) has a potentially major impact on the customer-supplier partnership, yet few of them are fully described in the formal business and technical documentation that defines the responsibilities of the customer and supplier.

Frequency of the seminars will vary with the complexity and dynamism of the technologies involved. Location of seminars will also vary. Bringing suppliers to the customer site allows for actual manufacturing-line tours during which suppliers learn about the environment in which their parts are used. This usually results in a better appreciation of the customer's requirements and the rationale behind them. Suppliers also have far greater access to all levels of the customer's personnel when seminars are held at the customer's location.

On the other hand, suppliers located far from the customer's site will be inclined to send only a small number of people to such a seminar, and key people will almost certainly be left behind. The way to overcome this, of course, is to periodically hold seminars at locations at which there are concentrations of several suppliers. Afterward, visits to actual supplier plants can provide the customer with a detailed understanding of the supplier's environment. The best solution, of course, is to alternate seminar locations between the customer's plant and supplier locations.

PROCESS CONTROLS

It is important to understand the distinction between the generic term "process control" and the very specific term "statistical process control." Both are gaining widespread use in manufacturing companies today, and it must be clearly understood that "statistical" process control, while extremely important, is only one part of a modern process control system.

The term "process control" covers the disciplines, controls, tooling concepts, staffing, and so forth necessary to assure virtually error-free output from a process without heavy dependence on inspection. Process control includes the staffing of a production program with appropriately skilled and trained people. It also includes the plans for training, certification, and periodic recertification of production operators and inspectors. Process control encompasses all the production and inspection tooling needed in the process, complete with plans for regularly assuring the capability of production tooling and the accuracy and repeatability of the inspection tooling. It provides for the correlation of measurement results between suppliers and customers and the traceability of measurement calibration standards to accepted international standards. It includes process documentation, from tool drawings and process specifications to all manufacturing and inspection procedures. Finally, process control includes all the data collection, data analysis, and auditing procedures necessary to assure that the entire system continues to operate as planned. It is very common for customers to require suppliers to submit process control data regularly, and to perform their own independent audits of critical supplier processes.

Quality systems based on process control differ fundamentally from systems based on final inspection. As we have seen, inspection is both too costly and too inefficient a way to assure quality. Even if it wasn't, the discovery of a defect at the final stage in a manufacturing process, especially a high-volume or long-lead-time process, often means that the process upstream is contaminated with hundreds of thousands of similar defects.

The abandonment of heavy final inspection can only be tolerated if it is replaced with stringent controls at every stage of the process. These controls provide for virtually real-time measurements of both the parts and the process and for immediate process adjustments when control limits are exceeded.

One of the most important parts of a process control system is statistical process control (SPC). This is a technique for assuring that unfavorable drifts in a manufacturing process are detected and corrected long before any actual defective product is produced. Thus, it provides a dependable method of determining that some factor which has crept into the process is causing variations outside the scope of the established normal variation of the process.

Inspection tooling for high-volume processes is usually "go/no go" gauging or "functional" gauging, which merely determines, quickly and inexpensively, whether an individual part falls within specification limits (attributes data). Unfortunately, though, these gauges tell the user nothing about how the process is varying; the user's first sign of trouble comes when the gauge starts rejecting parts. With variables data, however, SPC methods can detect an unfavorable process change long before defective material is produced. It is therefore advisable, whenever possible, to obtain variables data.

The choice of parameters to be controlled should be made jointly by customer and supplier. The customer knows far more about the intended function of the part or assembly and, therefore, which parameters are critical on the finished product. On the other hand, the supplier almost always knows more about the production process and, therefore, which process characteristics require the most attention.

As was pointed out in the previous chapter, the technical aspects of SPC are very well-developed. The area that has fallen behind is training. Both the engineers who set up processes and the process operators need to be well-versed in the concepts and techniques of SPC. Unfortunately, these groups usually receive only cursory training in SPC during their formal education. In addition, management—the people who must finance and support a conversion to SPC—must also have a solid enough understanding of the basic concepts and benefits to sustain their support when the going gets tough and progress seems painfully slow.

In many cases, manufacturing companies will not initially have the in-house resources to support the required training in SPC. Many consultants, classes, training tapes, and written materials are available on the topic, however. Unfortunately, though, these resources are sometimes of poor quality or inappropriately applied. A careful review of the material and of references—including multiple references of companies that have actually implemented statistical process control using the consultant or training materials, and not just companies that have sent a few people to a class or rented a videotape—is important. After a significant investment in training or consulting services, an initial failure can dampen management enthusiasm for the technique and even permanently stop the company from trying it again.

One last point. Inspection of the final product becomes less and less important in the process control environment. Nevertheless, audit inspections still take place for a variety of reasons, and it is important to implement sampling plans consistent with a commitment to zero defects. In particular, there is a gross shortcoming of the most commonly used sampling plans, the acceptable quality level (AQL) sampling plans of MIL-STD-105D. For large lot sizes and even very tight AQLs, these sampling plans allow lots to be accepted *even though defects are found in the sample.* If sampling inspections are done, the only sampling plans that are acceptable in a zero defects environment are "zero-one" plans, in which a lot is only accepted if zero defects are found in the sample—even a single defect means rejection.

INCENTIVE PROGRAMS

There are two types of incentive programs: positive (bonuses) and negative (penalties).

Bonuses

Some customers try to establish a positive tone by paying full price for quality less than but close to 100 percent, and paying bonuses as incoming quality gets closer and closer to 100 percent. There is a fundamental flaw with this approach, however. Issuing contracts that pay "full" price for parts less than 100 percent good flies in the face of any stated commitment to zero defects. Worse is the implied acceptance of the idea that 100 percent quality is impossible—a virtual guarantee that it will not be achieved.

Penalties

Penalty programs usually involve a sliding scale of discounts on the unit price if the quality received by the customer falls below predefined thresholds. Most modern penalty contracts are clearly geared toward a "zero-defects" philosophy and thus call for payment of full price only for defect-free shipments.

Some of the more aggressive contract provisions go beyond the idea of price reductions and actually call for payment of what amounts to consequential damages under some conditions. At the low end of the scale, it is quite common for customers to bill suppliers for direct costs, such as rework expenses, charges for screening inspections, and transportation costs incurred as a result of the return of defective material. Today, however, some provisions being developed obligate suppliers for hundreds of thousands of dollars if their defective material causes major problems for the customer. These include significant line shutdowns; major machine teardown, rebuild, and retest exercises; field rework or recall programs; and product liability problems. Small suppliers may have to obtain insurance coverage against these hazards.

This situation produces very interesting consequences. First, of course, the insurance company wants to be absolutely sure it is taking only a reasonable risk, requiring a very careful assessment of the supplier's capability of producing top-quality product over the long term. Once assured that the supplier has a sound control system in place, the insurance company will periodically audit the supplier, thus providing the customer with a regular unbiased second opinion of the state of the supplier's capability. In addition, the insurance company will offer more attractive premiums if the supplier's capability and history improve. Lower premiums mean lower overall costs, and lower costs mean more competitive pricing, so this form of contract provision can serve as a very broad incentive for suppliers to strive for the best possible manufacturing processes.

Overcoming Problems with Incentive Contracts

A number of problems go along with the incentive contracts described above. One is that penalty contracts, unless administered sensitively and fairly, can be a major impediment in efforts to develop a sense of partnership between customer and supplier.

Another series of problems stems from the level of administrative control necessary to enforce incentive contracts. First, there must be a very clear definition of how "quality" is to be measured. Lot acceptance rate is a rather coarse measure of parts quality, and it unfairly favors a supplier sending in large numbers of small lots over one sending small numbers of large lots. Measurements based on the number or percentage of acceptable pieces overcome this problem but typically require the customer to keep far more detailed data. Both methods imply that a large amount of inspection will be done *ad infinitum* for the purpose of maintaining accurate quality indices even though supplier inspection is something that both parties would like to reduce.

There is an approach to incentive contracting that overcomes most of these flaws. In the very high-quality environment being discussed, customers usually require suppliers to submit detailed documents describing the production process and control system. These documents cover such information as the operator training, initial certification, and periodic recertification system; the tool and inspection instrumentation calibration system; the manufacturing data collection and record keeping system; the statistical process control system; and so forth—in short, the full process control system described earlier in this chapter. Such documents are detailed enough to serve as the basis of an audit checklist which the customer can use for determining the degree to which the supplier is conforming to the documented process. It is possible for a supplier to deviate slightly from such a documented process without necessarily producing defective product. For example, an operator may have been recertified after 7 months instead of the 6 months called for in the checklist—a minor deviation. In this case, the customer can safely pay full price for a score that is slightly less than 100 percent while in no way implying that defective parts are tolerable. And the contract still has room to allow for bonus payments as the supplier gets closer to 100 percent on the periodic audits.

Finally, it should be noted that considerable incentive can be given to suppliers merely by handling rejected material in a firm manner. Halting all customer inspection upon the first discovery of a defect and requiring the supplier to send an inspector to screen the remainder of the lot, withholding payment until shipments are accepted, billing suppliers for transportation costs of returned material or rework costs, refusing to grant off-specs merely to salvage deviant parts that would be financially painful for a supplier to scrap or rework, and just plain removing work from poor performing suppliers are all things that motivate suppliers to provide error-free shipments.

SOURCE AUDITORS

Any company that has done defense-contract work is familiar with source auditors. These are representatives of the customer who perform parts inspection and process monitoring activities at the supplier's location, generally allowing the customer to reduce or eliminate receiving inspection. Source auditors are playing an ever-increasing role in commercial work as well.

Detection of a problem at the supplier's site prevents the defective material from getting into the customer's supply pipeline and gives the supplier somewhere between several hours and several days earlier indication of the problem. Corrective action is also faster and more effective because the defective material is immediately available for examination by those who produced it and those who have to implement the corrective action. Source auditors can also be very effective in helping supplier personnel to understand the customer's interpretation of subjective specifications such as those regarding cleanliness, surface texture, paint colors, and workmanship.

The optimum use of source auditors is to have them perform audits of the process control system and to do only enough actual inspection of the product to remain confident that the process control system is working effectively. This requires that the control system be very well-documented so that the source auditor can be provided with a very concise audit checklist, equivalent in detail and objectivity to the product inspection plans that inspectors are normally provided. The process audit system should also tell the auditor what to do in the event of various problems. These actions would range from simple written notifications to supplier management of minor shortcomings to withholding authorization for shipment in the case of major process control flaws that could allow defective product to go undetected.

Many source auditors today are parts inspectors and not truly process control system auditors, and an expanded role requires numerous skills that parts inspectors often lack. Significant training will normally be required. A process control auditor needs to understand statistical process control well enough to tell when the techniques are being used correctly and when they are being misapplied. The auditor must be a master at interpreting a wide variety of data patterns on control charts and knowing which patterns are normal and which signal trouble. A good understanding of probable causes for most unacceptable patterns is also essential because the auditor is required to judge whether the documented corrective actions make sense.

Numerous independent source-auditing services have become available in recent years. These outside services are frequently economical, especially in locations far from the customer's site and in situations not requiring a full-time auditor. An independent source auditor also provides an informal audit of the customer's specifications and procedures, pointing out those that are vague or unclear or that deviate from normal industry practice.

If a customer chooses to make use of source auditors, care should be taken that the supplier does not perceive this audit as taking the place of a control that they would otherwise provide themselves. The supplier's own control system should catch virtually all defects, either in the process controls or in the parts. If the auditor is finding defects on a fairly regular basis, that should be seen as a clear indication that the supplier is treating the audit as part of its own control system and that defective product could be regularly flowing into the customer's process in the absence of the audit.

SUPPLIER SURVEYS

A supplier survey is the systematic customer review of a supplier's business and technical capability. A typical survey team consists of a customer's buyer, manufacturing engineer, and quality engineer. Two or more of these roles may be performed by one individual, but any survey that does not cover all three disciplines is not adequate. Usually, each of these parties is armed with a checklist unique to his or her area of expertise. Many of these checklists are "cookbook" affairs that make it easy for the surveyor to assign numerical ratings to each of dozens of aspects of a supplier's operation. Most modern checklists assign different weights to each question, and some sort of weighted grand total can be calculated and compared to various threshold values, which correspond to general ratings such as "acceptable," "conditionally acceptable," and "unacceptable."

The most common shortcoming of these surveys is that they often consist of a mass of detailed questioning, followed by a brief plant tour. Most are completed in a few hours. Furthermore, most of the questions have obvious right answers, and most suppliers have become very adept at telling surveyors exactly what they want to hear. The bottom line is that traditional supplier surveys can consume enormous amounts of time and accomplish very little.

Improving Supplier Surveys

This process can be made more efficient in several ways. First, lists of candidate suppliers should be established through searches of standard industrial registers, trade association membership lists, financial rating services, and the like. With this information, a company can pare down the survey candidate list to only those companies that pass predetermined criteria such as size, financial strength, location, range of services, and so forth. Then a mail survey can be sent to the most promising candidates. This mail survey should cover the full range of questions asked on the traditional survey checklists and should also include questions about the supplier's willingness to handle various possible new orders in certain time frames.

The actual survey team can be dispatched to study only the most promising candidates. Since the majority of the checklist questions will already have been covered, only a minimum of time need be spent on this material. The bulk of the time should be spent instead on in-depth examinations of live evidence of the critical survey elements, such as conducting one-on-one interviews with the supplier's in-house technical support staff, examining actual process control charts on the shop floor, and seeing if the manufacturing operators are posting and interpreting the charts correctly. It is also very important to develop a good understanding of the supplier's commitment to quality and willingness to enter into a business and technical partnership with the customer.

Surveying Current Suppliers

A key element in the survey of current suppliers is the supplier history. The survey team should be very familiar with the supplier's performance for at least the preceding year, including all corrective actions based on rejected material. If the history looks good, is it due to a low number of receipts, very lax incoming inspection, or a solid control system at the supplier? Even if it is the last, it is very important not to avoid genuine critical examination. The good record may be due to fine capital equipment, now beginning to show signs of wear. Or perhaps the company is beginning a rapid expansion and less experienced employees are being added to the work force.

In the case of a supplier with a poor track record, has this poor record persisted over several years? Is there clear physical evidence that promised corrective actions are really in place and working effectively? Is there some underlying attitude problem, such as "we all make mistakes"? Or is there a chronic lack of skilled support people or adequate capital equipment or operator training? All of these issues can be studied in a much more focused way when there is a track record to look back upon.

Companies frequently become lax in keeping supplier surveys up to date. It is easy to lose sight of the fact that a supplier has not been formally surveyed for a long time when there is frequent contact. A good rule of thumb is to try to resurvey active suppliers at least annually.

INITIAL SUPPLIER QUALIFICATION

Once a supplier has been selected, but before authorization is given to ship large quantities on a regular basis, a series of product qualification criteria must be satisfied. These vary widely, and the complexity of the qualification process depends on the complexity of the product, the newness of the product technology, the importance of the product in the customer's intended application, and other similar factors.

The cycle begins with the submission of a few evaluation samples. These are subjected to physical, environmental, functional, and life tests, as well as being carefully measured for conformance to all requirements. The intent is to find out if the supplier is capable of producing an acceptable product. "Hard tooling," such as molds, dies, and machining fixtures, usually does not exist at this stage. The evaluation samples may even be from existing production jobs, to reflect the supplier's production capability.

Once the evaluation samples have been approved, authorization is given to the supplier to start producing the hard tooling. Upon completion of this tooling, the supplier usually makes several short production runs (often as short as one piece if the part is very complex or expensive), checking the product after each run and modifying the tooling and the process until an acceptable product is manufactured.

At this point, the supplier is ready to submit a "tool sample" for the customer's approval. Many serious problems have occurred as a result of taking this step too lightly. Tool samples should be fairly large in quantity and should be randomly selected from a production run that is truly representative of the anticipated full-volume production process. An absolute minimum of five pieces would be needed before any possible estimate of the variability of the process could be determined, and samples of about twenty are preferable for many processes. The requirement that the tool sample run be representative of the ultimate process is often very hard to achieve, especially if the ultimate process will be run over two or three shifts by several different operators. In any case, the customer needs to be aware of the conditions under which the tool samples were run and must be informed of significant deviations of those conditions from the ultimate process. The responsible customer manufacturing engineer should be present at the time the tool samples are run, to observe the process and randomly select the samples.

Violating any one of these guidelines can result in an inappropriate approval of a tool sample by the customer and the later discovery of large quantities of defects in high-volume production shipments. Tool samples as small as one piece are sometimes submitted. Very little can be learned from a single piece—and absolutely nothing can be learned about the variability of the process. A single part could be the *only* good piece produced after weeks of trying. Larger samples taken from a longer run could still be unrepresentative if the process was run by a model maker instead of a regular production operator. And failure to take the sample randomly increases the chance that major sources of process variation will not be reflected in the tool sample.

Once the tool sample is selected, it is sent to the customer, where it is subjected to very thorough inspection. (The supplier's inspection results should be submitted with the sample parts so that any inspection correlation problem between supplier and customer can be discovered and resolved at this time.) Even if the customer finds all parameters to be within specifications, modifications to the tooling may still be required. For example, all measurements of a parameter were within specification but were uncomfortably close to one of the tolerance limits, or the measurements of a parameter varied widely and covered nearly the entire allowable tolerance band. On the other hand, it might be either expensive or risky to make tool modifications that appear desirable from analysis of the data. In this case, the customer's design engineers may consider a minor design change if the function of the finished product would not be compromised. In any case, it should be clear that tool sample approval is far more than just a simple confirmation that all parameters meet their specifications. It involves a very detailed analysis of the data to confirm that the supplier is truly ready to begin volume production.

If the customer's product or manufacturing process is complex, the supplier's parts may have to be piloted in the customer's production line. In this case, a substantial quantity of parts (typically several dozen to several hundred) is built into the customer's product on a carefully controlled basis, and the finished products carefully observed in final test to establish that there is no degradation of the product. Pilot lots are also run through the process to be sure that the parts work well with the customer's assembly tooling, particularly if it is highly automated and potentially sensitive to small variations in component parts.

Some companies apply a final qualification criterion after volume production shipments begin. These take the form of granting "qualification" to a supplier on a given part after a predetermined number of error-free shipments or months. Such checkpoints can be dangerous. Granting qualification to a supplier may imply achievement of a goal, after which customer and supplier can devote their resources to more pressing problems. The danger is that controls will be relaxed only because the parts happen to be accepted by the customer and not because the process is known to have achieved long-term stability. The continuous maintenance of the process controls mentioned earlier is absolutely essential. Supplier qualification signals the beginning of the continuous improvement process, not the end of the need to improve.

SUPPLIER QUALITY REPORTS

It is incumbent upon customers to put considerable effort into assuring that suppliers receive a continuous flow of information about their performance that is prompt, clear, consistent, and communicated to the right people.

The definition of promptness depends on the type of information being communicated. Notification of the discovery of a defect should happen within minutes, or a few hours at most, after the discovery. There is nothing wrong with calling a supplier to alert them to a *suspected* problem, while making it clear that the investigation is still underway. At least the supplier has an early opportunity to check the process and halt production if a problem does exist. In addition, the supplier's opinion is often invaluable in directing the investigation toward the most likely causes and shortening the overall corrective action process.

It is also important to maintain good standards of promptness in reporting routine quality performance, even when no problems are being reported. Suppliers that routinely send in 100 percent good parts should be able to depend on a regular confirmation from the customer that this record is continuing. Such reports should be published at least monthly.

Documented reports should be as clear as possible, especially when defects are being reported. Shipment numbers covered, exact quantities involved, dates, and exact description of defects are all critically important in helping the supplier to take action. It is also important for the customer to maintain clear traceability from these reports to in-house records containing such information as the name of the inspector who discovered the problem or made the original measurements, the equipment or inspection methods used, and the ultimate disposition of the parts. This detailed information can be very useful in resolving recurring problems, monitoring long-term supplier performance, and investigating field performance problems with the finished product.

The requirement that supplier performance data be consistent can be more of a problem than it might first appear. It is not unusual for several different customer representatives—buyers, manufacturing engineers, quality engineers, product designers, and managers—to be in regular contact with a supplier. Few things can be more disruptive to a supplier than to receive conflicting or inconsistent information. This problem becomes most critical, unfortunately, at the very time when accurate information is most important—when trying to recover from a problem. The buyer plays the key role in assuring consistent information. This does not mean that technical people involved in supplier support activities should funnel all communications through the buyer or await the buyer's permission before contacting the supplier. But it does mean that all of these people are obliged to keep the buyer informed. Likewise, the supplier should be able to place a single call to the buyer to get any conflict resolved.

Long-term consistency is also important in supplier performance reports. As customers strive to continuously upgrade their systems for monitoring incoming parts quality, changes are made in sampling philosophies, disposition of rejects, inspection methods, and so forth. Many of these changes can produce a change in a supplier's quality rating when nothing has changed in the supplier's process.

Customers often fail to report supplier performance to the right people. Quality reports most commonly go to the supplier's quality people. This is certainly one of the places such data should go, but it is not the only place. Manufacturing and sales people are even more vitally affected by performance trends. Upper management is the group most frequently left out of the picture, and yet they are the people most influential in setting the tone for the whole organization with regard to quality standards. It is not at all unusual for customers to invoke the help of a top executive in a last desperate effort to resolve a chronic quality problem, only to find that this is the first that the executive has ever heard of the problem. Blame for such an occurrence rests at least as heavily on the customer as it does on the supplier.

SUPPLIER RATINGS

Quality is only one of three supplier performance criteria, the other two being delivery and cost. A truly comprehensive supplier rating system must include all three.

Many methods exist for calculating an overall supplier performance index, which assigns different weights to the three performance elements through algorithms of varying complexity. In general, though, care should be taken not to make the calculation too complex, lest the customer and supplier spend too much time haggling over the exotica of the algorithm and not enough time discussing the underlying phenomena the index is intended to reveal. It is preferable to use a simple weighted average method for calculating a single rating—if the customer insists on having a single number to represent overall performance—and to provide separate indices for quality, delivery, and cost performance so that the supplier can see the relative contributions of each.

Each of these three underlying indices can be complex in itself. In the past, quality ratings were frequently based on simple lot acceptance rates. In a zero-defects world, however, parts-per-million acceptance rates are more appropriate; but the massive parts inspection required to accurately estimate acceptance rates in parts per million is usually not economical. A quality index based on the results of regular audits of the supplier's process control system (described earlier in the chapter in the discussion of incentive programs) may be appropriate. It is also very important that the supplier quality index reflect any problems experienced with the parts after acceptance—problems discovered on the manufacturing line as well as those experienced in the field.

Quality ratings sometimes attach different weights to various types of defects: "critical," "major," and "minor" or "incidental." But incidental defects, such as incorrect or damaged packaging or minor deviations in "nonfunctional" dimensions, can jam up a robot; cause a materials handling system to go haywire; or trigger inordinate amounts of expediting, rework, or other special processing. Thus, it is less and less realistic to talk about classes of defects. *All* defects are potentially disruptive in high-efficiency manufacturing processes. Furthermore, the concept of a defect being minor is philosophically inconsistent with a commitment to zero defects.

The index of delivery performance is usually the easiest to calculate. Specific tolerance limits need to be established to define clearly what is meant by "on-time" performance. The simplest system could stop right there, merely rating deliveries as on time or not on time. A more complex system would add varying penalties to shipments based on just how early or late they arrived. (Notice that an early shipment is also not on time. Nowadays, an early shipment represents excess inventory, and there may not even be a convenient place to store it.) It is important to note that free-wheeling change in a customer's delivery demands necessarily creates havoc with suppliers' ability to maintain good delivery ratings, through no fault of their own.

A supplier cost index can be a very difficult and somewhat arbitrary thing to develop. An index comparing several suppliers' prices to that of the lowest-cost supplier sounds attractive, but this can lead to accidental revelation of confidential supplier data. In addition, the trend toward fewer suppliers makes such an index less important. Another approach would be to base the cost index on how well the supplier performs against a schedule of planned cost reductions if such provisions are contained in a long-term contract. For companies with good cost estimating skills, the best solution is to compare actual prices to estimated costs as an index of supplier cost performance.

One very practical problem in developing a composite supplier rating system is that the necessary data is usually spread among several organizations. Even if all the data is contained within an integrated computer network, the programming to bring it all together can be very tricky. The lesson here is to try to keep the rating system pretty simple, especially if the number of suppliers is very large.

10

Systems Assurance

INTRODUCTION

Since 1940, the quality assurance (QA) function has been given more and more assignments, including such activities as process control, failure analysis, process capability studies, equipment certification, workmanship standards, design review, corrective action, and many others. Many of the jobs quality assurance has been assigned can be accomplished much more effectively by other organizations, reducing quality costs and improving quality output, as we saw in Chapter 8.

Quality assurance is uniquely qualified to evaluate, measure, and report. This unique role means that QA should evaluate the adequacy of the plans and systems that control the company. They should measure the degree of conformance to these plans and systems as well as sample the output at various points throughout the process and in customer environments, then report their findings to management and the functions that can take action to correct identified problems. The functions that are responsible for developing the corrective action plans should be held accountable for the plans and for reporting their status. Quality assurance should evaluate the adequacy of these plans.

The QA function is changing in many of America's leading companies. When talking about the quality assurance function John Young, president of Hewlett-Packard, said,

> Today's HP quality manager gets evaluated on a much broader set of criteria, including complexity of the organization and cross-divisional linkages.
> They are motivated to create teams with other departments and to involve a wide range of people in quality efforts. QA managers at HP are well on their way to becoming facilitators and change masters, not policemen and administrators.

This type of approach—integrating many of the quality assurance activities into the areas in which they can be performed most effectively—will free up vast resources and allow part of them to be assigned to functions that have been ignored by quality assurance, functions such as sales, service, industrial engineering, accounting, personnel, and the like. It will allow quality assurance to provide the checks and balances to the total system that controls the company, thereby creating a new area within quality assurance called "systems assurance."

THE NEW QUALITY ASSURANCE ORGANIZATION

The result of integrating many of the quality assurance activities into other functions is the formation of a new quality assurance organization that consists of four major elements:

- Reliability and maintainability analysis
- Product assurance
- Quality laboratories
- Systems assurance

Only the activities that can be performed more effectively or that help to align accountability with responsibility were moved out of quality assurance. The resulting savings were used to create the new systems assurance organization.

Reliability and Maintainability Analysis

This group will provide the primary interface with the customer. Its mission is to develop a system that will predict product and service performance and measure how well customer expectations are being met. This group will

1. Make reliability predictions
2. Make maintainability predictions and spare parts provisioning
3. Make suggestions to product engineering on how to improve reliability and/or serviceability
4. Perform customer surveys
5. Respond to customer complaints
6. Report to management on customer satisfaction and product performance

Product Assurance

This group consists of both quality engineers and quality inspectors. Its mission is to ensure that the most effective and efficient quality system is used to provide product and/or service that meets customer expectations. To accomplish this, product assurance is responsible for

1. Qualifying product design by conducting independent performance evaluations in an off-line test laboratory
2. Qualifying the process by evaluating adequacy of the equipment, process documentation, production flow, and operator training
3. Vendor quality interface for the company
4. Maintaining the audit and measurement system that provides management with a measure of the in-process quality trends and identifies areas that require corrective action

Quality Laboratories

A number of support activities are often provided by quality assurance in the form of laboratories. Among these are standards laboratory, material analysis laboratory, failure analysis laboratory, calibration laboratory, and component laboratory.

SYSTEMS ASSURANCE ORGANIZATION

Up to this point, the quality assurance organizational structure has been pretty common, modified slightly to put quality assurance in the role of evaluating others' effort rather than performing the task itself, but the systems assurance activity puts quality assurance in a new role that is needed to direct its focus away from the production floor and to the business as a whole. The systems assurance group is focused on the systems used to control and direct the company business.

Mission of Systems Assurance

The mission of the systems assurance organization is to confirm that an effective anticipatory system of management controls exists throughout the organization and that exceptions are surfaced and resolved in a timely manner. To accomplish its mission, systems assurance is responsible for

1. Determining if adequate operational quality controls exist
2. Auditing to ensure existing controls are being adhered to
3. Anticipating internal control requirements
4. Monitoring management corrective action plans and solutions when controlled weaknesses are detected
5. Identifying systems that are cumbersome and/or overly bureaucratic
6. Coordinating self-assessment and audit readiness programs conducted by first-line managers
7. Coordinating department activity analysis programs (as defined in Chapter 5)
8. Developing and coordinating systems usage educational programs
9. Determining if systems and controls are in place to ensure the company is in compliance with good manufacturing practice (GMP) as required by regulatory agencies.

Characteristics of a Good Management Control System

Line management has the primary responsibility for the system that supports them and their employees. They are in the best position to measure the effectiveness and identify the weaknesses of the system. It is for this reason that they must be held responsible and accountable for the systems they use. When systems assurance audits an area, they look for the following as being representative of a good management control system:

1. The area's mission, business objective, and major assets are identified.
2. Measurement systems are in place to identify fluctuations in conformance. The system should be anticipative in nature so that changes can be identified before major costs or errors are created.
3. All major activities have documented procedures, including systems educational programs.
4. Effective control systems are in place. This means that control points for all major activities exist; that controls are placed directly in the work

area so that information can have the greatest effect; that controls are reasonable; and that controls cover key areas, including computer systems, safety, training, and interfunctional procedures. (Controls tend to be weakest when systems cross functional lines.) Management must know, understand, and feel responsible for the control systems.

5. Systems are in place that compare and reconcile differences in records. Mismatches almost always indicate a problem.

6. Systems should ensure that committed schedules are met and that missed schedules are highlighted to management with an appropriate corrective action plan. Missed commitments can cause serious problems to other areas.

7. Systems must be in place to reduce exposure to fraud and theft and to safeguard confidential information.

8. An internal audit system should be documented and followed to expose system and control problems or identify missing controls.

Systems Assurance Activities

The systems assurance group is a small group since it is not responsible for the company system but is only to provide management with an assessment of how effective the system is. In addition, systems change rather infrequently, making it unnecessary to evaluate each system each year. The systems assurance group is involved in such major activities as

1. Conducting system audits that span a number of functions
2. Conducting department audits
3. Coordinating management self-assessment programs
4. Providing systems education
5. Advising management on system control problems

System Audits.   The system audit is designed to evaluate the effectiveness and adequacy of a specific activity such as data integrity, shop floor control, controls over rejected materials, hiring process, safety, asset controls, and the like. They are directed at the location as a whole and involve many functions. They are costly and time-consuming to perform correctly, but the results have a major impact on the health of the business.

These detailed penetrating studies need not be conducted frequently because they are designed to evaluate the adequacy of the systems with only secondary emphasis placed upon how effectively they are being implemented. System audits are very important because they evaluate the effectiveness of the operational base that the company depends upon.

They also serve as the foundation for department audits. If the operational system is not based on sound business principles, there is little justification for requiring the individual areas to adhere to this system.

To get this audit program started, a list of key business systems should be prepared and each activity assigned a priority based on its importance to the company and its potential for change. Then an audit schedule for each key business system can be developed.

The success of the system audit is highly dependent upon the way the audit data is used by top management. There is really no excuse for any nonconformance to established systems, and management should assume that every deviation is important because even minor deviations are symptoms of a more serious disease that spreads like wildfire through the company if left unchecked. Proper control over the little things will ensure that big problems do not occur.

Department Audits.   In most companies, it is not practical to audit each department every year. The systems assurance group should select one department from each function to be audited each year as typical of the way a function is meeting its system control requirements. In selecting the representative department, priority should be given to departments that have recently had managerial changes or departments that have had a high influx of new employees since they are potential problem areas.

Department audits look at the total department activity. They are designed to determine how well the department is adhering to established procedures and its internal controls to ensure that there is no degradation in its output. It usually starts by reviewing the department's mission, its activity analysis record, and the manager's self-assessment checklist. From that point, the audit penetrates into the total business control system used within the department. The auditors will review work output, discuss controls and procedures with employees, and personally verify that the department is adhering to the approved systems. The auditors will also be alert to systems that need to be changed and/ or discontinued. The auditors will meet with the department's customers to determine the degree that the department is meeting customer expectations.

Based upon this evaluation, a detailed report is generated that discusses both the positive and negative results of the audit. The report is reviewed with the department manager before it is published so that he or she can have an opportunity to explain any false impression that the auditors may have acquired.

The report is then submitted to the functional manager, who investigates the report, applies its findings to all the departments within the function, and generates a corrective action plan that is presented to the appropriate vice president and the systems assurance group.

Management Self-Assessment Programs.   The systems assurance group coordinates management self-assessment programs (defined in Chapter 5). They review and approve each self-assessment checklist because they can readily detect missing controls and can also provide an unbiased judgment of the criteria used. They maintain a list of deviant conditions and corrective actions in order to identify chronic problems and seek permanent corrective actions.

Systems Education.   Systems assurance works with the functional managers to develop and conduct control systems educational programs. These programs provide management and employees with an understanding not only of the systems they are using but also why the systems must be adhered to. Careful attention is always given to pointing out that systems can become obsolete and cumbersome and that when this condition occurs, each employee involved has an obligation to get the system changed.

Advice to Management on System Control Problems.   The members of the systems assurance group become experts in the company's operating systems and frequently can identify system changes that will greatly improve overall effectiveness and quality of output. In addition, some management organizational changes will disrupt an effective system that has been in use for years. When this occurs, systems assurance has the responsibility to identify these problems as soon as each organizational change has been announced and obtain management commitment to correct them.

11

The Long and Short of It

INTRODUCTION

Sometimes we find ourselves in trouble because we don't always know where we're going or even where we've been. Our trouble occurs because we fail to look at all the options and make a long-range plan to direct our future or the future of our company.

No longer can companies react to the passion of the moment. A long-range company plan is needed, and all levels of management need to know, understand, and agree with it. This plan must set the direction and pilot the course, and it must have milestones along the way that can be used to mark progress. The long-range plan should change when there is a need, not when there is a change in management. It should be kept current, reflecting the needs of the organization. To accomplish this, a systematic company planning cycle must be established that includes both long-range and short-range plans. During a recent tour of the U.S., Kazuhiko Nishizawa, managing director of Sumitomo Metal Industries, pointed out that American businessmen are shortsighted. Japanese management looks 10 years ahead. Nishizawa stated, "I noticed that many companies were using the same factories I saw when I studied in the United States 30 years before. They need new plants, new production lines. From your national security point of view, steel going bankrupt is not good."

THE PLANNING CYCLE

Quality, like anything else worth doing, doesn't just happen. It's not like tomorrow; you can't just wait and it'll come to you. It requires a well-thought-out plan and probably some up-front investments. But these investments will pay off big dividends—twenty to one or even more.

The quality strategy has to be an integral part of the business strategy that supports the business mission and objectives. The planning cycle consists of six interrelated levels (see Figure 11.1):

1. *Mission.*   The stated reason for the existence of the company. The mission does not change frequently. Usually, it changes only when the organization decides to pursue a completely new market.

2. *Operating principles.*   These are the basic beliefs of the company, the principles that make up the culture of the organization. The operating principles rarely change.

3. *Business objectives.*   These objectives set the long-term direction the company will follow for the next 10 to 20 years. (Example: Increase the company share of the market in the flexible cable product lines.)

Figure 11.1   The planning pyramid.

4. *Performance goals.*   These goals normally are quantified measurable results that the organization wants to accomplish in a set period of time to support the business objectives. (Example: Increasing sales at a minimum rate of 12 percent per year from 1986 to 1996, with an average annual growth rate of 13.0 percent.)

5. *Strategy.*   The strategy defines the way the performance goals will be accomplished. (Example: The company will identify new customer markets within the United States and concentrate on expanding markets in the Pacific Rim countries.)

6. *Tactics.*   This plan defines the way the strategies will be accomplished. Normally, tactics are specific tasks that will be undertaken in the short term (1 to 3 years) to move the company toward the performance goals. (Example: Sales offices will be opened in Tokyo, Beijing, Hong Kong, and Singapore within the next 12 months, and a customer-needs survey will be conducted in the surrounding areas to define new product needs.)

To help understand the planning cycle, let's move through it from top to bottom, using a typical computer manufacturing company as a model.

Mission

The mission of the company should be developed by the company owners before they start the business. As the company develops, the mission statement may change slightly to meet changing market demands; but normally, the mission statement changes very little. Let us assume that the mission statement for our model company is: "To service worldwide information-handling needs." You can see that this mission statement is broad enough to allow for product and service growth but still is directed at a specific customer set.

Operating Principles

The operating principles set the culture of the company. To understand what I mean by operating principles, let's look at the operating principles for the IBM Corporation. The following are quotes from IBM's *Manager's Manual*:

> An organization, like an individual, must build on a bedrock of sound beliefs if it is to survive and succeed. It must stand by these beliefs in conducting its business. Every manager must live by these beliefs in making decisions and in taking actions.
>
> The beliefs that guide IBM activities are expressed as IBM Principles.

Respect for the Individual—Our basic belief is respect for the individual, for each person's rights and dignity. It follows from this principle that IBM should:

- Help employees develop their potential and make the best use of their abilities.
- Pay and promote on merit.
- Maintain two-way communications between manager and employee, with opportunity for a fair hearing and equitable settlement of disagreements.

Service to the Customer—We are dedicated to giving our customers the best possible service. Our products and services bring profits only to the degree that they serve the customer and satisfy customer needs. This demands that we:

- Know our customers' needs, and help them anticipate future needs.
- Help customers use our products and services in the best possible way.
- Provide superior equipment maintenance and supporting services.

Excellence Must Be a Way of Life—We want IBM to be known for its excellence. Therefore, we believe that every task, in every part of the business, should be performed in a superior manner and to the best of our ability. Nothing should be left to chance in our pursuit of excellence. For example, we must:

- Lead in new developments.
- Be aware of advances made by others, better them where we can, or be willing to adopt them whenever they fit our needs.
- Produce quality products of the most advanced design and at the lowest possible cost.

Managers Must Lead Effectively—Our success depends on intelligent and aggressive management which is sensitive to the need for making an enthusiastic partner of every individual in the organization. This requires that managers:

- Provide the kinds of leadership that will motivate employees to do their jobs in a superior way.
- Meet frequently with all their people.
- Have the courage to question decisions and policies; have the vision to see the needs of the company as well as the operating unit and department.
- Plan for the future by keeping an open mind to new ideas, whatever the source.

Obligations to Stockholders—IBM has obligations to its stockholders whose capital has created our jobs. These require us to:

- Take care of the property our stockholders have entrusted to us.
- Provide an attractive return on invested capital.
- Exploit opportunities for continuing profitable growth.

Fair Deal for the Supplier—We want to deal fairly and impartially with suppliers of goods and services. We should:

- Select suppliers according to the quality of their products or services, their general reliability and competitiveness of price.
- Recognize the legitimate interests of both supplier and IBM when negotiating a contract; administer such contracts in good faith.

- Avoid suppliers becoming unduly dependent on IBM.

IBM Should Be a Good Corporate Citizen—We accept our responsibilities as a corporate citizen in community, national, and world affairs; we serve our interests best when we serve the public interest. We believe that the immediate and long-term public interest is best served by a system of competing enterprises.

As you see, they are sound beliefs and there is a theme of excellence woven throughout all of them.

Business Objectives

Business objectives set the course that the company will follow for the next 10 to 20 years. They truly are the long-range strategy for the company. In the latter part of the 1970s, for example, IBM prepared "Business Goals for the 80s." They were

- To grow with the industry
- To exhibit product leadership across the entire product line—to excel in technology, value, and quality
- To be the most efficient in everything we do—to be the low-cost producer, the low-cost seller, the low-cost administrator
- To sustain the profitability that funds growth

The theme of improved productivity and quality runs through these goals; it is not directed only at the product or the services provided to the customer but is directed at every activity and employee within IBM.

In 1979 John A. Young, president of Hewlett-Packard, set the company's goals for the 80s. When discussing HP's business objectives, he said

> In 1979 I launched a new quality campaign by announcing what I call a "stretch" objective. I asked that our product failure rates be cut to one-tenth their current levels by the end of the decade of the 80s.
>
> Why ask for a factor-of-10 improvement number? If I'd called for an improvement of only 2 to 1, our people wouldn't have done anything until 1988. They wouldn't have been forced to radically rethink their operating procedures.

Motorola's objectives were even more aggressive. William J. Weisz, chief operating officer of Motorola, explains, "In 1981, we developed as one of the top ten goals of the company, the 5-Year, Tenfold Improvement Program. This means that no matter what operation you're in, no matter what your present level of quality performance, whether you are a service organization or a manufacturing area, it is our goal to have you improve that level by an order of magnitude in 5 years."

As it looks today both companies have a very good chance of meeting and exceeding these factor of ten objectives.

Performance Goals

To support these general philosophical objectives, additional quantitative goals need to be prepared by the individual units. Typical quality-related goals might be

1. To reduce the cost of quality as a percentage of sales by 10 percent per year from 1986 to 2000
2. To have three quality indicators in each department by 1988
3. To change the ratio of internal to external poor-quality costs from 1 to 4 to 1 to 2 by the year 2000
4. To improve the customer-satisfaction index from 92 to 98 percent by the year 2000

Each of these goals has a measurable end result that can be plotted and tracked. They are not "how to do" items but define what results are desired. Normally, these objectives are developed by middle management and approved by upper management.

Strategy

Middle management is responsible for developing the strategy that will be used to meet the agreed-upon objectives. Strategies may change based upon experience, changing environment, and customer requirements. The quality strategy that this book recommends is "To establish integrated quality systems that penetrate into all parts of the company." Or, in other words, to align quality responsibility with accountability. With a strategy of integrating quality responsibility, you can reduce the size of many quality assurance organizations rather than follow the present trend of expansion.

When discussing Avon's new quality strategy, James E. Preston said

An integrated quality process was a revolutionary concept in our functionally oriented environment. Individual departments had always pursued their vested interests and operated within their own departmental budgets. Rewards were given for quantity of output (despite rejects), for handling crisis, and for adherence to schedules rather than for solving problems and seeking causes so as to prevent problems from recurring. Traditionally, responsibility for quality and for implementing quality programs rested with the quality departments.

Tactics

The tactics are task-oriented activities that are developed and/or updated at least once a year. The tasks are the how-to required to edge constantly closer to the company's performance goals. Tactics are developed and implemented by the first-level managers and employees and then approved by middle and top-level management. Without this type of direction, people don't know how best to allocate their activities.

The Way to Plan

You will note that the planning cycle starts at the top, with upper management setting the mission, operating principles, and business objectives, and comes up from the bottom, with the departments and middle management setting the tactics, strategies, and performance goals. Then they meet in the middle with a joint agreement on the company's long-range plan. The object is to have everyone in the company involved in the planning cycle and to have everyone know and understand the results of the cycle. Total involvement in the planning cycle is critical because without it "someone up there" generates a plan that is passed down from manager to manager to employee but still very little happens because the managers and employees who must do the work are not committed to the plan, let alone involved in it.

SHORT-RANGE QUALITY IMPROVEMENT PLAN

Each year, every responsible business prepares an operating plan for the coming year. Historically this plan has included a production schedule, capital expenditure plans, marketing strategy, cost targets, human-resource assumptions, and new product plans. This strategic operating plan is reviewed, massaged, and approved by all areas of the business. Each area provides its inputs and eventually (sometimes after many cycles) the plan is accepted by all areas as the measurement plan for the coming year. The success or failure of the company is measured by how well each area meets the requirements outlined in the yearly strategic operating plan.

This strategic operating plan has one very important element missing—the quality improvement plan. In the past, this key element of the business has been missing from many strategic operating plans, but in today's environment this crucial part of the business cannot be left to chance. It is imperative that quality improvement plans be included in the company's yearly strategy. This is important because cost, human resources, equipment requirements and profits are all closely linked to product quality. For example, it is just plain poor business to invest 10 percent more money in capital equipment to meet a 10 percent increase in production demands if the quality improvement program is going to provide a 15 percent yield improvement. Without the quality improvement plan, capacity plans have questionable meaning.

Each area of the business must develop and commit to a quality improvement plan for the coming year. These plans must be specific, defining exactly what will be investigated and what the expected returns on the investment will be. The improvement steering council or quality assurance function pulls all these individual quality improvement plans into a company strategy, ensuring that they are complete and mesh together smoothly with no suboptimization. This is accomplished in much the same manner that production control pulls together the production schedules and compares them with the ship demand projections. This method of establishing a yearly quality improvement plan has the advantage of aligning responsibilities with accountabilities. It places the quality program in the hands of the people who can do the most about making it work. Quality assurance's role is to measure compliance to the plan and report the degree of compliance to upper management throughout the year.

Oliver C. Boileau, president of General Dynamics Corporation, stated

> Research has shown that these key success factors (business objectives) must be addressed in business planning and implementation strategies if meaningful quality improvement is to occur. Each key success factor is complemented by a series of objectives that should be reflected by all units of the organization as they continue to strengthen their quality improvement plans and implementation strategies. It seems to me that no real progress in quality and reliability is possible unless an organization shares a strategic vision of the task ahead. Without such a vision, neither resolve nor resources can be expected to produce much headway.

12

Recognition

INTRODUCTION

People need to be accepted by other human beings and recognized for their efforts. Love is a form of recognition. It indicates that an individual is different, special. Your salary is recognition of what your time is worth to your company. A baby cries to get attention, to be recognized. The whole competitive society we live in is driven by people striving to be recognized. Often recognition is simply having someone else acknowledge your worth. It is something everyone wants, needs, and strives to obtain. Studies have shown that people classify recognition as one of the things they value most.

INGREDIENTS OF A COMPANY RECOGNITION PROCESS

A good recognition process has six major objectives:

1. To provide recognition to employees who make unusual contributions to the company to stimulate additional effort for further improvement.

2. To show the company's appreciation for superior performance.

3. To assure maximum benefits from the recognition process by an effective communication system that highlights the individuals who were recognized.

4. To provide many ways to recognize employees for their efforts and stimulate management creativity in the recognition process. Management must understand that variation enhances the impact.

5. To improve morale through the proper use of recognition.

6. To reinforce behavioral patterns that management would like to see continued.

Why does recognition matter? George Blomgren, president of Organizational Psychologists, puts it this way, "Recognition lets people see themselves in a winning identity role. There's a universal need for recognition and most people are starved for it."

A National Science Foundation study made the same point. "The key to having workers who are both satisfied and productive is motivation, that is, arousing and maintaining the will to work effectively—having workers who are productive not because they are coerced but because they are committed." The NSF study continues, "Of all of the factors which help to create highly motivated/highly satisfied workers, the principal one appears to be that effective performance be recognized and rewarded—in whatever terms are meaningful to the individual, be it financial or psychological or both."

There are five major types of recognition:

1. Financial compensation
2. Monetary awards
3. Personal public recognition
4. Group public recognition
5. Private recognition

FINANCIAL COMPENSATION

A study by the Public Agenda Foundation revealed that

- Employees are not rewarded for putting out extra effort.
- Almost two-thirds of the employees would like to see a better connection between performance and pay.
- Over 70 percent of the employees feel that the reason work effort has deteriorated is because there is no connection between pay and performance.

Bell Atlantic is trying a new pay-for-performance system. They are holding back pay from their 23,000 manager-level employees and at the end of the year will distribute this money to the managers, with more of it going to the high-performing managers.

Salaries are important, and means for relating quality and productivity to salary have been discussed in Chapter 3. But other types of financial compensation can also motivate improvements in productivity and quality. In addition to salaries, typical financial compensations are

1. Commissions
2. Piecework pay
3. Employee stock plans
4. Cash bonuses and gain sharing

The January 1979 issue of *Training HRD* journal reported that a study of 400 plants in the U.S. revealed that productivity was 63.8 percent higher in plants that used incentive plans compared to those that do not have a work-measurement system.

Commissions

Have you ever noticed how enthusiastic your Avon salesperson or that Fuller Brush representative is when he or she knocks on your door? Did you see the same degree of enthusiasm in the order clerk in your company the last time you placed an order for a gross of paper clips? The difference is that the clerk in the order department is working for a salary, while the door-to-door salesperson is working for a commission. The better the service to customers, the more return sales made and the more money earned. The successful salesperson is always turned on because he or she looks at the last sale made as additional compensation that was not there before the client was found. But the clerk in the order department looks at the new order of paper clips as additional work that wasn't really needed and that has no impact upon personal financial status.

Customers in the service industry are being turned off today, not by price but by carelessness, discourtesy, and disinterest. Customers want a caring and friendly salesclerk, a cheerful "Good morning, may I help you?" They want to be treated as valuable individuals who are important to the clerk and to the company. If you show them this type of consideration, they will buy more and come back again and again. Commissions provide a means to motivate certain employees to do more and better work. Commissions work to improve the salesperson's productivity. This same principle can be applied to other white-collar activities. For example a design engineer could receive a percentage of the profit from a product he or she designed.

Piecework Pay

Piecework was a popular method of increasing productivity in the first part of the twentieth century and still is widely practiced in some parts of the world. In essence, this system pays the employee a portion of the value added to the item being processed, based upon the effort, skill, and time required to complete the task. Along with the sweatshop, piecework has slowly been phased out of the American scene because although it did increase raw productivity, it did not stress quality, and it resulted in a great deal of suboptimization.

Employee Stock Plans

Employee stock plans are becoming increasingly popular because they provide an effective means of focusing the employees' attention on the business aspects of the company and allowing them to share in the profits. They also help to break down the "we and they" feeling many employees have about the company because from their standpoint the stockholders are the ones that make all the money from their hard work.

In commenting about the stock purchase plan used at Hewlett-Packard, John Young, its president, said, "The company contributes $1 for every $3 an employee puts in. More than three-fourths of our people participate in the plan. The result has been that since employees own part of the company, they feel ownership for some of the company's problems and successes."

More than ten million American workers already belong to employee stock plans, and within 15 years over 25 percent of all American workers will join the parade. The number of new employee stock plans is growing at 10 percent per year, spurred on by the 1984 U.S. tax incentive.

A recent study of 360 high-technology companies, conducted by the National Center for Employee Ownership, concluded that companies that share ownership with their employees grew 2 to 4 times faster than companies that did not have employee stock plans.

The object of an employee stock plan is literally to make capitalists out of all employees. Many plans have been developed and used to directly tie the employees' economic future into the success of the company. One of the more popular plans that is now in use is called the "Employee Stock Ownership Plan." The theory behind this kind of plan was developed by Lewis O. Kelso, a San Francisco lawyer.

Cash Bonuses and Gain Sharing

HRD Training journal reports that over 75 percent of the manufacturing companies in the United States have an executive bonus plan. A study of 1100 companies revealed that companies with executive bonus plans average better than 40 percent pretax profit.

Cash bonuses and gain sharing are not new—they can be traced back to the Roman civilization. In modern times, they have been a proven effective way for a company to share its profits with its employees. Suggestion awards should be separate from the bonus system and should be paid directly to the employee who makes the suggestion.

The bonus concept is used extensively in Japan, where many companies give bonuses twice a year, once just before summer vacation, and another during the first part of December. In very good years, the bonus has been known to almost equal the employee's salary. In bad years, the employees don't expect a bonus, and they are not disappointed when they don't get one.

In the U.S., bonus-incentive plans are becoming more widely accepted. A Sibson national survey revealed that 32 percent of the companies surveyed are considering using them, compared to 23 percent just 12 months earlier.

As John Young explains, his company has "Profit-sharing among all employees, where everyone gets the same percentage of base salary as a bonus. The amount people receive depends on our profitability, and that really helps get everyone in the organization pulling in the same direction." Companies that use gain-sharing programs find their employees starting to think differently, starting to learn and use a new vocabulary—words like "profits," "gross sales," and "production costs" start to slip into their conversation because they see for the first time a direct correlation between their well-being and the well-being of the company.

At General Motors, managers tell employees about the plant's direct labor costs, scrap and rework costs, and profits compared to targets the company has set for itself. This is information that only top management had in the 1970s. General Motors feels that providing the employees with this kind of information is helping to close the gap between management and labor. It has proven to be an effective way of aligning company and employee goals and developing a partnership between the two groups that until recently were in opposition to each other.

In an international survey on productivity conducted by Louis Harris and Amitai Etzioni, nearly two-thirds of the employees surveyed indicated that they would be happy to have their salaries linked to higher productivity. To take advantage of this opportunity for employee involvement over the years, different kinds of bonus and gain-sharing programs have been developed. Most of them focus on an equal division of a pool of money among the employees, tied to their base salary. Of these programs, the best known are

- Scanlon plan
- Rucker plan
- Improshare plan

A government study of thirty-six companies that are using productivity-sharing plans (seventeen Scanlon, eleven Improshare, eight Rucker) revealed the work-force savings averaged 17.3 percent for companies with less than $10 million annual sales and 16.4 percent for companies with over $100 million in annual sales.

Scanlon Plan.   The Scanlon plan is a financial reward system that is directly related to improved productivity. It is the outgrowth of work done by Joseph Scanlon in the mid-30s at Empire Steel and Tin Plating Company. The company was on the verge of bankruptcy. In an effort to put the company back on its feet, Scanlon derived a formula for sharing profits with all employees. In addition, a special program was introduced to increase union-management cooperation; it was directed at reducing costs and increasing productivity. The ensuing teamwork and cooperation helped to rebuild the financial soundness of the failing company.

The Scanlon plan is a companywide productivity strategy made up of three key elements:

1. Cooperation and teamwork between employees, labor unions, and management
2. Employee involvement through a suggestion network
3. Sharing the benefits of productivity gains directly with the employees

Most profit-sharing plans distribute a portion of the company's profits to the employees on an annual or biannual basis. The Scanlon plan shares changes in productivity normally on a monthly basis, keeping the employee very aware of the company's ups and downs.

In the Scanlon plan, monthly bonuses are based upon improvement to a historical measure of labor productivity. Commonly, a base labor productivity ratio is calculated for the coming 12 months based on historical data and planned capital improvements. The most commonly applied formula is

$$\text{Base ratio} = \frac{\text{total personnel cost}}{\text{sales value of production}}$$

The formula shows the historical relationship between human resource costs (including payroll and benefits) and by the value of production (including adjustments to variations in inventory). The formula is designed to focus employee and management attention on the variables that have an impact on productivity of the company.

The actual positive and negative variation to the agreed-to base ratio is then shared between the company and the employees. In most applications, the employees receive 50 to 75 percent of the variation, and the company receives 25 to 50 percent.

Scanlon Suggestion System. The other major activity of the Scanlon plan is a suggestion system that encourages the employees to submit written ideas to improve productivity and quality and to reduce costs. Each department forms a production committee made up of the department manager and at least one employee elected by the people in the department. Employees prepare written suggestions and submit them to the manager or their representative on the production committee. Suggestions are evaluated to determine their impact on productivity and their potential return on investment. Suggestions that are not accepted are returned to the employee with a written explanation of why they were rejected. Accepted suggestions that do not affect other departments, do not exceed a predefined expenditure, and will improve productivity or quality and/or reduce costs are implemented by the production committee. Suggestions that cannot be accepted by the production committee because of the cost of implementation or because they affect other areas of the business are referred to a higher-level screening committee which is made up of employees and managers and is usually chaired by the plant manager. The screening committee is responsible for evaluating suggestions and setting the monthly bonuses (or deficit).

In the Midland-Ross plant in Tennessee, following the implementation of the Scanlon plan, the effectiveness of the direct labor force went up 8 to 10 percent. They had a 16 percent increase in productivity, using the same equipment. Grievances dropped by 50 percent, and absenteeism dropped far below the national average to an all-time-low record for the plant. A turnover rate that had been as high as 30 percent dropped to below 5 percent. From the employee standpoint, morale improved as they received monthly bonuses that ranged between 12 and 20 percent.

Dana Corporation, a manufacturer of industrial equipment and motor vehicle parts, has also implemented the Scanlon plan. As a result, some employees earn 10 to 25 percent more a year in the form of bonuses. Dana has discovered that the bonuses are not the only important part of the Scanlon plan. Some plants, because of the depressed auto market, have not paid bonuses for a number of years, but the employees still vote in the plan each year, attend monthly meetings, submit suggestions, and feel that they are part of the company.

Other Bonus and Gain-Sharing Plans.   The Rucker and Improshare plans also use formulas to share profits, reduce costs, and increase quality and productivity with the total employee population. The Rucker plan was developed by Alan W. Rucker in the late 1940s, based upon his observation that there was a relatively constant ratio between payroll cost and value added. Material costs are deducted from sales in the Rucker formula. This is a group plan with everyone except top management sharing in a percentage bonus. There are no individual awards. The Rucker plan is similar to the Scanlon plan, but the employee-management committees are less structured and formalized. It also does not use a formalized suggestion system. Robert C. Scott, vice president of the Eddy-Rucker-Nickels Company, when describing the Rucker plan, observed that, "It gives you something on the order of 20 percent free gain in productive capacity."

The Improshare plan, whose name means IMproved PROductivity through SHARing, has a goal to produce more final products in fewer employee hours. The plan was developed by Mitchell Fein in the 1970s to eliminate some of the problems that the other incentive plans were having in collecting the data for their formulas. The Improshare plan uses hours rather than dollars to calculate the employee bonus. It is a group plan that covers both direct and indirect personnel. It normally excludes staff and management. A suggestion program is not normally included in the Improshare plan. The Improshare plan uses a ceiling on bonus earnings. When the bonus payment becomes limited by the ceiling for a long period of time, management can make a lump payment to the employees that will allow them to adjust the standards so that the bonus earnings will be below the ceiling. The best bonus formula is a combination of the ones now used, including productivity ratios, scrap ratios, and warranty ratios. This approach provides the proper balance between productivity and quality. If quality is low, even if productivity is up, the calculated bonus is low or even negative. This type of formula combines all the improvement activities that are controllable by the employee. It also has the advantage that it focuses management's and employee's attention on the improvement activities that need it most. The company's poor-quality cost system can provide the additional data needed to implement this type of profit-sharing system called "improvement gain sharing."

Individual or Team Bonus Systems

Individual incentive or bonus programs are difficult (but not impossible) to administer in nonsales activities in large corporations. In small companies, individual incentive programs have very definite advantages. They require a lot of management attention and emphasis, but the resulting improvement is well worth the effort. Delta Business Systems Incorporated, a $32 million company with headquarters in Orlando, Florida, had thirteen different incentive programs that applied to their 2000 + nonsales positions. For example

- Warehouse workers divide up to $400 every 2 months for filling out orders on schedule, processing paper so that the company receives the allowed cash discount, and keeping the operation working smoothly.
- For retaining their customer base, giving sales personnel leads, and getting maintenance agreements renewed, the field service technicians can increase their salaries by 3 to 25 percent.
- People in accounts payable were offered up to $200 a quarter to reduce outstanding unpaid bills. As a result, the long-term accounts payable were reduced by 50 percent.

Bryan King, president of the company, put it this way: "If we can see how fast someone's canoe moves in the water, we provide an incentive for him to improve."

MONETARY AWARDS

Another class of recognition is monetary awards. The word "award" indicates it is a unique recognition of an individual or small group for unusual contributions to the company's goals. Monetary awards are one-time bonuses paid to the recipient immediately following an unusual or far-exceeds-expectations contribution. They may also be given to individuals for long-term, continuous, and high-level performance or unique leadership. The award should be specific, and the person or persons who receive the award should be perceived by management and fellow employees as "special." The amount of the monetary award should vary based upon the magnitude of the contribution.

Exceptional Contributions

Ten basic categories of exceptional contributions should be considered for monetary awards:

1. *Economic value.*   An activity that results in a significant cash saving or increased income should be considered for a monetary award if it required exceptional performance to achieve or was achieved in an area of the business not directly related to the employee's assigned task.

2. *Managerial excellence.*   This award recognizes managerial excellence in leadership, managers who use participative management methods to effectively improve their employee's ability to contribute to the success of the company. It reflects outstanding ability to attract, hold, and develop good personnel.

3. *Engineering or scientific contributions.*   Employees should be rewarded when their ideas and/or activities result in a significant improvement in the product or process specifications that they are not responsible for or in activities that extend the state of the art.

4. *New concept activities.*   This award category recognizes individuals or groups who develop new concepts, work out the details so they can be implemented, and sell the ideas to management.

5. *Commercial or industrial achievements.*   Awards that are given to individuals in this category recognize contributions to increasing the sellability of the product or service, increasing the prestige of the company in the eyes of the public, increasing target markets, or developing new products for internal or external use. They also include activities that extend product performance, decrease product failure rates, or improve customer satisfaction.

6. *Demonstrated initiative or resourcefulness.*   This category of awards is used when a significant achievement is accomplished as a result of action taken by an individual without management direction—action that required resourcefulness and possibly reasonable risk but accomplished a major contribution to the business.

7. *Exceptional effort.*   On occasion, employees and managers are called upon to give more than their fair share to meet critical business needs and business fluctuations. These people who step up to meet these needs to help the company out over difficult periods should be considered for a monetary award.

8. *Patents or disclosures.*   Employees who generate new and unique ideas are the lifeblood of every company. Often truly unique ideas result in the filing of a patent disclosure and eventually in a released patent. Because of the major impact these activities have on the business, it is important that an award program be developed to provide recognition and incentive to the people who are responsible.

9. *Improvement achievement.* This type of award is given to individuals and/or teams whose activities have a significant impact on the quality of products or services, or whose activities result in a major productivity improvement.

10. *Prevention activities award.* It is far better and less expensive to prevent problems than to react to them. This award is used to recognize individuals who anticipate problems and take steps to prevent them from occurring. Recognizing this type of individual is probably one of the biggest challenges facing management today. It is easy to observe the employees who are out fighting fires because their activities are very visible to management. It is much more difficult for management to identify the person who picked up the match from the floor and thereby avoided a fire. Frequently the person who never has any problems doesn't just have an unlimited supply of blind luck but is making his or her own luck by anticipating and preventing problems.

Typical Monetary Awards

There are many types of monetary awards that reflect differing degrees of contribution. The following three are typical:

1. Suggestion awards (discussed in Chapter 7)
2. Patent awards
3. Contribution awards

Patent Awards. This type of award may present a problem to management. In most cases, the people who are applying for patents are being paid to develop them. Nevertheless, you want to encourage the individual who is generating new creative ideas that are generating hundreds of jobs and large sums of revenue for the company. The answer used by some companies is a plateau award system. In these systems, the employee accumulates points based on the number of patents received and the potential contribution that each patent makes to the company. As the employee moves up from one award level to the next level, more meaningful awards are given.

Contribution Awards. An effective contribution award system must provide flexibility or recognition to management and equity to all employees. It must be based on actual contributions of the person and must be administered in all areas using the same ground rules. For purposes of discussion, let's use the following contribution award system.

Award name	*Dollar amount*
Outstanding contribution award	1000 to 50,000
Recognition award	500 to 1000
Weekend on the town award	400
A night out for two award	85

As the contribution to the company increases, the value of the monetary reward increases, and it becomes increasingly difficult to obtain management approval to give the award. For example, a line manager should be able to give one of his employees a night out for two when the occasion warrants it. On the other hand, the outstanding contribution award should be supported with a very detailed written description of the contribution and its impact on the company. It should be reviewed by a company recognition review board to ensure that the award system is being interpreted equitably in all areas of the company. The award should be presented at a formal meeting with the total function in attendance. In addition to the money, the employee should receive some special award jewelry (tie tack, ring, pin, etc.) and a framed certificate. The jewelry provides a continuous reminder to people that the program is viable and available to them.

Remember, the award system is designed to recognize people who have achieved something over and above what they are normally expected to accomplish. It is not given for a normal job well done. Only the truly outstanding people should receive contribution awards.

INDIVIDUAL PUBLIC RECOGNITION

There is an almost endless list of types of recognition that do not directly involve money. The following are some ideas that should stimulate your thinking and give you something to build on:

1. Promotions
2. Office layout, size, or possibly view
3. Trips to customer locations
4. Company recognition meetings
5. Annual improvement conferences
6. Jewelry
7. Special parking spaces
8. Articles in newsletters
9. Public notice posted on the bulletin board (One plant in New York City has a huge billboard on top of the plant that flashes the names and accomplishments of special individuals.)
10. Employee's picture on a poster

11. Verbal recognition at a department, division, or company meeting
12. Special job assignments
13. Plaque presented in front of fellow workers
14. Plaque in the company entrance way with the employee's picture and name on it

At Stacoswitch Corporation in Costa Mesa, California, all the supervisors were provided with badges that read "We do it right or we don't do it at all." Supervisors with the lowest reject rate had gold stars on their badges. Harry E. Williams, vice president of operations, wrote, "Supervisors soon took pride in being able to achieve the smallest number of rejections, and requests for refurbished tooling, drawing changes, and capital equipment increased notably."

National Car Rental uses commemorative plaques with individual employee names on them, hung in the business offices around the United States. A typical plaque would read: "Carrie Harrington deserves national attention for outstanding performance, second quarter, 1986."

GROUP RECOGNITION

Recognition of the group makes the group feel that it is a winner and the members of the group get a sense of belonging that leads to increased company loyalty.

Again, there are an unlimited number of ways for management to recognize a group for contributions. Typical ways are

1. Articles about the group's improvement in the company's newsletter, accompanied by photographs of the group
2. Department luncheons to recognize specific accomplishments
3. Family recognition picnics
4. Progress presentations to upper management
5. Luncheons with upper management
6. Group attendance at technical conferences
7. Cake and coffee at a group meeting, paid for by the company
8. Department improvement plaques
9. Top management attending group meetings to say thanks for a job well done
10. Group mementos (pen sets, calculators, product models, etc.)

PRIVATE RECOGNITION

Of all the recognition categories, this is one of the most important because it directly relates to the interface between management and the employee. The one-on-one interface is very important in stimulating improvement and keeping morale high.

There are many unpleasant jobs that have to be performed, jobs that can't be automated, that cannot be ignored, that have no prestige associated with them; but without them, the company could not function effectively. What makes these unbearable jobs bearable for the employee is a manager who appreciates the individual's contribution and lets the employee know that the effort being put forth is appreciated. This is the type of manager who makes a good job great and a great job fantastic. Such a manager always seems to "luck out" and have the best employees. It's that department that always seems to get out the work on schedule, exerting seemingly no effort; and when the company has a problem, it's that area that is first to step forward and volunteer to help. This area's absenteeism is down and productivity is up. Why? Because the manager remembers asking an employee to do something and follows up to see that it was accomplished, not looking over the employee's shoulder but showing that the assignment was important and that the effort the employee invests is noticed.

A lot of managers feel strange telling employees they are doing a good job, and frequently the employee has a hard time accepting compliments and reacts with comments like: "Ah, knock off that bull!" "Don't give me compliments, give me money!" But comments like that do not mean that they don't need the manager's appreciation. So don't let it prevent you from expressing your honest appreciation for a task well done. Employees need encouragement and need to have their good acts reinforced through management appreciation. A sincere pat on the back at the right time is much better and more effective than a swift kick in the pants at any time.

Typical ways that private recognition is provided to an employee are

1. A simple, honest thank you for a job well done, given immediately after the task is completed.
2. A letter sent to the employee's house by his manager or upper manager, thanking him for his specific contribution.
3. Personal notes on letters or reports, complimenting the originator on content or layout.
4. Sending birthday cards and work anniversary cards to an employee's house, thanking the employee for the contributions that were made

over the past year, not with general statements but with specific examples that let the employee know that management knows that the employee is there and what he or she is doing.

5. The performance evaluation that takes place every 3 months is an ideal time to give private feedback to the employee about accomplishments. It should not be the first time you will have expressed your appreciation, but it should be used to reinforce the favorable work patterns and summarize employee accomplishments. The most basic rule of performance evaluations is "no surprises."

A

Reporting and Using
Measurement Data

Measuring the health of the process is only the start of the cycle. The problem that now faces the quality engineer is how to use the data to maximize its benefit to the process and the company. Essentially measurement data can be used for three purposes:

1. Process control
2. Engineering problem analysis
3. Management reports (fully discussed in Chapter 12 of the text)

PROCESS CONTROL

Measuring Defects

Several easy-to-use methods exist for identifying, measuring, and displaying defects. Figures A.1 through A.8 illustrate the various techniques.

Portions of this appendix were prepared by Lester D. Kaye of IBM General Products Division in San Jose, California.

1. *Check sheets.* Used for data collection and organization (see Figure A.1).

2. *Graphs.* Used to display data. There are several kinds, including line graphs, bar graphs, and pie graphs. Figure A.2 is an illustration of a line graph.

3. *Histograms.* A type of bar graph, used to display distribution of whatever is being measured (see Figure A.3).

Week number

Reason for E/C	1	2	3	4	5	6	7	Total
Functional	‖	‖	‖‖	‖‖		‖‖‖‖	‖‖	16
Error correction	‖	‖‖	‖‖		‖‖‖‖ ‖		‖	14
Manufacturability	‖‖	‖	‖‖	‖‖‖	‖	‖‖‖	‖‖‖‖	18
Cost reduction		‖			‖‖‖		‖‖	6
Reliability	‖‖	‖‖‖	‖‖‖	‖‖‖‖	‖‖	‖‖‖‖	‖‖‖‖	22
Safety			‖	‖	‖‖			4
Disposition	‖‖‖	‖‖‖‖ ‖‖	‖‖‖‖		‖‖	‖‖‖	‖‖‖‖	24
TOTAL	10	16	16	12	16	16	18	104

Figure A.1 Check sheet.

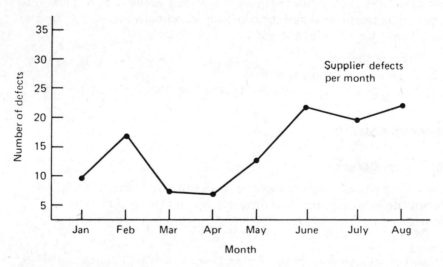

Supplier defects per month

Figure A.2 Line graph.

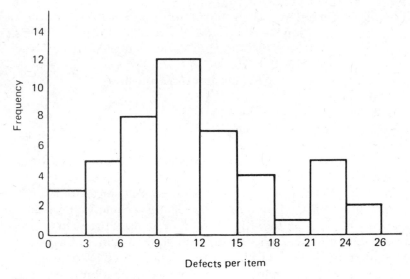

Figure A.3   Histogram.

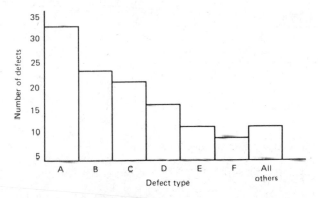

Figure A.4   Pareto diagram.

4. *Pareto diagrams.*   Another type of bar graph, showing data classifications in descending order from left to right (see Figure A.4).

Measuring Processes

To measure the effectiveness of a process or how it is meeting requirements, it is necessary to use statistical methods. Several are briefly described and illustrated below.

1. *Sampling.*   A method used to obtain information from a portion of a larger population when it is too expensive or time-consuming to measure the total population. Utilizes sampling tables (see Table A.1) and random number tables.
2. *Data collection.*   A method that has three purposes:
   a. Analyze a process
   b. Determine if a process is in control
   c. Accept or reject a product
   The two types of data used are
   a. Attributes, to identify "yes/no," "go/no-go," "accept/reject" units or parts
   b. Variables, to identify variations between units measured
   After data is collected, one or more of the techniques described below is used to analyze information and identify problem areas.
3. *Stratification.*   A special sampling technique utilizing information from subgroups (strata) of a larger population. Used in conjunction with histograms that indicate an abnormal distribution, as in Figure A.5.

TABLE A.1   Sampling Table Example

Lot size	Number of parts required for sample
500–1200	80
3200–10,000	200
35,000–150,000	500

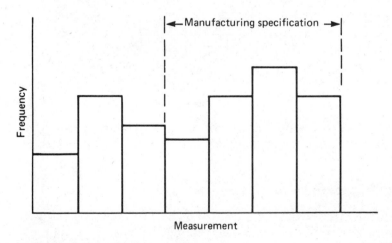

Figure A.5   Stratification.

4. *Frequency distribution (data arrangement).* Used to measure and analyze variations between items produced by a process (see Figure A.6).
5. *Scatter diagrams.* Used to display the relationship between two different variables, as shown in Figure A.7.

PROCESS CONTROL CHARTS

A great deal of time and effort was spent to evaluate and bring the process under control as it was qualified. The problem now is how to keep the process from degrading and going out of control. One of the best ways to accomplish this is through the use of control charts. A control

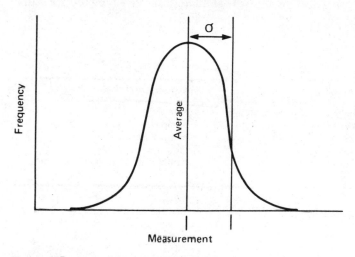

Figure A.6   Normal frequency distribution.

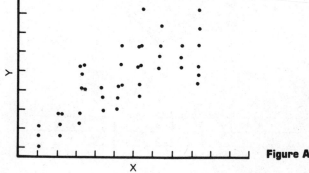

Figure A.7   Scatter diagram.

chart graphically portrays a running picture of the process performance at a specific point in the process. These charts are used to detect negative trends before a serious out-of-control condition develops. There are basically two types of control charts, attributes (go or no-go) control charts, and variables data control charts. Table A.2 lists four control charts that use attributes data. You will note that constant and variable sample sizes can be used to plot attributes control charts. Figure A.8 is a typical $n\bar{p}$ control chart. The central line $(n\bar{p})$ is calculated by summing the total numbers of defective units detected in the lots inspected and then dividing this sum by the number of lots inspected to provide the average or mean defectives per lot.

The upper control limit (UCL) and lower control limit (LCL) are used to evaluate each point on the graph to determine if the process is statistically under control. The UCL is calculated by the following formula:

$$UCL = n\bar{p} + (3\sqrt{n\bar{p}})(\sqrt{1 - \bar{p}})$$

TABLE A.2   Attributes Control Charts

Name	Description	Sample condition
U chart	Number of defects per unit	Sample size can vary
c chart	Number of defects in a sample	Sample size must stay the same
P chart	Percentage of defective units in a sample	Sample size can vary
$n\bar{p}$ chart	Number of defective units in a sample	Sample size must stay the same

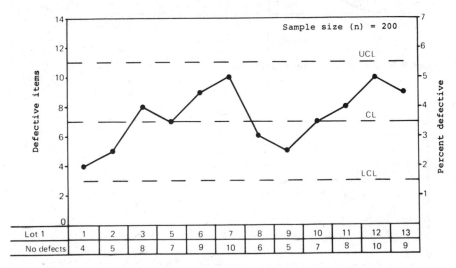

Figure A.8 $n\bar{p}$ control chart.

$\overline{p}$ is calculated by dividing the central line value $n\overline{p}$ by the constant sample size. LCL is calculated by the following formula:

$$LCL = n\overline{p} - (3\sqrt{n\overline{p}})(\sqrt{1 - \overline{p}})$$

The second basic type of control chart makes use of variables data. Normally control charts that use variables data provide much more detailed information about the process under evaluation. $\overline{X}$ and R charts are the most frequently used variables data control charts (see Figure A.9). By carefully examining Figure A.9, you will note that an $\overline{X}$ and R chart is not one but two related charts. The top chart plots the mean value, or $\overline{X}$, of the sample; the lower graph plots the range, or R, for the sample. This chart is particularly useful because it shows on one page changes in both the mean value and the process distribution.

To be effective, process control charts should be plotted by the manufacturing operator as the assigned tasks are performed. The operator should also be provided with a set of firm guidelines that will help him or her analyze the chart and react appropriately. For example

1. Each time a point is outside of either control limit, shut down the process and correct the problem. Record on the control chart what was done to correct the problem.

2. If seven points in a row or nine out of eleven points are on one side of the central line, contact the manufacturing engineer, who will record action taken on the control chart (see Figure A.10).

3. If six consecutive points increase or decrease in the same direction, notify the manufacturing engineer, who will again record the corrective action on the control chart (see Figure A.11).

The basic concept behind control charts is to enable one to decide when to take action and when to leave things alone. Control charts identify statistically when unnatural patterns occur so they can be investigated.

ENGINEERING PROBLEM ANALYSIS

The manufacturing and quality engineers need two types of reports—one that highlights problem areas and a more detailed report for analysis of specific problems so that appropriate action can be taken to improve the process. Probably one of the most valuable reports that engineers receive is a yield report. The yield report should include both first-time and throughput yields. In addition, the engineers need to be supplied

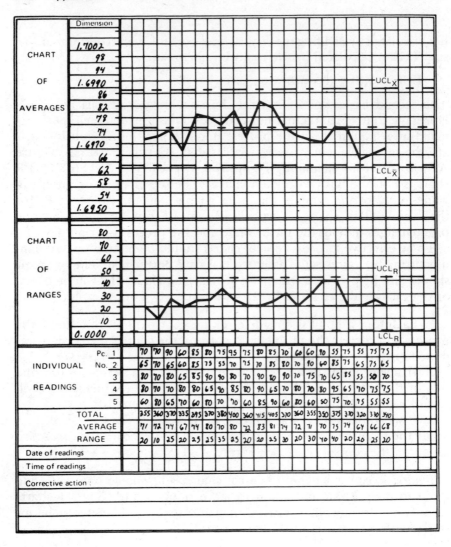

Figure A.9 X̄ and R control chart.

with the data collected at the QA measurement point. This is normally reported to them as a percent defective and is portrayed as a running history by problem type. The data system should also allow them to obtain detailed error-by-error information about each process step that needs to be improved. The engineering community also needs to be provided with error-rate reports for product and/or service that has been accepted by the customer.

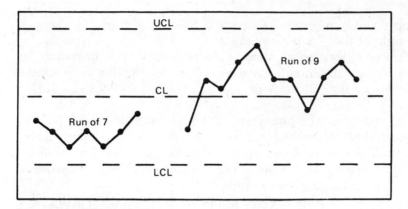

Figure A.10   Runs of 7 and 9.

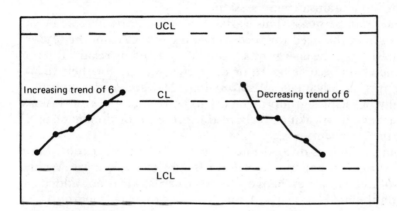

Figure A.11   Trends of 6.

TECHNIQUES USED IN TEAM AND CIRCLE MEETINGS

Several participative decision-making techniques are available for problem identification, solution identification, and prioritization of problems.

Brainstorming

1. *Standard session.*   In a round-robin fashion, the leader asks each member to state a problem that he or she feels is affecting the department, the process, the equipment, the environment, or any other aspect of the work that is done together. Each problem statement is listed on

chart paper and numbered. As a page is filled, it is posted on the wall in clear sight of the group members.

Criticism or evaluation of ideas is not permitted. It is important to maintain a supportive, nonthreatening atmosphere so that all members feel free to state their ideas. A person is permitted to "pass" (not offer an idea).

The quantity of ideas is important. Don't be concerned with "quality" at this point; that will come later. Everyone is encouraged to participate. "Off the wall" ideas are encouraged; they often prove to be not as irrational as they first appear. Combining and improving on previous ideas (known as "piggybacking") is essential.

If ideas are not flowing readily, an option is to end the meeting and reschedule it in a day or two. This allows ideas to incubate.

Figure A.12 illustrates a hypothetical problem list that might be developed during a brainstorming session.

2. *Round-robin session.* This variation fosters participation by all members without the need for verbal encouragement from the leader. It can be used when the energy of a group is inhibited by relatively large size (i.e., members become bored or distracted waiting for their turn). It has the further advantage of improving ideas and generating new ones. Finally, it enables group members to be free of any reservations they might have in speaking freely in the presence of dominant individuals or management.

The team or circle is divided into subgroups of three or four. Each individual writes, on paper or 3 × 5 cards, two or three ideas. Within a subgroup, individuals exchange sheets or cards; ideas are added or modified on the cards received. After three passes, each subgroup lists its ideas on chart paper. The entire team or circle is reassembled and subgroup reports are given.

3. *Setting priorities in brainstorming.* The list of ideas generated by brainstorming is usually quite lengthy (twenty or more). The following method has proven to be very effective in establishing priorities:

All ideas, listed on chart paper, are posted on the wall and made clearly visible. All ideas are numbered.

Each member is given five votes, which may be allocated in any way: one vote for each of five ideas, all five for one idea, two votes for one idea plus one each for three other ideas, etc. Explain that this approach permits an individual to express strong preference for certain ideas. (Note: The number of votes per member can be varied, based on the number of ideas listed, size of the group, and preference.)

Each idea is called off numerically and read to the group; members raise their hands, indicating how many votes they are casting for that idea. The scribe counts the number of fingers held up by each member

PROBLEMS AFFECTING OUR QUALITY

1. Too many changes
2. Not enough tools
3. Specifications not stable
4. Schedules too tight
5. Too much re-do
6. Too many approvals needed
7. Don't know what the overall goals are
8. Too many procedures
9. Turnaround time too long
10. System down too much

11. Shortage of parts
12. Everything around here is rush-rush
13. Can't get my typing done
14. Missing procedures
15. Red tape
16. People are separated; isolation
17. Lack of instructions
18. Can't read the documents
19. Need more terminals
20. No quality control

21. No planning
22. No way to test
23. Too many meetings
24. Inaccurate documentation; down level
25. Too many mistakes
26. Don't know what's going on in the real world
27. Our work is rejected for no good reason
28. Personality conflicts
29. No time for training
30. No recognition
31. Commitments not kept

Figure A.12   A brainstorming problem list (hypothetical).

voting, verifies it verbally, and posts the summary count on the chart. After all votes have been cast, the scribe ensures that the total number of votes equals the vote allotment (i.e., eight members with five votes each should yield forty votes cast).

A second vote is taken, considering only those items that received a minimum number of votes. The group decides this minimum by reviewing the spread of votes cast and agreeing, by consensus, that only those ideas that received the minimum (say, three votes) or higher be considered in the runoff. This enables the votes that were cast for the other ideas (the "ones" and "twos") to be redistributed. This process is repeated as many times as necessary to establish a clear priority.

A final check is made to ensure that the group is in agreement regarding the selection of the no. 1 priority. The charts are saved for further use. (After resolving the no. 1 priority, the group should subsequently address the remaining items.)

Nominal Group Technique (NGT)

1. *The method.*   NGT has advantages similar to the round-robin technique. It, too, gives the leader increased control of the group process. If the group is particularly energetic and vocal, verbal brainstorming may prove to be inefficient, as individuals may feel compelled to recount their own experiences or require a great deal of elaboration.

The leader states the issue or topic and writes it on chart paper. The issue can be a global one, such as "What problems inhibit the effectiveness of our department?"

Members are asked to work on their own, writing out problems or solution statements that address the original issue. After 5 to 10 minutes, the leader asks each member to publicly read one suggestion. These are listed on chart paper and numbered. This procedure continues, in round-robin fashion and without criticism or comment, until all ideas are listed.

The next phase is that of clarification. Each idea is reviewed; the originator responds to questions so that each item is well-understood by all members. Ideas are then ranked.

2. *Ranking the items.*   Group identification of high-priority items can be done differently than for brainstorming. The following procedure retains the advantage of enabling individuals to feel free to express their opinion in the presence of dominant members.

The group chooses the top five (or seven or eight, etc.) ideas. Working independently, each individual lists, on separate 3 × 5 cards or sheets of paper, the numbers of the items and a short phrase summarizing each one. The participants then spread their cards out before them. They choose the most important item and assign it the highest rank. They write down the rank, circle it, and turn the card over. Then the least important item is selected; a "1" is placed on the card, circled, and the card turned over.

In succeeding steps, the next most important item is selected, then the next, and so on. The cards are passed to the leader, who reads the item number, the summarizing phrase (to ensure that the item selected corresponds to the item on the chart) and the rank number chosen. The rank numbers are posted beside the appropriate items.

This process is continued until all ranking numbers from all cards have been listed. Both the number of votes and the numerical summary of the rankings are reviewed by the members to determine the high-priority ideas.

Force-Field Analysis (FFA)

This technique can be used when the group is fairly large (about twenty), when the topic concerns a global process or situation that can be assigned a quantitative value based on intuition or "gut feel," and when group discussion or interaction is desired. The following steps describe FFA (see also Figure A.13).

Draw a vertical axis; index it 0 to 100 percent in increments of 10. Poll the group for its estimate of "level of performance" of the process or situation.

Plot each estimate, making a scatter diagram. Estimate the mean and draw a horizontal line, labeling it with the original question. Draw arrows "pushing up" the horizontal line (driving forces) and other arrows "pushing it down" (restraining forces).

In round-robin fashion, ask the group to identify the restraining and driving forces. List these on chart paper.

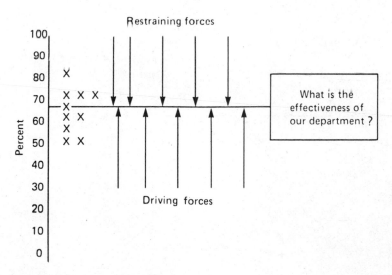

Figure A.13   Force-field analysis.

In subsequent meetings, the group establishes priorities for the restraining forces, which are then addressed as problems to be resolved. In addition, driving forces can be strengthened, of course.

Cause and Effect Diagrams

These are sometimes known as "fish-bone" diagrams because of their shape. Cause and effect diagrams are generally used to identify problem solutions. They portray the relationship between a problem and its possible causes and provide an opportunity for the group to graphically develop, explore, and analyze this relationship.

To begin, write the problem statement on chart paper. This could be a problem that the group identified during an excellence-circle brainstorming session, or it could be a problem given to an excellence team by its manager. Draw a box around the statement and draw a horizontal arrow pointing to it (see Figure A.14).

Add the four or five major sources of the problem (categories) above and below, connected to the horizontal arrow. Some of the more common categories are

- Methods, procedures, processes

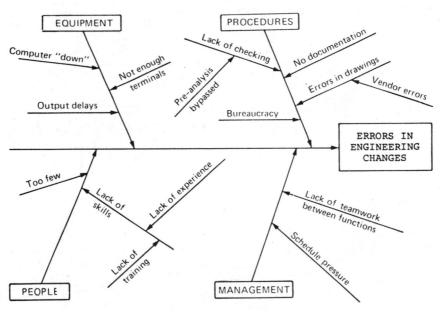

Figure A.14 Cause and effect diagram (hypothetical).

- People
- Material
- Machines, equipment
- Measurement
- Management
- Money

Through group discussion, identify specific causes and group them by category. Develop or modify categories as needed. Encourage participation and idea generation. Don't criticize; enter every idea on the diagram.

Ensure that the group understands each possible cause as it is listed. Use the 5W-1H approach:

Why
What
Where
When
Who
How

If one cause category begins to dominate, establish it as a separate cause and effect diagram on a separate chart.

After all ideas are exhausted and understood, the group identifies the most likely causes. These are circled on the diagram. Causes that are quantifiable should be measured using the techniques described in the next section. This will validate the existence of a problem, indicate its relative size, provide a basis for prioritization, and provide a basis for a later "before and after" evaluation of solutions that are implemented.

The final step is for the group to identify the one or two most likely causes and to develop, recommend, and implement solutions.

Follow-up evaluation of the problem, quantifiable if possible, should be performed to determine if the implemented solutions have corrected the actual most likely causes. If not, the group should continue to identify the most likely causes and solutions until it is agreed that the original problem has been solved.

Mind Maps

A mind map is an unstructured cause and effect diagram. It is used by groups that prefer a more free-wheeling examination of a complex problem and its causes.

The problem statement is written in the center of chart paper. Members of the group offer their opinions about possible causes, using brainstorming. These are drawn on the chart paper as "spinoffs" from the problem statement (see Figure A.15). After all causes have been identified, the group selects the most significant cause. A new mind map is created, with this cause now becoming the problem statement.

This process is continued until two or three suggested causes are at a low enough level that they can be modified or corrected (see Figure A.16). Solutions and action plans are developed.

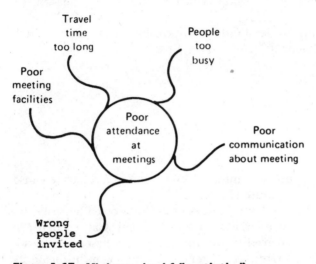

Figure A.15   Mind map—level 1 (hypothetical).

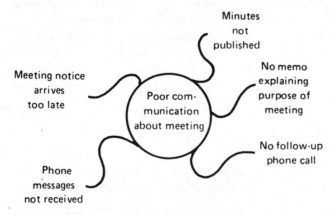

Figure A.16   Mind map—level 2 (hypothetical).

Guidelines for Conducting Meetings

It is essential that all group members feel a sense of accomplishment as a result of their activities. Meetings should, therefore, be supportive (nonthreatening) and well-focused. Listed below are several guidelines for group members to observe to ensure productive team or circle meetings.

1. Establish an agreed-to agenda. Keep the energy focused on the desired objective of the meeting.
2. Don't criticize ideas; all contributions are valuable.
3. Encourage participation and idea generation.
4. Keep it positive; do not speculate on "why this idea won't work."
5. Observe the personal rights of individuals:
   a. The right to "pass."
   b. The right to be put "on hold."
   c. The right to take time.
   d. The right to revise, restate, clarify.
6. Keep discussion focused on the topic being discussed.
   a. When discussing causes, avoid discussing solutions.
   b. Avoid debates, philosophical discussions, or "war stories."
7. Be aware of the general level of detail being discussed; keep comments at that level. If the level of detail seems to change, the group should acknowledge it and agree that the level has changed.
8. Listen attentively to each contribution.
9. Be aware of the level of familiarity of other members.
10. Allow only one conversation during the meeting unless the group agrees to break up into subgroups.
11. Have each member take responsibility for group productivity.
12. Summarize the meeting. Identify what was accomplished and what could have been improved.
13. Document all meetings through charts and minutes.

ANALYSIS TOOLS

Systems engineering is one approach to analyzing and improving established systems and processes. Other effective techniques include value analysis, work simplification, paperwork simplification, PERT, business systems planning (BSP), process analysis technique (PAT), and structured analysis and structured design (SA/SD).

B

Statistical Process Control

Statistical process control is an effective method of ensuring through the process that the process output will conform to the desired requirements. Appendix A described the statistical process control tools and how to plot control charts. This section provides an introduction to how they should be used.

Statistical process control is a method of evaluating a process to identify both desirable and undesirable changes. Each measured characteristic should be evaluated to determine if statistical process control methods are applicable.

Once the characteristics to be controlled have been identified, preliminary limits are set for each characteristic based on technical judgment and past experience and/or the specification limits. These are the limits within which natural variation is expected to drift randomly. Control sample size and frequency are also determined at this time. In the best implementations, the measurements are taken right at the workstation

Appendix B was written by P. J. McMahon and H. J. Harrington, Project Managers, IBM Corporation, San Jose, California.

by the person performing the task. This individual will record the data and plot data points on control charts. It is also important that the person performing the activity be the one to do the primary analysis of the updated control charts since he or she is the one who needs to be most sensitive to the state of the process on a continuous basis.

Once the preliminary control limits are in place and the measurement and data recording system is working, the process is monitored to see if the process sample data remains within the control limits for at least twenty-five samples. If not, causes of process variation must be identified and eliminated until this test is passed, finally indicating that the process is stable enough to perform a process capability study.

It is, of course, possible to have a very stable, repeatable process that is producing unsatisfactory output. The purpose of the process capability study is to determine if the controlled characteristics of a stable process are also close enough to their desired nominal values that the statistically predictable proportion of those characteristics falling outside the specification limits is below a predetermined limit. Once again, if the process does not satisfy these predetermined criteria, causes of the deviations must be identified and eliminated, process stability established once more, and new process capability studies performed.

By the time a proper process capability study has been successfully completed, sufficient real process data will be available to allow the replacement of the original preliminary control limits, with ongoing process monitoring limits statistically determined from the real data of the stable capable process. These are called the "natural" limits of the process.

From this point on, failure of the process sample data to remain within these limits, or the appearance of nonrandom variations within these limits, is an almost sure sign that a "special cause of variation" has crept into the process. Examples of such causes include tool wear, changes in raw material, introduction of an improperly trained employee, and even subtle seasonal changes such as ambient temperature, relative humidity, etc.

In the event that a control-chart sample point indicates the process has gone out of control, two actions must immediately be taken. First, all output since the last in-control sample was taken must be screened to assure that any deviant output is found and either corrected or eliminated. At the same time, the people responsible for finding and eliminating the cause of the unfavorable variation must be notified immediately because the process should not be allowed to continue until it has been brought back in control. If there is an overriding reason to keep the process going, such as customer demand or economic necessity, all output must be screened until the process is back in control. It is only

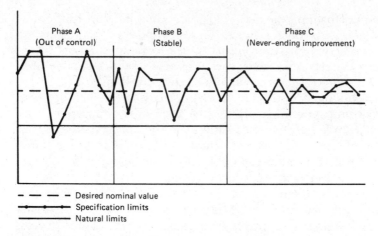

Figure B.1 Process control cycle.

through disciplines such as these that there is any hope of developing processes whose error rates will be in the world-class range. In no case should the process be allowed to continue in the hope that a few more samples will show that the process has magically corrected itself.

As the process improvement team and process employees become more and more familiar with the process and become very adept at continually reducing variation, a very interesting pattern will begin to show up in the control charts. The charts will literally show that the sample data are becoming so tightly clustered about the desired nominal condition that the control limits are no longer representative of expected process random variations. This is the point at which new natural limits for the process need to be calculated and placed on the control charts to be sure that the process does not drift away from this improved state. This iteration can go on continuously, and this is the state referred to as "never-ending process improvement." It is an extremely desirable state, and companies that reach it find themselves in strong competitive positions, continually able to beat their cost objectives and bid aggressively for new work.

Figure B.1 shows a typical cycle process improvement. During phase A the process is unstable and the output should be inspected 100 percent. In phase B the process is able to produce output to specification, and output only needs to be measured on an occasional basis to prove there are no negative trends. During phase C the specification limits are easily met and measurements are made to ensure the process does not degrade.

Suggested Readings

Note: The items are listed in alphabetical order. This is not intended to be a complete list; it only directs your attention to some of the materials that I have found to be useful and interesting.

VIDEOTAPES, FILMS, AND SLIDE PROGRAMS

"Casablanca Nights," 17 minutes (film), Revlon Corporation. (*This entertaining film dramatizes, in the Bogart tradition, the identification and solution of quality problems. It also emphasizes the importance of individual responsibility for quality.*)

"If Japan Can, Why Can't We?" 77 minutes (tape, film), NBC White Paper. (*This is a contrast of recent industrial innovations and economic gains made by the Japanese with the current economic productivity status in the U.S.*)

"Japan vs. U.S.A.—High-Tech Shootout," 52 minutes (tape), Films Incorporated for NBC Reports. (*An NBC News correspondent examines the Japanese threat to America's high-tech industry and its possible economic effects. Quality is addressed in general terms as one of many things contributing to the Japanese success.*)

Nashua Seminar, 160 minutes (tape). (*A presentation by William Conway, president and CEO of Nashua Company, to executives of Ford. He describes the introduction of control charts into the Nashua Company. Mr. Conway is an engaging speaker with an interesting story to tell. An illuminating and enjoyable presentation.*)

"On the Line," 37 minutes (film), King Arthur Productions for National Semiconductor. (*An acclaimed film on the challenge of Japanese productivity and how it works. The film follows the actual experiences of four American workers who visited a Japanese factory. The film is outstanding for motivation and consciousness-raising.*)

"Pluto," 6 hours, Intertek, Rolling Hills, California. (*A computer-based learning program for simple statistical process control.*)

"Quality Control Circles," W. S. Reiker. (*Two sets of slides and cassettes with supporting training materials. One set has ten training classes for basic team problem-solving techniques. The other set has eight training classes on advanced statistical measurement techniques.*)

"Quality Is Free," 23 minutes (tape). (*Phil Crosby discusses the basic principles of his quality management program.*)

"Reliability Engineering," "Quality Planning," and "Engineering Statistics," Colorado State University videotape courses. (*Each course has ten 30-minute color tapes. Typical subjects are economics of quality, designing quality into a product, developing quality-mindedness, quality data collection and analysis, and lot acceptance sampling.*)

"Survival Run," 20 minutes (film). (*Two runners team up to overcome serious handicaps when they compete in a difficult cross-country race.*)

"Type Z: An Alternative Management Style," 105 minutes (film), Professor William Ouchi. (*American versus Japanese styles of management. The American response to the Japanese challenge.*)

BOOKS AND ARTICLES

"American Manufacturers Strive for Quality Japanese Style," *Business Week*, March 12, 1979.

Crosby, Philip B.: *Quality Is Free*, McGraw-Hill Book Company, New York, 1979. (*How to manage quality so that it becomes a source of profit for your business.*)

Crosby, Philip B.: *Quality without Tears*, McGraw-Hill Book Company, New York, 1984. (*How cooperation can achieve quality and eliminate problems. Well-written and fun to read.*)

Deming, W. E.: *Japanese Methods for Productivity and Quality*, George Washington University, 1981. (*A good motivational tool with real and readable examples for statistical quality control. Especially good to show the power of control charts in running a business.*)

Feigenbaum, Armand V.: *Total Quality Control*, McGraw-Hill Book Company, New York, 1983. (*In the new (third) edition, Dr. Feigenbaum has put together the latest concepts on a total quality control system. For readers with a background in engineering.*)

Grant, E. L.: *Statistical Quality Control*, McGraw-Hill Book Company, New York, 1952. (*The book upon which present statistical quality control systems are based. Very understandable.*)

Ishikawa, Kaoru: *Guide to Quality Control*, Asian Productivity Organization, 1984. (*How quality control is practiced in Japan. Easy to understand.*)

Juran, J. M.: *Quality Control Handbook*, McGraw-Hill Book Company, New York, 1979. (*A reference book on quality control for managers, supervisors, engineers, and others.*)

Juran, J. M., and Frank M. Gryna, Jr.: *Quality Planning and Analysis*, McGraw-Hill Book Company, New York, 1980. (*A textbook on quality, covering several broad areas including quality costs, controlling defects, designing for quality, statistical aids, process control measurement, and sampling.*)

Ouchi, William G.: *Theory Z*, Addison-Wesley Publishing Company, Reading, MA, 1981. (*How American business can meet the Japanese challenge.*)

"Overhauling America's Business Management," *New York Times*, January 4, 1981.

Peters, Thomas J., and Robert H. Waterman, Jr.: *In Search of Excellence*, Harper and Row, New York, 1982. (*An examination of America's best-run companies and the deep-seated values that have shaped their long-term success.*)

Squires, Frank H.: *Successful Quality Management*, Hitchcock Publications, 1980. (*A collection of Squires' articles that have been published in* Quality *magazine, covering many aspects of quality management.*)

"The New Industrial Relations," *Business Week*, May 11, 1981.

Western Electric: *Statistical Quality Control Handbook*, Mack Publishing Company, Easton, Pennsylvania, 1977. (*Prepared to assist Western Electric employees, this book may also be used as a general guide for applying statistical quality control.*)

Index

About the Author

H. James Harrington, M.B.A., Ph.D., is currently chairman of the board pro tem of the American Society for Quality Control (ASQC), the leading quality professional association. A senior engineer and project manager in quality assurance at IBM Corporation in San Jose, California, he has a wealth of experience ranging from manufacturing and test engineering to reliability engineering and quality assurance.

Among his many honors, Dr. Harrington has been named lifetime honorary president of the Asia Pacific Quality Control Organization. He also serves as national vice president for the International Management Council, and he is the official advisor on quality methods to the China Quality Control Association of the People's Republic of China.